# ADVANCED

# BUILDING CONSTRUCTION

*A MANUAL FOR STUDENTS*

BY THE AUTHOR OF

"NOTES ON BUILDING CONSTRUCTION"

*NEW EDITION*

1893

# PREFACE

THIS volume contains all the information required for the examination in the Second Stage or Advanced Course of Building Construction held annually under the direction of the Science and Art Department, and forms a sequel to "Elementary Building Construction and Drawing" by Mr. E. J. Burrell, which deals with the First Stage.

It is a reduced edition of Part II., "Notes on Building Construction," prepared by omitting certain important portions, which, though useful to the more advanced student or in practice, are not required for this special examination. Chapters IX. and X. have been added in an abridged form from Part I.[1]

The syllabus for the Second Stage on Advanced Course is as follows.

The figures in brackets show the pages of this volume in which the different subjects are treated.

---

## "SECOND STAGE, OR ADVANCED COURSE.

"In addition to the subjects enumerated for the Elementary Course—in all of which questions of a more complicated nature may be set, combining work done by the different trades—the knowledge of the students will be tested under the following heads, viz.:—

"1st. Freehand sketches explanatory of any details of

[1] In the following pages the letters E.B.C.D. denote the book "Elementary Building Construction and Drawing," and N.B.C. denote "Rivington's Series of Notes on Building Construction." Both books are published by Messrs. Longmans.

[2] Taken from the Directory of the Science and Art Department of the Committee of Council on Education, 1891.

construction, such as the joints of iron and wooden structures, and other parts requiring illustration on an enlarged scale [Chaps. IV., V., VI., VII., VIII., XII.]. These sketches may be roughly drawn, provided they are clear and capable of being readily understood.

"2nd. The nature of the stresses to which the different parts of simple structures are subjected [p. 2], as follows:—

"In the case of beams either fixed at one or both ends, or supported or continuous, the student should know which parts of the beam are in compression and which in tension [p. 5].

"He should be acquainted with the best forms for struts, ties, and beams, such as floor joists, exposed to transverse stress [p. 9].

"He should know the difference in the strength of a girder carrying a given load at its centre, or uniformly distributed [p. 8].

"In the ordinary kinds of wooden or iron roof trusses, and framed structures of a similar description, he should be able to distinguish members in compression from those in tension [p. 12].

"He should be able, in the case of a concentrated or uniform load upon any part of a beam supported at both ends, to ascertain the proportion of the load transmitted to each point of support [p. 15].

"3rd. The nature, application, and characteristic peculiarities of the following materials in ordinary use for building purposes, viz.:—

"Bricks of different kinds in common use [p. 19], York, Portland, Caen, and Bath stones [p. 22] (or stones of a similar description) [p. 22], granite [p. 21], pure lime, hydraulic lime [p. 23], Portland and Roman cements [p. 24], mortars [p. 25], concretes [p. 25], grout [p. 25], asphalte [p. 26], timber of different kinds in common use [p. 26], cast and wrought iron [p. 32], lead [p. 37].

"4th. Constructive details, as follows:—

"The ordinary methods of timbering excavations, such as for foundations to walls, or for laying down sewers [p. 39];

the erection of bricklayers' and masons' scaffolding [p. 41]; the construction of travellers [p. 44]; the use of piles in foundations [p. 47], hoop iron bond in brickwork [p. 74], diagonal and herring-bone courses in ditto [p. 69], damp-proof courses [p. 60], bond timber in walls and the objections to it [p. 74].

"He should know how bricks are laid in hollow walls [p. 61], window or door openings with splayed jambs [p. 70], flues [p. 77], chimneys [p. 77], fireplaces [p. 83], and arches up to about 20 feet span [p. 71]; how mortar joints are finished off, and the thickness usually allowed to them [p. 65].; why bricks and stones ought to be wetted before being laid [p. 66].

"He should be acquainted with the construction of brick ashlar walls [p. 56], rubble ashlar walls [p. 57], stone stairs [p. 146], wooden stairs (both dog-legged and open newel) [p. 159], skylights [p. 136], fire-proof floors [p. 133] (such as brick arches supported on rolled or cast-iron girders) [p. 180], Fox and Barrett's [p. 190], and Dennett's patent concrete floors [p. 183]), circular and egg-shaped drains [p. 75], roofs of iron [p. 95] or wood [p. 90], for spans up to 60 feet; the fixing of architraves [p. 116], linings [p. 120], and skirtings to walls [p. 117], shutters to windows [p. 127], lath, plaster, and battening to walls [p. 209], roof coverings of tiles [p. 102] and zinc [p. 107], slate ridges and hips [p. 112].

"Written answers will be required to some of the questions."

# CONTENTS

## CHAPTER III.

### EXCAVATIONS—SHORING—SCAFFOLDING—PILE FOUNDATIONS.



## CHAPTER IV.

### BRICKWORK AND MASONRY—

## CHAPTER VIII.



## CHAPTER IX.



## CHAPTER X.



## CHAPTER XI.

## CHAPTER XII.



## CHAPTER XIII.



## APPENDIX.

# ADVANCED BUILDING CONSTRUCTION

SEVERAL works on different subjects were consulted in the preparation of the Notes from which this volume has been abridged, among which may be mentioned the following:—

Adams' Designing Cast and Wrought Iron Structures.
Dobson and Tarn's Guide to Measuring.
Fairbairn's Application of Iron to Buildings.
Hurst's Architectural Surveyor's Hand-Book.
Latham's Sanitary Engineering.
Latham's Wrought Iron Bridges.
Laxton's Examples of Building Construction.
Matheson's Works in Iron.
Maynard's Bridges.
Molesworth's Pocket-book of Engineering Formulæ.
Newland's Carpenter's and Joiner's Assistant.
Nicholson's Works.
Pasley's Practical Architecture (Brickwork).
Proceedings of the Institute of Civil Engineers.
Proceedings of the Royal Institute of British Architects.
Rankine's Civil Engineering.
Reed on Iron Shipbuilding.
Seddon's Builders' Work.
Stoney on Strains.
Thwaites' Factories, Workshops, and Warehouses.
Transactions of the Society of Engineers.
Tredgold's Carpentry (1870 edition); also a new, valuable, and greatly extended edition, by Mr. Hurst, C.E.
Unwin's Wrought Iron Bridges and Roofs.
Woodbury's Fire Protection of Mills.
Wray's Application of Theory to the Practice of Construction (revised by Seddon).
The Professional Journals.

The assistance derived from the above-mentioned works and others has been acknowledged, as far as possible, wherever they have been quoted or otherwise made use of.

*Caution.*—Some of the figures which appear to be isometrical projections are purposely distorted in order to bring important points into view.

# ADVANCED
# BUILDING CONSTRUCTION.

## CHAPTER I.

### *STRESSES ON STRUCTURES.*

THIS chapter will give merely the information called for by the Syllabus for the Advanced Course. The subject is fully gone into in Part IV. of N.B.C.

The headings in this chapter, marked A to F, are quoted from the Syllabus (see p. vii), and mention the points required to be understood in the Advanced Course.

*Subjects required by Syllabus,*[1] *and* (*in brackets*) *the pages at which they are treated upon.*

A. *The nature of the stresses to which the different parts of simple structures are subjected* [p. 2], *as follows:—*

B. *In the case of beams either fixed at one* [p. 7] *or both ends* [p. 7], *or supported* [p. 5] *or continuous* [p. 8], *the student should know which parts of the beam are in compression and which in tension.*

C. *He should know the difference in the strength of a girder carrying a given load at its centre, or uniformly distributed* [p. 8].

D. *He should be acquainted with the best forms for struts* [p. 9], *ties* [p. 10], *and beams, such as floor joists exposed to transverse stress* [p. 10].

E. *In the ordinary kinds of wooden or iron roof trusses* [p. 12], *and framed structures* [p. 13] *of a similar description, he should be able to distinguish the members in compression from those in tension.*

F. *He should be able, in the case of a concentrated* [p. 15] *or uniform load* [p. 15] *upon any part of a beam supported at both ends, to ascertain the proportion of the load transmitted to each point of support.*

**Stress and Strain.**—When a load or any force acts upon a structure or piece of material, it produces a change of form which is called the *strain.* The internal forces called out in the material to resist this strain are called the *stress.*

[1] The order of paragraphs C and D has for convenience been altered.

Thus a load hanging from a bar of iron lengthens it, causing a *strain*, and calls out in it the resistance of the fibres, which are under a tensile *stress*.

These two terms are sometimes used indiscriminately, but it is more accurate to make the above distinction between them.

## A. "The Nature of the Stresses to which the different Parts of Simple Structures are subjected."

These stresses are as follows :—

**Tension** is the stress produced by pulling; it elongates the body upon which it acts, and tends to cause rupture by tearing it asunder.

Thus if a rope or a bar of iron is subjected to a sufficient pulling or tensile stress it will break or tear across.

**Compression** is the stress produced by pressure; it shortens the body to which it is applied, and tends to cause rupture by crushing.

Thus a block of stone bearing a weight is under compression, and if the weight is sufficient it will be crushed.

Fig. 1.

**Transverse Stress** is one caused by bending the body on which it acts, and it tends to break it across.

Thus the weight in Fig. 1 bends the beam as shown, until, if the weight is sufficiently increased, the beam will break across as in Fig. 2.

Fig. 2.

**Shearing Stress** is that produced when one part of a body is forcibly pressed or pulled so as to tend to make it slide over another part.

Thus when two plates riveted together as in Fig. 3 are separated by

Fig. 3. Fig. 4.

pulling (or pushing) in opposite directions one plate slides upon the other and the rivet is sheared as in Fig. 4.

**Bearing Stress** is that which occurs when one body presses against another so as to tend to produce indentation or cutting.

FIG. 5. FIG. 6.

In Fig. 5 the plates *a* and *b* being pulled in opposite directions, the rivet *c*, being of harder iron than the plate, has borne upon it, making the hole larger, as shown at *d*, Fig. 6.

**Load.**—The load or weight upon a beam may be either concentrated at the centre as in Fig. 7, or uniformly distributed over the whole beam as in Fig. 8

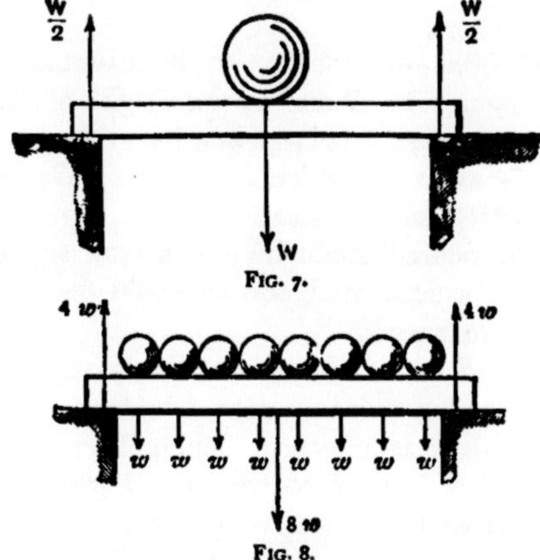


FIG. 7.

FIG. 8.

There may be concentrated loads at any point or points in the length of the beam, as in Figs. 9 and 10; or the load

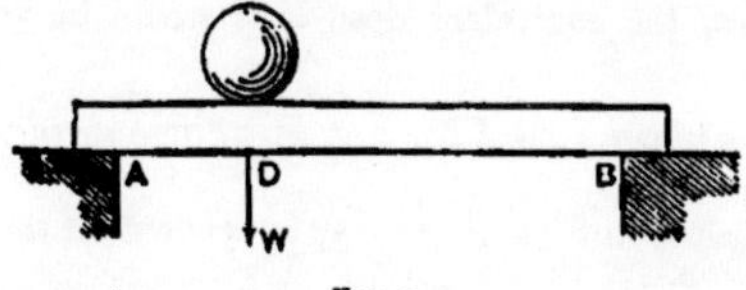


FIG. 9.

may be uniformly distributed over a portion only of the beam, as in Fig. 11.

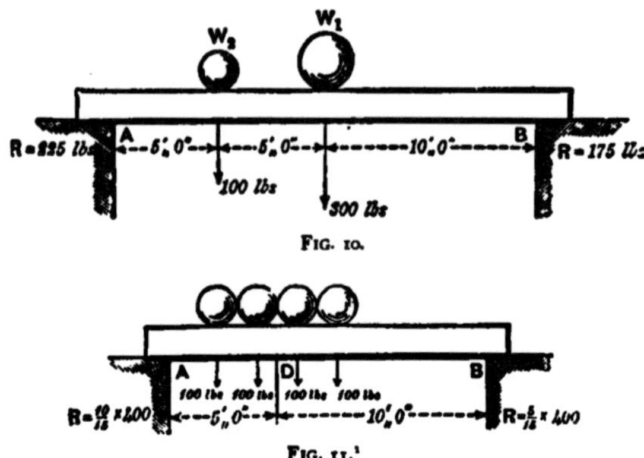


Fig. 10.

Fig. 11.[1]

*Weight of Beam.*—In addition to the external loads represented in the figures by W and *w*, the weight of the beam or girder itself must, when it is large and heavy, be considered.

**A Dead Load** is one which is very gradually and steadily applied, and which remains steady.

Thus water poured gradually into a tank supported by a girder would be a dead load, and so would the tank and the weight of the girder itself.

**A Live Load** is one which is suddenly applied, as in the case of trains coming suddenly upon a bridge. It is generally taken as equivalent in effect to double its amount of dead load. Thus a live load of 10 tons would produce the same amount of stress as a dead load of 20 tons.

**A Mixed Load,** consisting partly of live load and partly of dead load, may be reduced to an equivalent amount of dead load by doubling the live load and adding it to the dead load.

Thus, if a girder weighs 500 tons (dead load), and is subject to a live load of 900 tons, the equivalent dead load would be $500 + (2 \times 900) =$ 2300 tons.

**The Breaking Load** for any structure or piece of material

[1] The dimensions in Figs. 10 11 may be ignored for the present. They are explained at pp. 17, 18.

is that dead load which will just produce fracture in the structure or material.

**The Working or Safe Load** is the greatest dead load which the structure or material can safely be permitted to bear in practice.

**The Breaking Stress** is that caused by the breaking load; it is sometimes called the *ultimate stress.*

**The Working Stress** is that caused by the working or safe load; it is sometimes called the **Limiting or Safe Stress.**

It is evident that structures intended to stand must not be subjected to breaking loads or breaking stresses, but only to safe loads and working stresses (see Table, p. 36).

**The Factor of Safety** is the ratio in which the breaking load or stress exceeds the working load or stress.

That is, it is the figure by which the breaking load or stress is divided to obtain the working load or stress.

Thus if the breaking tensile stress of a bar of iron is 20 tons per square inch, and it is subjected to a working stress of only 5 tons, the factor of safety is $\frac{20}{5} = 4$.

---

## B. "Beams supported at Ends, fixed at one or both Ends, or continuous," and Cantilevers "to know which Parts of the Beam are in Compression and which in Tension."

### Supported Beams.

Beam supported at both Ends with a Breaking Load in the Centre.—A rectangular wooden beam, supported at the ends, when subjected to a concentrated load greater than it can bear, breaks as shown in Fig. 12.

Fig. 12.

The beam bends, sinking most just under the weight, and

the fibres of the upper portion of the beam are crushed, and those of the lower portion torn asunder, as shown on a larger scale in Fig. 13.

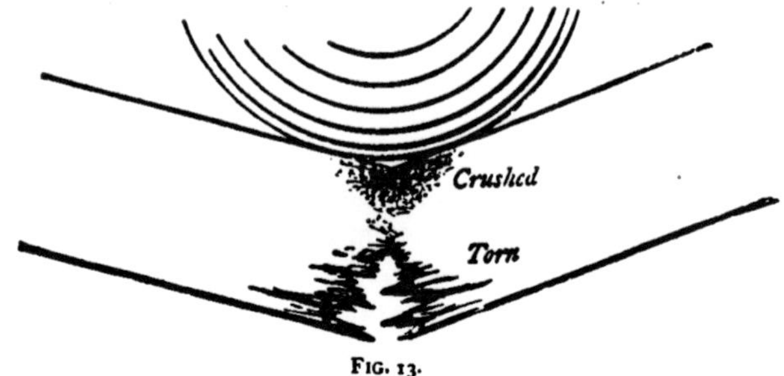


FIG. 13.

BEAM SUPPORTED AT BOTH ENDS AND WITH A UNIFORMLY DISTRIBUTED LOAD.—A load uniformly distributed over the beam would produce rupture in the same way, but the form of the beam before rupture would be slightly different.

A BEAM SUPPORTED AT BOTH ENDS AND SUBJECT TO A SAFE LOAD—that is, one much smaller than is required to

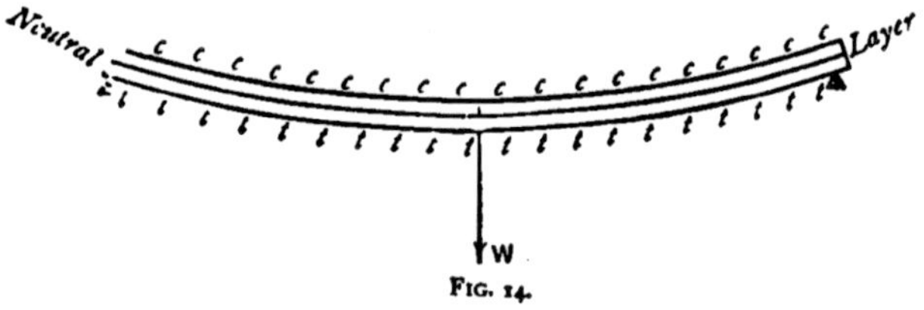


FIG. 14.

break it—will bend to a certain extent, and the fibres of the upper part of the beam will be in compression, and those of the lower part in tension, as shown in Fig. 14. There is a layer between the upper and the lower fibres, in which there is neither compression nor tension, which is called the *neutral layer.*

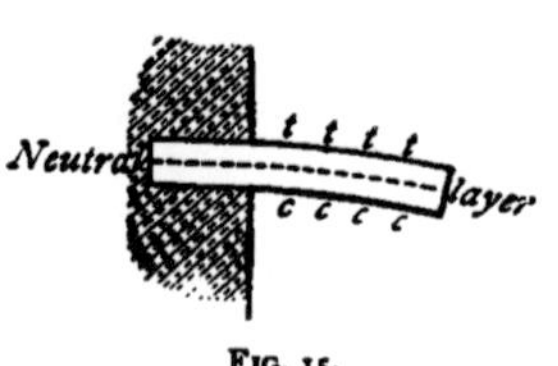


FIG. 15.

**A Cantilever**, however it may be loaded, has the upper fibres in tension and the lower in compression, as shown in Fig. 15.

## Fixed Beams.

A Beam fixed at Both Ends—that is, so fixed that the ends cannot tilt up when the beam is loaded—is shown in Fig. 16.

Such a beam is in the condition of two cantilevers, A*f* and B*i*, carrying a beam *fi* between them, which is supported at its ends *f* and *i* by hanging from the ends *f* and *i* of the cantilevers.

From the figure it will be seen that the upper portion of the beam is in tension from A to *f* and from B to *i*; the remainder from *i* to *f* is in compression.

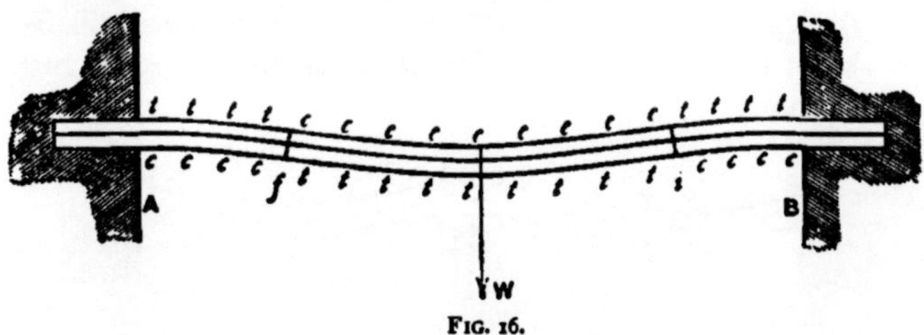


Fig. 16.

The lower portion of the beam is under compression from A to *f* and B to *i*, the central portion *if* being in tension.

It will be noticed that at the points *i* and *f* the nature of the stress in each case changes; *i* and *f* are called the *points of contraflexure*, and their distances from A and B depend upon the form of section of the beam, and the distribution of the load, etc. Roughly speaking, the points of contraflexure are generally distant about ¼ of the span from the abutments.

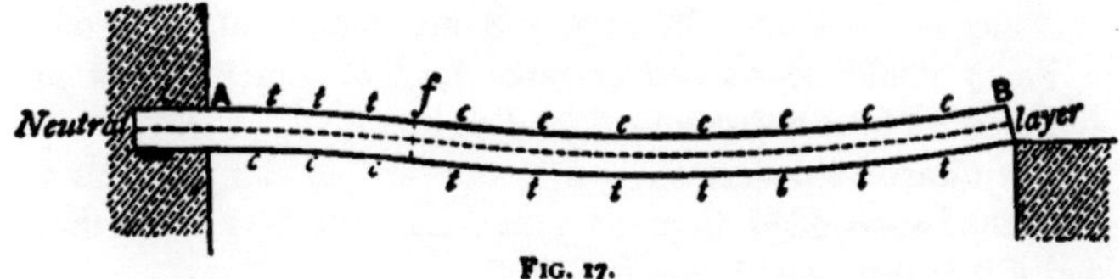


Fig. 17.

A Beam fixed at one End and supported at the other (Fig. 17) is like a combination of a cantilever A*f* and a supported beam *f* B; and the portions in tension and compression respectively are shown by the letters *t t t* and *c c c*.

A CONTINUOUS BEAM is one that extends without break in itself over two or more spans.

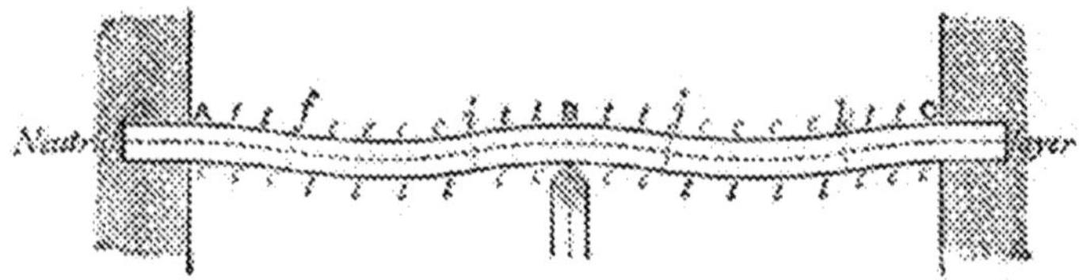

FIG. 18.

*If the ends are fixed* the compressions and tensions will be as shown by *c c c* and *t t t* in Fig. 18, resembling those of two fixed beams

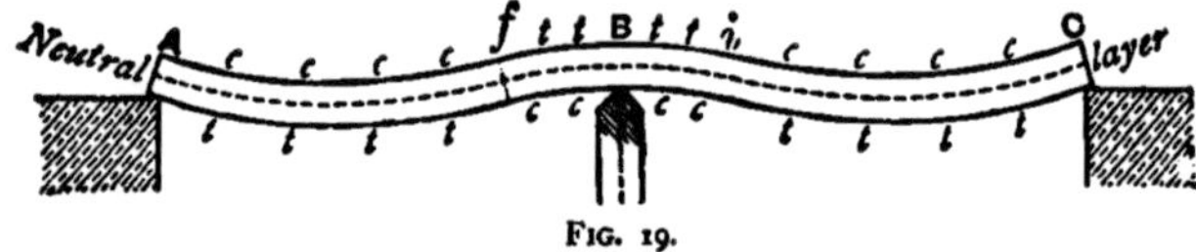


FIG. 19.

*If the ends are supported* the stresses will be as shown in Fig. 19, the arms in each span being like those of a beam fixed at one end and supported at the other (Fig. 17).

## C. "Difference in Strength of a Girder carrying a given Load at its Centre or Uniformly Distributed."

*On Beams.*—A beam that can bear a given load concentrated at its centre can bear twice that load uniformly distributed over its length.

Thus if the beams in Figs. 7, 8 are similar, and the one in Fig. 7 could bear a concentrated load of 400 lbs., that in Fig. 9 could bear a distributed load of 800 lbs.

*On Cantilevers.*—Similarly a cantilever that can just bear a given load suspended from its outer end can bear twice that load if it is distributed over its length.

**Difference in Strength between Beams of uniform Section supported at both Ends and those fixed at both Ends, or fixed at one End and supported at the other.**

*A beam fixed at both ends, with a concentrated load at the centre,* is *twice* as strong as the same beam supported at both ends and similarly loaded.

*A beam fixed at both ends, with a uniform load throughout its length,* is 1½ times as strong as the same beam supported at both ends and similarly loaded.

*A beam fixed at one end, and supported at the other, with a concentrated load in the centre,* is 1½ times as strong as the same beam supported at both ends and similarly loaded.

*A beam fixed at one end and supported at the other, with a uniform load throughout its length* is of the same strength as the same beam supported at both ends and similarly loaded.

---

## D. "Best Forms for Struts, Ties, and Beams, such as floor joists exposed to transverse Stress."

### Best Form for Struts.

*Timber Struts* should be rectangular in section, and of the same section throughout.

*Cast-Iron Struts* may be of these cross sections, and tapering in their length, widening from one end to the other as in a column, or from both ends.

FIG. 20.  FIG. 21.

*Wrought-Iron Struts* are often of these cross sections:

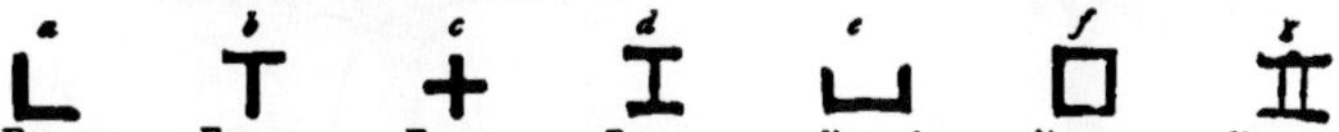

*a* FIG. 22. *b* FIG. 23. *c* FIG. 24. *d* FIG. 25. *e* FIG. 26. *f* FIG. 27. *g* FIG. 28.

Of these *c*, *d*, and *g*, are the best. Fig. 29 is an elevation of *g*, for the other forms the section is uniform throughout the length of the strut; *g* is very useful for struts of roofs.

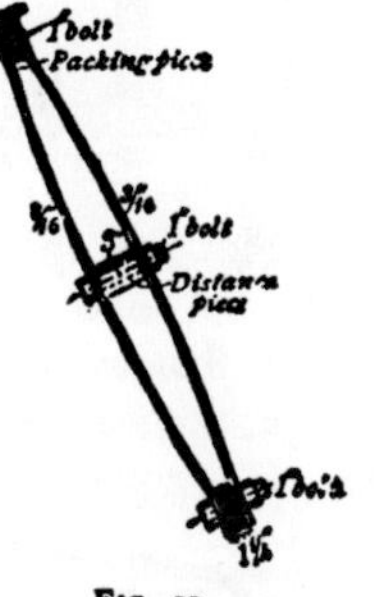

FIG. 29.

**Long Struts or Compression Bars** are those which are so long in proportion to their width that they fail by bending before crushing.

**Short Struts or Compression Bars** are those which do not bend under the load, but fail by actual crushing.

**Long Struts fixed at the Ends** are much stronger than those of which the ends are hinged or rounded. If both ends are fixed they are 3 times, if one end only is fixed, 1½ times, as strong.

### Best Form for Ties.

Any cross section is suitable for a rod or bar in tension, whether it be made of timber or wrought iron. Cast iron should never be used for ties.

### Best Form for Beams subject to Transverse Stress.

TIMBER BEAMS may be of rectangular cross section uniform throughout their length. The deeper they are the better both for strength and stiffness.

IRON GIRDERS are of a section roughly resembling an I, the upper and lower horizontal portions are called the *flanges*, and the upright portion the *web*.

CAST-IRON BEAMS should have a cross section in which the lower flange to resist tension should have an area from three or four to six times as great as that of the upper flange which is to resist compression (see E.B.C.D.).

Fig. 30 shows a section with flanges having areas as 6 to 1, and Fig. 31 with flanges as 4 to 1.

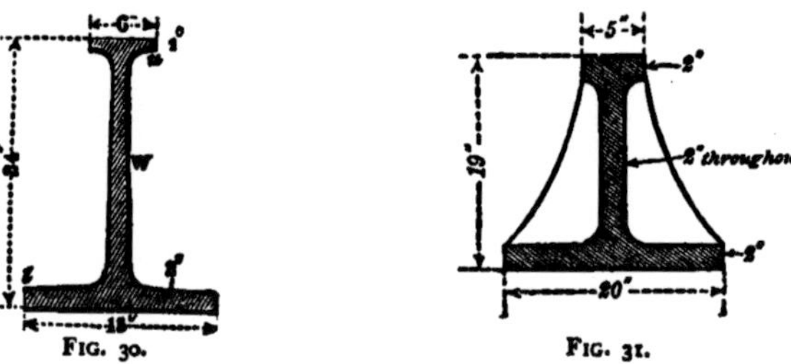

FIG. 30. FIG. 31.

And Figs. 32 to 35 show plans and elevations of cast-iron girders for uniformly distributed loads.

The flanges are sometimes made to differ in thickness as in Fig 30, the web tapering from one to the other, or the metal may be of equal thickness throughout as in Fig. 31.

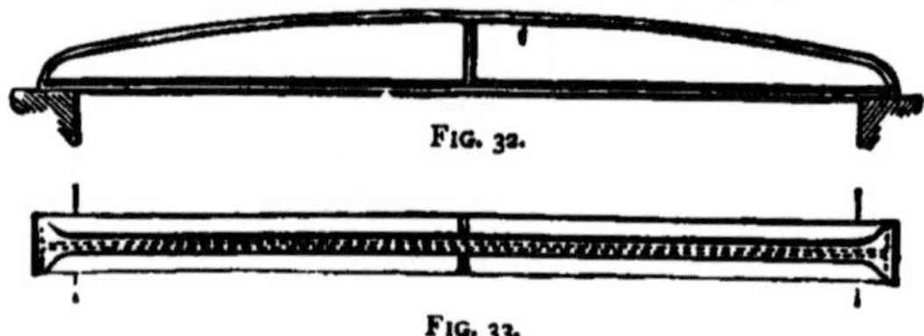
FIG. 32.

FIG. 33.

Figs. 32, 33, are the elevation and plan of a girder of uniform width, the depth being varied according to the stress

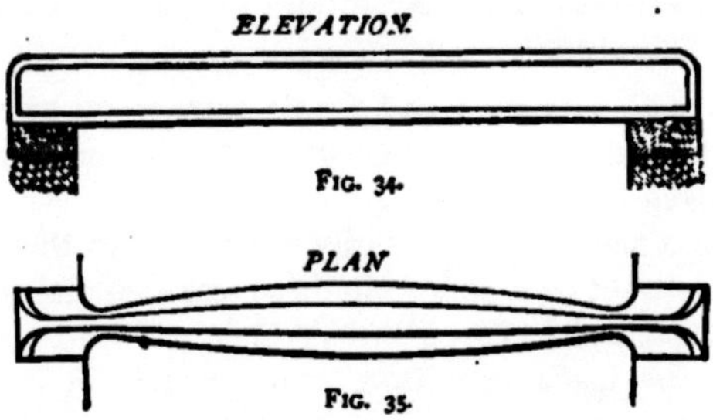


Fig. 34.

Fig. 35.

to be borne. Figs. 34, 35, are the elevation and plan of a girder of uniform depth, the width of the flanges being varied to suit the stress.

Rolled-Iron Joists are of uniform section like Fig. 36 throughout, the flanges being similar and of equal area (see p. 179).

Fig. 36.

Plate Girders are also of a general I form, built up with a plate and angle irons, riveted together as in Figs. 37, 38, or, where additional strength is required, with one or more plates in the flanges (one plate is shown in Fig. 39), and stiffeners to support the web.

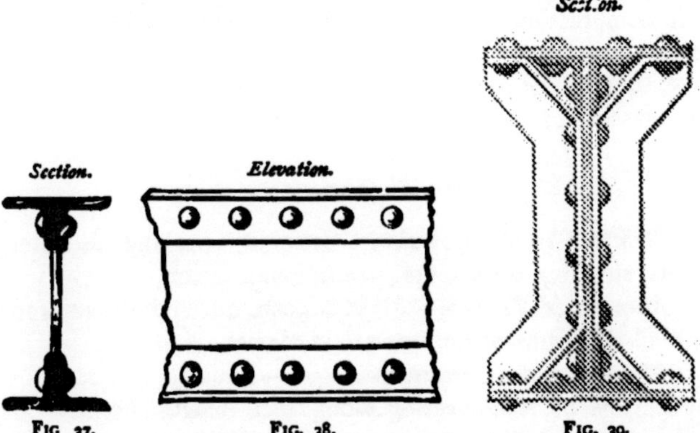


Fig 37. Fig. 38. Fig. 39.

**E. "In the ordinary kinds of Wooden or Iron Roof Trusses and Framed Structures of a similar description, to distinguish the Members in Compression from those in Tension."**

There is no very short and simple method for ascertaining whether the members of a truss are in tension or compression under a given load in any position.

The information can be easily obtained, but the methods employed cannot be explained in these very short notes. They are fully explained in Part IV., N.B.C.

When the loads vary from time to time in position, a member which may with one position of the loads be in tension may with another position of the load have no stress upon it, or even one of an opposite nature.

Thus in an ordinary king-post roof (see Fig. 43) the wind blowing from the right causes a compressive stress upon the strut on that side, but no stress whatever on the other strut, and when the wind is from the left, the stresses on the struts are just reversed.

The student can, however, easily learn and carry in his head the nature of the stresses to which each member of a roof truss is practically subjected.

In Plate III. and in Figs. 40–44, which give a great many forms of roof trusses, each of the members shown in thick lines is in compression, and each of those shown in thin lines is in tension, under all loads that can practically come upon the roof, such as the weight of the roof, of snow lying upon it, and the pressure of the wind upon both sides in turn.

## Roofs Generally.

*Members in Compression.*—Generally speaking all rafters, struts, straining beams, etc., are in compression.

*Members in Tension.*—All king posts, queen posts, and rods, and all tie beams or tie rods are in tension.

*Members under Transverse Stress.*—Principal rafters loaded by purlins or roof-covering along their length, between the points at which they are supported, as in Fig. 43, are subject to transverse stress as well as compression, and tie beams carrying ceiling joists are also subject to transverse stress.

TIMBER ROOFS.—Figs. 40–44 give skeleton diagrams of ordinary roof trusses (see also Plate IV.).

FIG. 40. FIG. 41.

*Couple Roof* (Fig. 40) *and Tied Couple Roof* (41).—The rafters are in compression, and the tie in Fig. 41 is in tension.

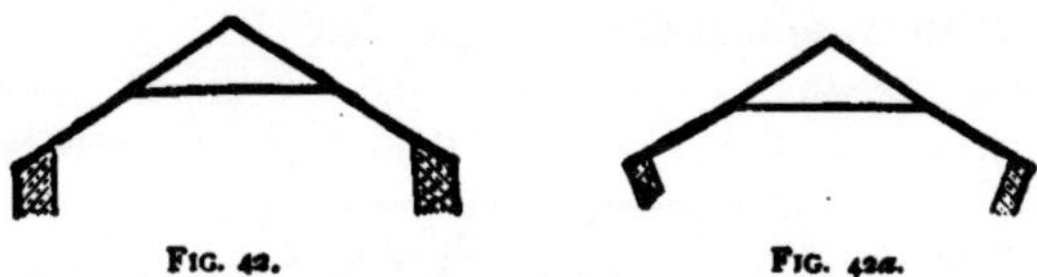

FIG. 42. FIG. 42*a*.

*Collar Beam Roof.*—In this, so long as the walls stand firm (Fig. 42), the beam is a strut and supports the rafters, but if the walls are weak and give way, the beam becomes a tie as shown in Fig. 42*a*.

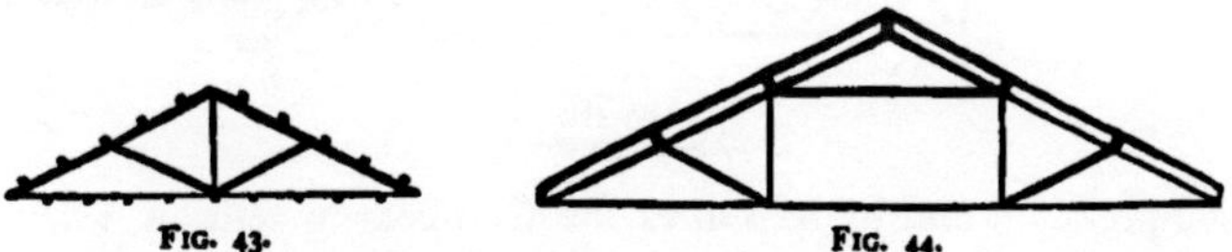

FIG. 43. FIG. 44.

*King-Post Roof and Queen-Post Roof* (Figs. 43, 44).—Nothing need be said about these, except that in Fig. 43 the principal rafters being loaded by the roof-covering between their points of support are subject to transverse stress, as well as the compression upon them, and the tie beam being loaded by the ceiling is also subject to transverse stress as well as tension.

When the purlins are only at the points at which the principal rafter is supported, as in Fig. 44, it is not subject to transverse stress, nor is the tie beam, where there is no ceiling.

### Other Framed Structures.

*Trussed Beams.*—The diagrams, Figs. 45, 46, show by thick

lines the members in compression, and in thin lines the members in tension in trussed beams.

These will be the same in nature though not in amount,

Fig. 45. Fig. 46.

whether the load be distributed along the upper surface or concentrated at points.

When the load is distributed between the points where the bracing joins the upper beam, the latter is of course subject to transverse stress as well as to compression.

*Braced Girders.*—Figs. 47–50 are common forms of braced girders, and they show by thick lines the members in

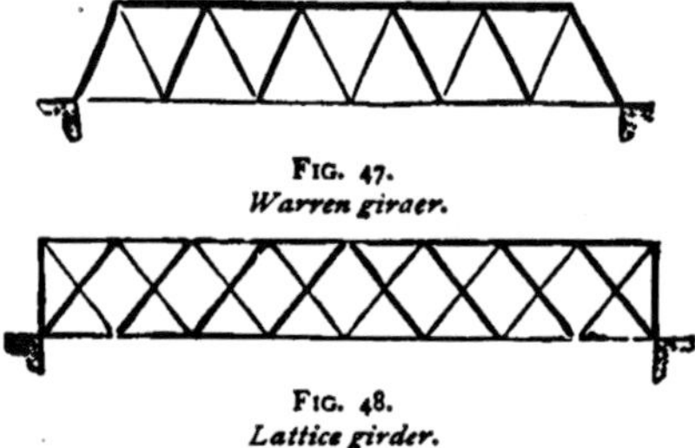

Fig. 47.
*Warren giraer.*

Fig. 48.
*Lattice girder.*

compression, and by thin lines the members in tension, when the girders are carrying loads uniformly distributed along the lower flange or at the points where the braces join that flange.

The stresses will be similar in character when the load is on the upper flange, but in Fig. 49 an additional bar will have to be introduced as dotted, and it will be in compression.

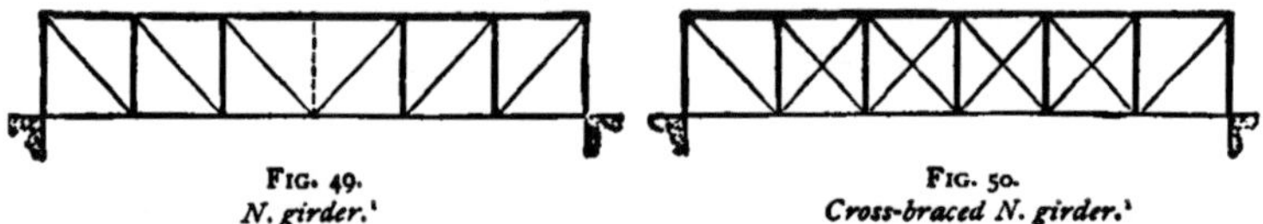

Fig. 49.
*N. girder.*[1]

Fig. 50.
*Cross-braced N. girder.*[1]

Such girders are frequently suspended between their abutments from the ends of their upper flanges; in such a case the construction at the ends of the girder is slightly

[1] Sometimes called *Whipple-Murphy* girder.

different, but the nature of the stresses is practically the same as shown in the Figures.

F. **"In the case of a concentrated or uniform load upon any part of a beam supported at both ends, to ascertain the proportion of the load transmitted to each point of support."**

CONCENTRATED LOAD IN CENTRE OF BEAM.—If a concentrated weight W be placed upon the centre of a beam

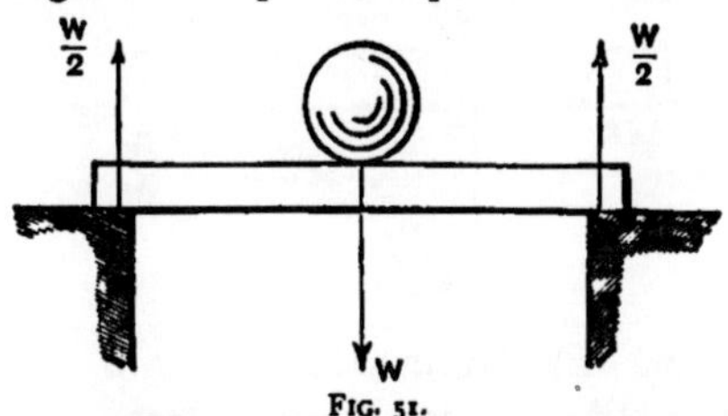


FIG. 51.

supported at the ends, then half the weight is borne at each end. Thus in Fig. 51 half the weight W is borne on each abutment.

LOAD UNIFORMLY DISTRIBUTED OVER WHOLE LENGTH OF BEAM.—If a load, 8 *w*, Fig. 52, is uniformly distributed over

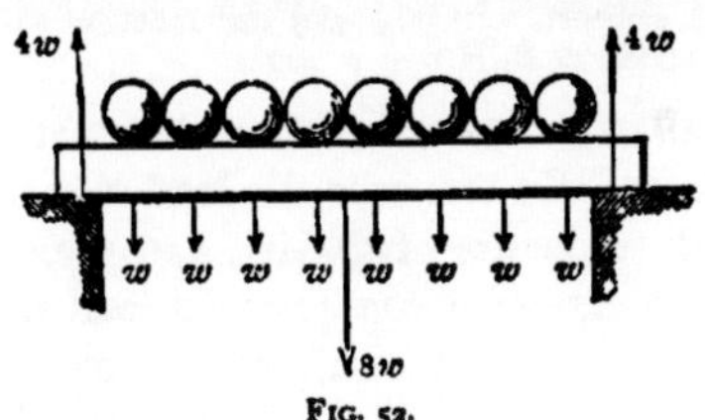


FIG. 52.

a beam, then again half the load (in this case 4 *w*) is borne by each abutment.

WEIGHT OF THE BEAM ITSELF.—The weight of the beam itself is like a uniform load, and half that weight is supported by each abutment.

LOAD AT ANY POINT OF BEAM.—The proportion of the load borne by each support may, avoiding formulas, be found by the following rule:—

RULE.—*If a load is placed anywhere on a beam supported at both ends, then the proportion of the load borne by either support is equal to the load, multiplied by the distance from its centre of gravity to the other support, and divided by the length of the beam between the supports.*

CONCENTRATED LOAD.—Thus in Fig. 53 the load W is 400 lbs., and it is distant 5′ from A and 10′ from B.

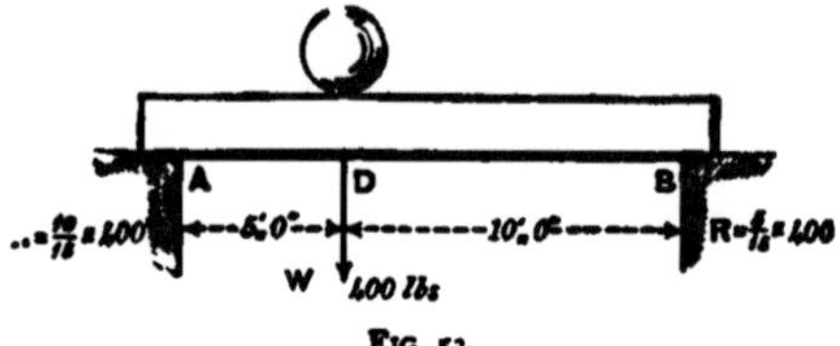


FIG. 53.

The proportion of W borne at A is equal to

$$\frac{\text{W} \times \text{distance DB}}{\text{Length AB}}, \textit{i.e.} = \frac{400 \text{ lbs.} \times 10 \text{ feet}}{15 \text{ feet}} = 266\tfrac{2}{3} \text{ lbs.}$$

The proportion of W borne at B is equal to

$$\frac{\text{W} \times \text{distance DA}}{\text{Length AB}}, \textit{i.e.} = \frac{400 \text{ lbs.} \times 5 \text{ feet}}{15 \text{ feet}} = 133\tfrac{1}{3} \text{ lbs.}$$

**Reaction.**—The proportion of the load borne by each support is called the reaction at that support. In Fig. 474 the reaction at A is shown as $R = \frac{10}{15} \times 400$. Reaction at B, $R = \frac{5}{15} \times 400$.

LOAD UNIFORMLY DISTRIBUTED OVER CENTRAL PART OF THE LENGTH OF A BEAM.—In this case the load may be considered as acting through its centre of gravity, and then its reactions are found as in the case of a concentrated load at the centre.

Thus if the load were uniformly spread over an equal distance on each side of the centre of the beam as in Fig. 54, then half the load is borne by each support.

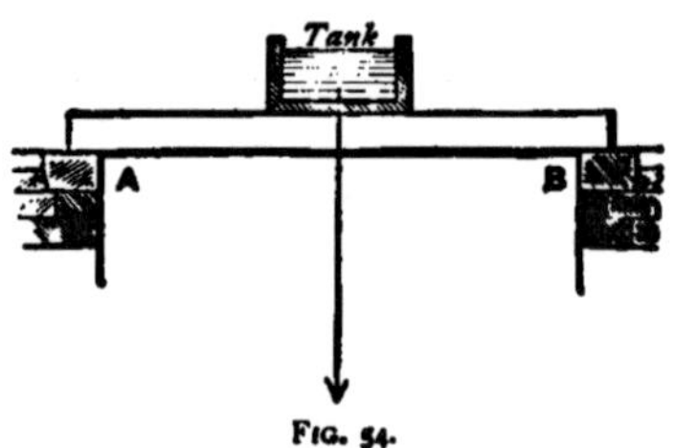


FIG. 54.

Similarly, when the uniform load is made up of a number of weights 4 *w*, then each support takes 2 *w*.

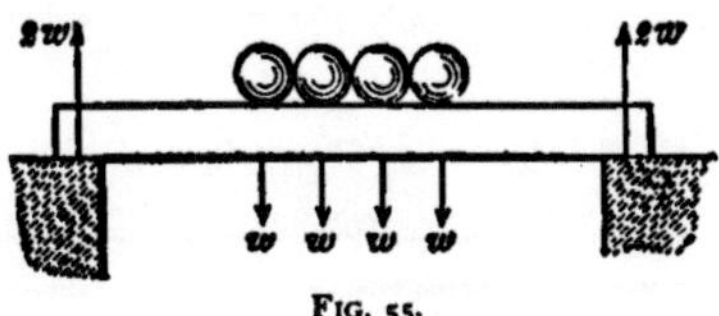


Fig. 55.

## Load uniformly distributed over any Part of the Length of a Beam.

In this case the load is equivalent to a single concentrated load at the centre of gravity of the distributed load.

Thus in Fig. 56 the weight of the tank which is distributed over EF may be taken as acting at D through its centre of gravity.

The reactions are then just the same as in the case illustrated in Fig. 53.

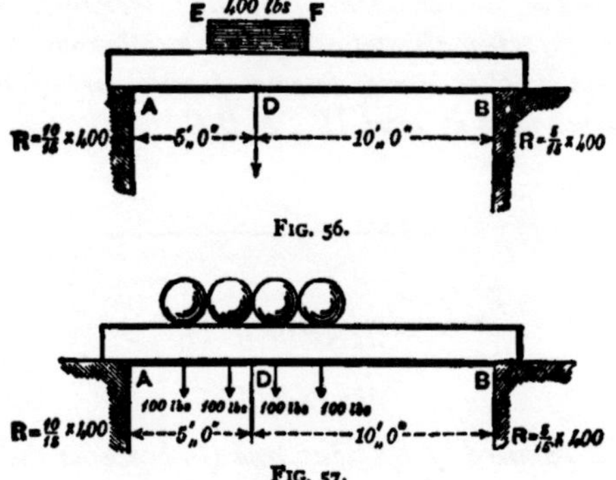


Fig. 56.

Fig. 57.

Again, when the distributed load is made up of separate weights as in Fig. 57, they may be considered as acting through their common centre of gravity, and the reactions are again the same as shown in Fig. 53.

**Any Number of Concentrated Loads on a Beam.**—When the loads are unequal, and placed unsymmetrically, the reaction of each at each support is found in turn. The total reaction at either support will be the sum of the reactions produced by each weight at that support.

Take a simple case, with only two unequal weights placed unsymmetrically, as shown in Fig. 58.

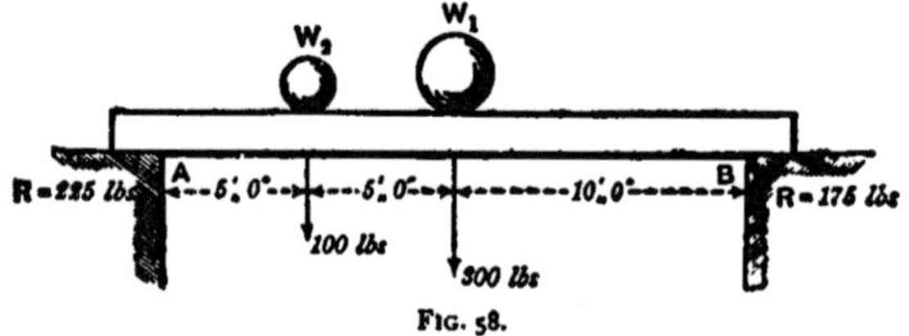


Fig. 58.

Applying the rule given above for a single weight not in the centre of the beam, we have—

| | at A | at B |
|---|---|---|
| Reaction produced by $W_1$ | $\frac{10}{20} W_1 = \frac{10}{20} \cdot 300 = 150$ | $\frac{10}{20} W_1 = \frac{10}{20} \cdot 300 = 150$ |
| " " $W_2$ | $\frac{15}{20} W_2 = \frac{15}{20} \cdot 100 = 75$ | $\frac{5}{20} W_2 = \frac{5}{20} \cdot 100 = 25$ |
| Total reaction produced by $W_1 +$ " *i.e.* by 300 + 100 lbs. | 225 lbs. | 175 lbs. |

---

N.B.—*The consideration of bending moments, moments of resistance, shearing stresses, etc., and calculations for strength, even for the simplest beams, does not form a part of this Course, but is entered upon in Part IV., N.B.C.*

---

## CHAPTER II.

### *MATERIALS.*

*Subjects required by Syllabus, and (in brackets) the pages at which they are treated upon.*

*The nature, application, and characteristic peculiarities of the following materials in ordinary use for building purposes, viz. :—*

*Bricks of different kinds in common use* [p. 19]; *York, Portland, Caen, and Bath Stones* [p. 22] (*or stones of a similar description*) [p. 22]; *granite* [p. 21], *pure lime* [p. 23], *hydraulic lime* [p. 23], *Portland and Roman cements* [p. 24], *mortars* [p. 25], *concretes* [p. 25], *grout* [p. 25], *asphalte* [p. 26], *timber of different kinds in common use* [p. 26], *cast and wrought iron* [p. 32], *lead* [p. 37].

This chapter will contain only so much information about the materials used in the construction of buildings as is necessary to meet the above requirements of the Second Stage or Advanced Course. Full information on the subject is given in Part III., N.B.C.

BRICKS.

**Manufacture.**—Ordinary building bricks are made of clay or other earths subjected to various processes, such as clearing from stones, grinding if necessary, and mixing in some cases with chalk. These vary somewhat according to local practice, influenced by the nature of the material. The clay is formed, after mixing with water to a plastic condition, to the required shape by hand in moulds, or by machines, dried, and then burnt either in *kilns* (large ovens) or *clamps* (piles of the dried bricks themselves).

HAND-MADE BRICKS have a *frog*, or indentation, on one side, which lightens the brick and forms a key for the mortar.

MACHINE-MADE BRICKS are generally denser and heavier than those made by hand. In some machines the bricks are cut off by a wire—they then have no frog; in others the clay is pressed when nearly dry in a mould, and these generally have a frog, and are often pierced through with holes to make them lighter.

**Classification of Bricks.**—This differs in various localities, but in some brickfields near London there are three general classes :—

*Malms*, in which the clay is mixed with about $\frac{1}{16}$ chalk, and cinders.

*Washed*, in which less chalk is added to the clay.

*Common*, in which no chalk is added.

These classes are divided into several varieties, the principal of which are—

*Cutters* or *Rubbers* of even texture and very soft, so that they can be cut and rubbed to accurate shapes and to a smooth face.

*Facing Paviors*, hard-burnt malm bricks of good shape and colour, used for facing superior work.

*Hard Paviors* are more burnt, slightly blemished, and used for copings, superior facing, etc.

*Stocks*, good hard bricks, used generally for ordinary good work.

*Grizzles* and *Place Bricks*, which are weak, under-burnt, inferior bricks.

*Chuffs* are bricks on which the rain has fallen when they were hot, making them full of cracks and useless.

*Burrs* are lumps of over-burnt bricks vitrified and run together.

MACHINE-MADE BRICKS may be classed as *Pressed* or *Wire-cut*, of each of which there are several varieties.

**Characteristics of good ordinary Bricks.**—They should be well burnt, hard, ringing well when struck together, free from cracks and lumps, especially lumps of lime, regular in shape and uniform in size, not absorbing more than $\frac{1}{8}$ of their weight of water.

**Size and Weight.**—This varies; but near London ordinary bricks are about $8\frac{3}{4}$ inches long, $4\frac{1}{4}$ inches broad, and $2\frac{1}{2}$ inches thick, and weigh about 7 lbs. each.

In order to obtain good brickwork, the length of each brick should just exceed twice its breadth by the thickness of a mortar joint.

**Varieties of Bricks.**—Besides the ordinary bricks above described there are innumerable varieties in the market, the most important of which are—

WHITE BRICKS, made from peculiar clays, sometimes with the addition of a large proportion of chalk. The best known are the *Suffolk* and *Beaulieu* bricks.

*Gault Bricks* are from the clay between the upper and lower greensand. They are white, and generally very dense and heavy, being to some extent lightened by a large frog, or by holes through their thickness.

STAFFORDSHIRE BLUE BRICKS are made from the local clays, which contain some 10 per cent. of oxide of iron, converted under great heat into the black oxide. They are of a dark blue colour or nearly black. They have an enormous resistance and compression, are very hard, non-porous, very durable, and much used for paving, copings, etc.

FAREHAM RED BRICKS are made near Portsmouth, and are much used for superior face-work.

ENAMELLED BRICKS have a white china-like surface, and are used for lavatories, dairies, etc.

DUTCH CLINKERS are very small, well-burnt hard bricks, used for paving.

MOULDED and PURPOSE-MADE BRICKS may be obtained of every possible form, and not only save much labour in cutting ordinary bricks, but weather much better, being as a rule of better material.

**Fire Bricks** are made from "fire clays," found generally in the coal-measures. They are capable of withstanding very high temperatures, and are much used for lining furnaces, etc.

**Terra Cotta** is made from mixtures of peculiar clays with ground glass, pottery, and sometimes sand. It is apt to warp in manufacture, but is much used for building, is very hard, strong, and durable in any atmosphere.

**Pipes and Clay Goods.**—These are innumerable in form, but it is important to distinguish between the material of which they are made.

*Unglazed ware* is made from ordinary clays, weak, and unable to resist frost.

*Fire-clay ware*, made from fire clays and glazed, used for common work.

*Stoneware*, made from Lias clays, glazed, is very strong, durable, and used for the best work.

*Terra Cotta*, made from the material above described. It is inferior to stoneware, being more absorbent, but better than fire-clay goods.

## STONE.

**Characteristics of good Building Stone.**—Stone is found of many different descriptions and qualities, but the chief characteristics required in a good stone for building are as follows:—

DURABILITY, which depends chiefly upon chemical composition; for a large proportion of lime will render the stone unfit to resist the acid atmosphere of towns—a stone that is not durable out of doors is said to "weather" badly. The durability is, however, to some extent influenced by its PHYSICAL STRUCTURE, thus marble is more durable than chalk, though chemically the same. HARDNESS (for quoins, etc.), FACILITY FOR WORKING (for carvings, etc.), and APPEARANCE, have sometimes to be considered.

**Classification of Building Stones** may be taken as follows:—

Granites and other igneous rocks.
Slates.
Sandstones.
Limestones.

**Granite** is composed of quartz, felspar, and mica. It is, as a rule, very durable and hard to work, and is used for heavy engineering structures and for massive buildings, also in the parts of ordinary buildings, such as steps, that undergo most wear. Mica and some kinds of felspar are liable to decay, but quartz is always hard and durable; therefore the more quartz a granite contains the better.

The best-known granites are found in Scotland and Cornwall.

**Slates** for roofing are well known as regards appearance, and need not be described. They should be fine-grained, hard, with a metallic ring; not friable at the edges; tough, so as not to splinter when cut or holed; and non-absorptive. The best varieties come from Wales. Slate is also used in slabs of from one to three inches thick for cisterns, sills, skirtings, landings, etc.

**Sandstones** are found in great variety. They consist of grains of sand held together by cementing material, upon the nature of which latter depends their durability.

The best-known sandstones are as follows:—

YORKSHIRE SANDSTONES.—These have a coarse grit, are very strong, can be obtained in large blocks of a light brownish-white colour, and are much used for heavy engineering work. The best-known quarries are *Bramley Fall*, *Bradford*, *Scotgate Ash*, etc., etc.

MANSFIELD STONE is found in Nottinghamshire in two colours, red and white, and is well adapted for ashlar work, columns, etc.

CRAIGLEITH STONE, found near Edinburgh, is the most durable sandstone in the country, and useful for any good masonry.

**Limestones** consist of grains of carbonate of lime cemented together by the same substance, or by the same mixed with silica.

They vary greatly in texture, being either *granular*, with grains varying much in size, or *compact*, not showing grains.

The principal varieties are—

BATH STONE.—An even-grained, comparatively soft white stone; some of it weathers badly. It is obtainable in large blocks, and much used for mouldings and carved work. There are several quarries, such as Box, Combe, Corsham, etc.

PORTLAND STONE.—Several distinct kinds are found in the quarries. *Roach and Whitbed Roach* are full of shell casts, and not much used in ordinary buildings. *Whitbed* and *Basebed*, known also as "*Bestbed*," are most valuable white building stones, of even texture, and durable in most positions. Both descriptions present the same appearance, but Whitbed is harder to work and more durable than the other.

KENTISH RAG is a hard, compact, non-absorbent gray stone, very difficult to work, and used chiefly for rubble.

YELLOW MANSFIELD STONE is a magnesian limestone, composed almost entirely of carbonate of magnesia and lime, and is an even-grained stone fit for ashlar and carving.

CAEN STONE is found in Normandy, but much used in this country. It is of a cream colour, very soft when just quarried, easily worked and carved, but weathers badly.

**Marble** is a very dense, compact form of limestone that will take a polish; some varieties are beautifully marked, and are used chiefly for decorative purposes.

**Natural Bed.**—The importance of placing stones in walls with their natural beds—*i.e.* the layers in which they were geologically deposited, horizontal—has been mentioned in

E.B.C.D.; in cornices or overhanging work the natural bed should be vertical and at right angles to the face.

## LIMES AND CEMENTS, MORTAR, GROUT, CONCRETE, ETC.

### LIME.

**Quicklime** is produced by burning limestone in a kiln, the carbonic acid is driven off, and the result is quicklime.

**Slaking** is effected by thoroughly wetting a quicklime and covering it up. It then swells, becomes hot, gives out puffs of steam, and falls to powder, which is called *slacked lime.*

The slaking process is very violent with rich limes, less so with poor limes, and very slight in the case of hydraulic limes.

**Setting.**—When a lime or cement is made with water into a pat, and exposed to the air, it will harden less or more according to its quality, until in most cases it becomes quite hard throughout its bulk. With hydraulic limes and cements the hardening will take place even better if the pat is placed under water.

**Pure, Rich, or Fat Lime** is that produced from pure limestones, such as marble or chalk, containing nothing but carbonate of lime. Such a lime slakes furiously, but a pat made from it will never thoroughly set or harden, even in the air, and if placed under water it will simply dissolve away. Rich limes cannot, therefore, make good mortar or concrete, but are the best for whitewashing and sanitary purposes.

**Poor Lime** is from limestone containing useless impurities, and it shares all the defects of rich limes.

**Hydraulic Limes** are produced from limestones which contain from 5 to 30 per cent. of clay in a peculiar form. They slake with more or less difficulty, but will set, becoming quite hard in air or under water, and are therefore adapted for making good mortar and concrete.

TEST.—To ascertain whether a limestone is hydraulic, it should be made red hot, to drive off the carbonic acid. The resulting quicklime should be slaked, made up with water into a pat, and then placed under still-water, to see if it will set there. If it does not set, but dissolves or becomes disintegrated, it will show that the lime is not hydraulic.

## CEMENTS.

Cements are either natural or artificial.

**Roman Cement** is the best-known natural cement in this country. It is made by burning nodules containing some 30 to 45 per cent. of clay, found in the London clay. This cement is of a rich brown colour, and weighs about 75 lbs. a bushel. It sets in about 15 minutes, and is valuable for tide-work or stucco, but its ultimate strength is very small.

**Other quick-setting Cements.**—For the names and uses of other somewhat similar cements see p. 209. They are not used for mortar or concrete, but chiefly for plasterers' work.

**Portland Cement** is an artificial compound made by mixing chalk and clay in water in the proportion of about 75 per cent. chalk to 25 per cent. clay, drying and burning the mixture in kilns, and grinding the resulting "clinker" to such a fineness that 90 per cent. of it will generally pass a sieve of 2500 meshes to the square inch, and it will weigh about 115 lbs. per bushel.

The result is a fine powder of greenish gray colour, which when mixed into a pat will set either in the air or under water, becoming hard in twenty-four hours, attaining considerable tensile strength in seven days, and in course of time a strength far greater than that of any other cement.

Fig. 59.

TESTING.—The tensile strength of samples of Portland cement is ascertained by forming the cement into *briquettes* or blocks, of the form shown in Fig. 59, the section at A being generally 1½ inch square. These are broken in a machine which applies slow tension upwards and downwards at K and K.

A good cement after setting seven days under water is expected not to break under a less weight than of about 800 lbs. on the area A (2¼ square inches), *i.e.* 355 lbs. per square inch.

COOLING.—It is of the utmost importance that Portland cement should be thoroughly *cool* when used—all the lime in it thoroughly air-slaked—otherwise it may swell in the work when used, and cause much damage. In order to cool it, it should be spread out on a floor protected from the weather, and turned over daily for some weeks, so that every part of it may become thoroughly air-slaked.

## MORTAR—CONCRETE.

**Mortar** is made by mixing, to the consistency of soft porridge, limes or cements with clean sands, the proportion of which depends upon the description of the lime or cement.

PROPORTION OF SAND.—*Rich and Poor Limes* may be mixed with a large proportion of sand (3 or 4 measures of sand to 1 of lime), for in any case they make mortars with very little strength. *Hydraulic Limes* make a good mortar with 2 of sand to 1 of lime. *Roman Cement Mortar* should not have more than 1 or 1½ sand to 1 cement, and is then a very weak mortar. *Portland Cement* will make a very strong mortar when mixed with 2 or 3 of sand, and even with 5 of sand—a mortar better than any of those made from lime.

**Grout** is a weak mortar made liquid by the addition of water, and used to pour into joints and interstices which cannot be got at with the stiffer material.

**Concrete** is a conglomerate or thorough mixture of shingle, broken stones, or similar material, with lime or cement, sand and water, which form a mortar filling the interstices between the pieces of stone. The proportions of ingredients mixed determine the quality of this mortar, which in its turn governs the strength of the concrete.

PROPORTIONS OF INGREDIENTS.—Concrete is generally described with reference to the bulk (when dry) of the materials comprising it. Thus for an important work the concrete might be 1 Portland cement, 2 sand, and 5 of shingle or broken stone; for less important work, 1 Portland cement, 3 sand, and 8 shingle.

LAYING CONCRETE.—This should be carefully done in horizontal layers, about 12 inches thick, well rammed, the surfaces being kept clean, and the material not disturbed when setting.

## PLASTER AND ASPHALTE.

**Plaster** for common work is a sort of mortar spread over surfaces to make them smooth. It is laid on in successive coats, the composition of which varies, and is given at pp. 209, 210.

PLASTER OF PARIS, or calcined gypsum, is a very quick-setting material, the basis of several cements, for which see p. 209.

**Asphaltes** are combinations of bituminous and calcareous matter. The best are natural—found chiefly in Switzerland—but there are many artificial imitations made with pitch and chalk.

The material is generally heated, and poured in a molten state over the surface to be covered. Some kinds are laid as powder and compressed by ramming.

The best varieties of asphalte are from Seyssel, and Val de Travers in Switzerland.

## TIMBER.

**Appearance of Cross Section.**—The timber used in engineering and building works is obtained from a class of trees which grows by the deposit of successive layers of wood outside under the bark, while at the same time the bark becomes thicker by the deposit of layers on its under side.

ANNUAL RINGS.—The cross section of such trees (see Fig. 60) consists of several concentric rings or layers, each ring consisting in general of two parts—the outer part being usually darker in colour, denser, and more solid than the inner part. The difference between the parts varies in different kinds of trees.

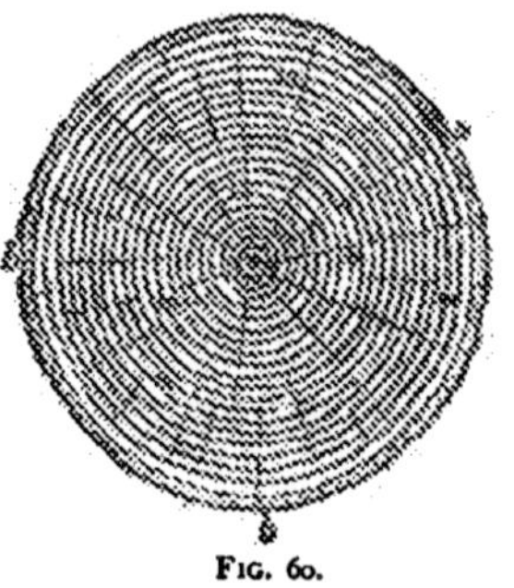

FIG. 60.

These layers are called *annual rings*, because one of them is, as a rule, deposited every year. Sometimes, however, a recurrence of exceptionally warm or moist weather will produce a second ring in the same year.

MEDULLARY RAYS AND SILVER GRAIN.—In the centre of

the tree is a column of pith *p*, from which planes, seen in section as thin lines *m m*, radiate toward the bark *b*, and in some cases similar lines *m m* converge from the bark toward the centre, but do not reach the pith.

These radiating lines are known as "medullary rays" or "transverse septa." In many woods they are not discernible by the eye, but when they are of large size and strongly marked, as they are in some kinds of oak, they present, if cut obliquely, a beautiful figured appearance, known as "silver grain" or "felt."

HEARTWOOD AND SAPWOOD.—As the tree increases in age the inner layers are filled up and hardened, becoming what is called "heartwood," the remainder being called "sapwood." The latter is softer and lighter than heartwood, and can generally be easily distinguished from it.

This is important, as the heartwood is in most trees far superior to the sapwood in strength and durability, and should alone be used in good work.

**Felling.**—While the tree is growing the heartwood is the strongest, but after the growth has stopped the heart is the first part to decay. It is important, therefore, that the tree should be felled at the right age. This varies with the soil, climate, and description of tree.

Tredgold recommends the following ages at which the undermentioned trees should be felled: oaks, 60 to 200 years (100 years the best age); ash, larch, elm, from 50 to 100 years; spruce, Scotch fir, 70 to 100 years. The best season for felling is at midsummer or midwinter in temperate climates, or during the dry season in tropical climates, when the sap is at rest. Oak bark is sometimes stripped in the spring, when it is loosened by the rising sap, and the tree felled in the winter.

**Characteristics of Good Timber.**—Good timber should be from the heart of a sound tree—the sap entirely removed. The wood, uniform in colour and substance, straight in fibre, free from large or dead knots, flaws, shakes, or blemishes of any kind.

The annual rings should be regular in form; close and narrow rings indicate strength, porous and open rings are signs of weakness. Good timber is sonorous when struck. A dull heavy sound betokens decay.

**Classification of Timber.**—For practical purposes timber may be classed as—

SOFT WOOD, including fir, pine, spruce, larch, and all cone-bearing trees.

HARD WOOD, including oak, beech, ash, elm, mahogany, teak, etc.

**Market Forms of Timber.**—The following are the most common forms in which timber is sold:—

*Logs*, being trunks of trees with the branches lopped off.

*Balks* or *square timber*, being the trunks roughly squared, generally by the axe, sometimes by the saw.

*Planks*, being parallel-sided pieces 2 to 6 inches thick, 11 inches wide, and from 8 to 21 feet long.

*Deals*. Similar pieces 9 inches wide, and not more than 4 inches thick.

*Battens*, being like deals, but only 7 inches wide.

## DESCRIPTIONS OF DIFFERENT KINDS OF TIMBER.

### SOFT WOODS.

**Red or Yellow Fir**, or *Northern Pine*,[1] is obtained chiefly from the Baltic or Russia.

Its cross section shows distinct annual rings, the hard portions of which are much darker than the others; the wood is resinous, and there are no medullary rays visible.

The best timber of this description comes from *Memel*, *Dantzic*, and *Riga*, the balks being from 18 to 45 feet long and 12 to 16 inches square.

*Yellow Deals* come from the same ports, the best from *St. Petersburg*, *Archangel*; and others from *Christiania*, and from *Gefle* and other Swedish ports.

All these are used for carpenters' work, and the best of the deals for joinery.

**American Pine.**—*Red Pine*,[2] so called from the colour of its bark, very like Memel timber, and *Yellow Pine*,[3] of a brownish-yellow colour when seasoned, are imported from Canada.

AMERICAN YELLOW PINE is of a very soft and even grain, and can be easily recognized by short, detached, dark, thin hair-streaks running in the direction of the grain, which show upon a planed surface.

It is invaluable for joinery, but is not so strong or durable for carpenters' work as Baltic timber.

**Pitch Pine**[4] also comes from North America. It has very strongly marked annual rings, is full of resin when it has not been "bled," hard to work and to wear, very durable except in a moist atmosphere.

It is much used for heavy engineering structures, also for ornamental joinery and for parts, such as heads of steps, sills, etc., subjected to much wear.

---

[1] Obtained from the *Pinus sylvestris*, or *Scotch fir*.

[2] Known also as *Canada Red Pine*, *Pinus rubra*, or *Pinus resinosa*.

[3] *Pinus strobus*. [4] *Pinus rigida*.

**Spruce**,[1] or *White Fir*, comes both from the north of Europe and from North America.

The wood is of a yellowish white, with clear annual rings and hard glossy knots, by which it is easily recognized.

It shrinks and warps very much, and is fit only for common joinery and floors, packing-cases, and other common work.

**Larch** is found in various parts of Europe, the best being in Russia.

It is of a brownish-yellow colour, the hard parts of the rings being reddish. The wood is tough and durable, but shrinks and warps, and is used chiefly for posts and palings.

## HARD WOODS.

**Oak** is found both in this country and also in America, Holland, and the Baltic.

BRITISH OAK is found in three principal varieties,[2] which need not be described in detail.

It is in section of a light brown colour, with a hard surface, narrow and regular annual rings, and clearly marked medullary rays.

The timber is very strong, hard, tough, and durable; is used for all purposes where strength and durability are required in engineering structures, and in buildings for sills, treads, superior joinery, keys, wedges, etc.

AMERICAN OAK[3] has a straighter and coarser grain than English oak, but is not so strong or durable.

DANTZIC, RIGA, and ITALIAN OAKS are chiefly used for ship-building. FRENCH OAK is very like British oak.

WAINSCOT is a form of oak that comes chiefly from Holland and Riga, is easily worked, and is so converted as to show the *silver grain*.

**Beech** is of a whitish-brown colour, with very distinct medullary rays and perceptible annual rings. The wood is hard, compact, and smooth, not difficult to work, very durable if always dry or always submerged, but decays quickly under alternate wet and dry or in damp places. It is used chiefly for piles, wedges, and carpenters' tools.

**Ash** is of a brownish-white, with yellow streaks, each annual layer separated from the next by a ring of pores. The sapwood is not generally distinguishable. The timber is tough, flexible, and durable when dry. It is too flexible for building purposes, and is used chiefly for tool handles and felloes and spokes of wheels.

**Elm** is found in several varieties. The heartwood is reddish-brown and the sapwood yellowish. No medullary rays visible. The wood is very fibrous, dense and tough, durable—the sapwood as well as the heartwood, except when alternately wet and dry. It is very useful for work under water, such as piles, and for various carpenters' purposes.

**Mahogany** is imported chiefly of two descriptions, *Honduras* or *Bay Mahogany* and *Spanish Mahogany*, the latter from Cuba.

The wood is of a golden-brown colour, often very veined and mottled, capable of receiving a good polish, and durable when dry and not exposed

---

[1] *Abies excelsa*.

[2] Stalk-fruited or Old English oak, *Quercus robur* or *Quercus pedunculata*. Cluster-fruited or Bay oak, *Quercus sessiliflora*. Durmast oak, *Quercus pubescens*.

[3] White oak (*Quercus alba*) or *pasture oak*. Other kinds are also imported.

to weather. The *Spanish* is distinguished from the *Honduras* by a chalk-like substance in its pores. Both descriptions are used for handrails and furniture.

**Teak** or *Indian Oak* comes chiefly from Burmah. It somewhat resembles English oak, but has no visible medullary rays. It is stronger and stiffer, but splinters easily. It contains an aromatic resinous oil, which makes it very durable.

This timber is too expensive for general use in buildings, but is sometimes employed for treads of steps, floors, etc.

**Greenheart** comes from South America. Its section is full of pores, like that of a cane, of a dark green colour, the sapwood not distinguishable from the heart, and the annual rings not perceptible.

It is the strongest timber in use, and contains an essential oil which preserves it for a time from the attacks of worms. These qualities make it very valuable for marine work, in which it is much used.

**Seasoning.**—Timber is best seasoned, and the sap dried up, by being stacked under cover with the air circulating freely round it. There are methods of seasoning by hot air, also by boiling and steaming, and other special processes, which cannot here be described.

**Decay.**—When timber is in positions where it is alternately wet and dry, or not well ventilated, it soon decays, the sapwood being generally the first affected.

*Dry Rot* takes place in confined positions. A fungus eats into the timber, makes it change colour, smell disagreeably, become brittle, and eventually reduces the fibres to powder.

*Wet Rot* occurs in the growing tree, and in positions where the gases generated can escape.

**Preservation.**—The best method of preserving timber from decay is to have it thoroughly seasoned and placed in well-ventilated positions.

*Painting* or *Charring* preserves timber if it is thoroughly seasoned; if not, it does harm by confining the moisture and causing rot.

*Creosoting* consists in forcing creosote (oil of tar) into the pores of the timber, by which the albumen of the wood is coagulated, worms repelled, and rot prevented.

There are many other methods of preserving timber, which are described in Part III. N.B.C.

## IRON AND STEEL.

Iron is produced by smelting different ores with a flux, which extracts from them most of their impurities. The liquid iron runs out of the blast furnace into rough bars called "*pigs*."

*Hot Blast Iron* is that produced by furnaces into which the air is admitted at a high temperature. When the air is not thus heated the resulting metal is known as *Cold Blast Iron*. There are but few cold blast furnaces now in the country.

## PIG IRON

**Carbon in Pig Iron.**—The bars or pigs run from the blast furnace are not pure iron, but contain several impurities, such as carbon, silicon, sulphur, phosphorus, and manganese.

Of these carbon is the most important. It is sometimes free, being visible as black specks; sometimes chemically combined, when it is not visible.

EFFECT OF CARBON.—The effect of the *uncombined or free carbon* is to give a fractured surface of the iron gray colour, and to render it easily fusible.

The *combined carbon* does not show in the fractured surface, which is white and bright, the iron being very hard, brittle, and forms when fused a pasty mass, which will not freely fill a mould.

DIFFERENCE OF CARBON IN IRON AND STEEL.—It is important to remember that the materials produced from pig iron differ considerably as to the amount of carbon they contain, upon which depend many of their characteristics.

These materials are—

*Cast Iron*, containing from 2·0 to 6·0 per cent. of carbon—a comparatively large percentage.

*Steel*, containing about ·15 to 1·8 per cent.—a small percentage.

*Wrought Iron*, containing, if perfectly pure, no carbon, but practically containing a trace.

## Classification of Pig Iron.

*Bessemer Pig*, a distinct variety, free from impurities, but containing a little manganese and silicon; made for the Bessemer process (see p. 35).

*Foundry Pig*, having a fracture of a gray colour, and useful to the iron founder.

*Forge Pig*, being almost devoid of free carbon, not fit for superior castings, but only for conversion into wrought iron.

Besides the above varieties, the pig iron of commerce is divided into six or eight classes.

## CAST IRON.

Cast iron is obtained by remelting pig iron with a little limestone flux to get rid of its impurities, and running it into moulds.

**Classification.**—GRAY CAST IRON is made from foundry pigs. No. 1, the darkest in colour, contains a large proportion of free carbon; is soft, very fluid when melted, and useful for very delicate castings. No. 2 is lighter in colour, less fluid, but is harder than No. 1 when cold, and good for casting girders, etc. No. 3 is of a still lighter colour, harder, more brittle, and adapted for heavy castings.

WHITE CAST IRON is made from forge pigs; is very bright, hard, and unfit for castings, except the commonest, such as sash weights.

MOTTLED CAST IRON contains both gray and white, which can easily be distinguished on a fresh-fractured surface.

**The Structure of Cast Iron** is highly crystalline; a bar broken across shows no sign of fibre—nothing but crystals close together.

**Castings** are made by running molten cast iron into sand, in which an impression of the article to be cast has been formed by means of a wooden pattern.

The shape given to castings is important. There should be no sudden changes of thickness, or sharp angles as in Fig. 61, but the thickness should change gradually and the angles be rounded off as in Fig. 62.

If these precautions are not attended to the casting will crack at the angles, or at any rate have a tendency to do so.

FIG. 61.

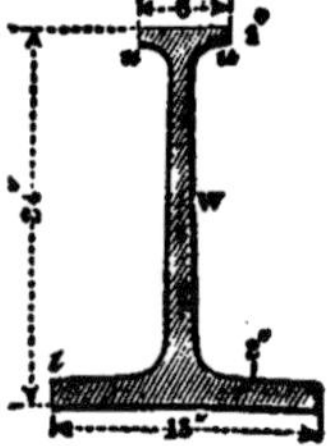

FIG. 62.

All castings should be smooth in surface, free from air-bubbles or flaws, with perfect edges.

**Chilled Iron** is a very hard substance like white cast iron; it is produced on parts of castings which are required to be especially hard by placing pieces of cold iron against those parts when the metal is being run in.

Thus the running surface of a cast-iron wheel may be chilled and made hard, the rest of the wheel being of a tough gray cast iron.

**Malleable Cast Iron** is made by extracting some of the carbon from cast iron, thus making it more like wrought iron in composition, which produces its toughness.

This is done for small castings by embedding them in oxide of iron and raising to a red heat.

Iron so heated is softened to a certain depth all over the surface, and can be hammered or bent to a certain extent.

## WROUGHT IRON.

**Manufacture of Wrought Iron.**—Wrought iron is manufactured from forge pig by the following processes.

*Refining*, or exposure when fused to a strong current of air, which removes part of the carbon.

*Puddling*, by which the molten metal is still further exposed to a blast of air and oxidizing substances in a reverberatory furnace. The remainder of the carbon is thus removed, and clotty lumps or "*puddle balls*" of pure iron appear.

*Shingling*, or hammering of these puddle balls so as to squeeze out the cinder and form them into "*blooms*."

*Rolling*, or passing the blooms while red hot between grooved rollers which convert them into *puddled bars*.

The effect of rolling is to elongate the crystals of the pig iron into *fibres*, giving the iron great strength and toughness.

**Bar Iron** is classified as follows :—

PUDDLED BARS, as obtained by the processes just mentioned, have but little tensile strength, and are used only for manufacture into better descriptions.

MERCHANT BAR or *Common Iron* is made by piling up short lengths of puddle bars, raising them to welding heat, and re-rolling. This improves the fibre of the iron, which is, however, still very hard, brittle, and useful only for the commonest purposes.

*Best Bar* is produced by cutting up merchant bars, piling, reheating, and rolling. It is tougher and more easily worked than merchant bar, and is generally used for ordinary good work.

*Best Best* and *Best Best Best* iron bars are those that have been submitted to three and four repetitions of the processes of piling, welding, and rolling.

**The Market Forms of Wrought Iron** are very various. Besides square, round, half-round, flat, and other sections of bars, the sections shown below are the most common, and Figs. 63 to 67 are useful in building up iron structures of all kinds. The name of each is given below it.

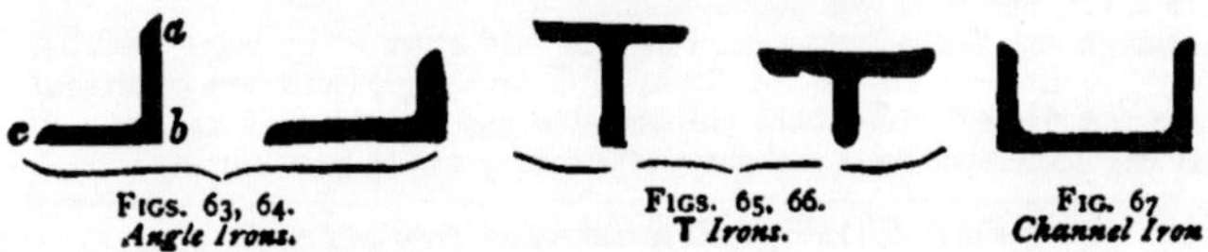


FIGS. 63, 64. *Angle Irons.*  FIGS. 65, 66. T *Irons.*  FIG. 67 *Channel Iron*

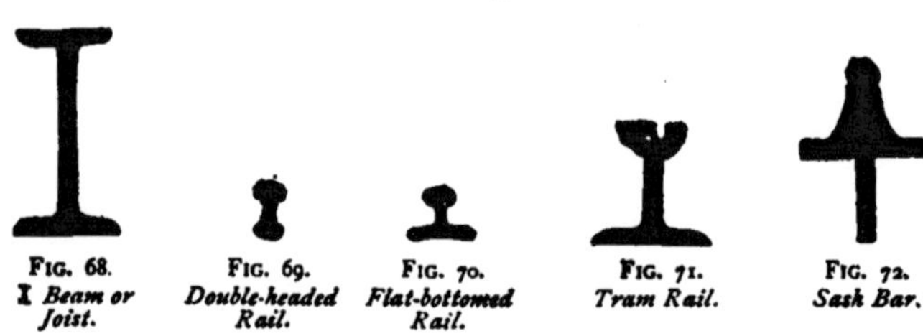

Fig. 68. I *Beam or Joist.* Fig. 69. *Double-headed Rail.* Fig. 70. *Flat-bottomed Rail.* Fig. 71. *Tram Rail.* Fig. 72. *Sash Bar.*

**Corrugated Sheet Iron** is made by passing sheets through grooved rollers which force them into waves or corrugations that immensely increase their stiffness and make them useful for roofing and other purposes.

**Galvanized Iron** is iron covered with a coating of zinc, which protects it from oxidation.

**Tests for Wrought Iron.**—For all structures of any degree of importance the tensile strength of the wrought iron used should be tested.

A good iron should not only be strong but ductile, in order that it may not snap suddenly, but stretch slightly under the shocks to which it may be subjected.

Such iron, when torn asunder by slow tension in a testing machine, should not break off short as in Fig. 73,[1] but draw out

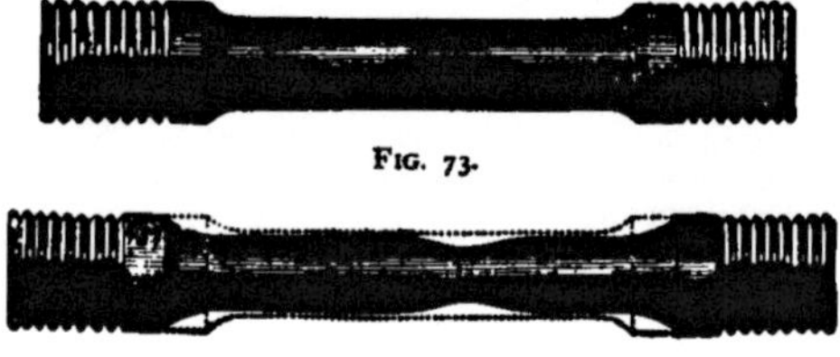

Fig. 73.

Fig. 74.

as in Fig. 74,[1] not only becoming longer, but also being reduced in sectional area at and near the point of rupture.

**Tensile Strength and Elongation.**—In order that both strength and ductility may be secured, engineers generally specify that iron bars for important work should bear a tensile stress of 23 or 24 tons per square inch, with an elongation of 30 to 40 per cent. Angle irons, T irons, and plates have lower, and rivet iron higher tests.

**Rough and Forge Tests.**—Iron may be further tested by being bent hot or cold to different angles, the limbs of T and angle irons being flattened down and rivets doubled cold without showing any signs of fracture. If they can stand such tests without cracking they are of good quality.

---

[1] From Kirkaldy's *Experiments on Iron and Steel.*

**Fractured Surface.**—"Whenever wrought iron breaks *suddenly*, a crystalline appearance is the invariable result; when *gradually*, invariably a *fibrous* appearance."[1]

Small uniform crystals or fine, close, silky fibres indicate a good iron. Coarse crystals, flaws, blotches of colour, loose and open fibres, are signs of bad iron.

## STEEL.

**Steel** varies very much in its characteristics according to the amount of carbon it contains.

Thus *Mild or Soft Steel* contains from ·2 to ·5 per cent. of carbon. When more carbon is present it becomes *Hard Steel.*

CHARACTERISTICS.—Speaking generally, the following are the characteristics of steel.

*Hardening.*—When raised to a red heat and suddenly cooled it becomes hard and brittle, thus differing from wrought iron, upon which this treatment has no effect.

*Tempering.*—After hardening as above, the steel may be softened again to any degree by reheating and again cooling; in this it differs from cast iron.

*Other characteristics* of steel are its sharp *metallic ring* when struck, its great *elasticity*, and its *retention of magnetism.*

**Methods of making Steel.**—Steel is generally made by adding carbon to pure wrought iron (see p. 31).

**Blister Steel** is produced by heating bars of the purest wrought iron with charcoal (carbon).

It has a crystalline structure, is covered with blisters and full of cavities, which render it unfit for edge tools, and it is used chiefly for conversion into better descriptions of steel.

**Shear Steel** is made by piling short lengths of blister steel and welding them together under the hammer, which closes the cavities, removes the blisters, and produces a more uniform material known as *Single Shear Steel.* A repetition of the piling and welding produces *Double Shear Steel.* Shear steel is used for large knives, plane irons, shears, etc.

**Crucible Cast Steel** is made by melting blister steel in crucibles, or by melting wrought iron with the addition of the necessary carbon in the form of charcoal. It is used for the best tools and cutlery.

**Bessemer Steel** is produced direct from pig iron which, when melted in a "converter," is deprived by a blast of air through it of all its carbon, the amount necessary to convert it into steel of the softness required is then added in the form of *spiegeleisen*, a variety of cast iron rich in carbon. The resulting metal is run out into ingots, which are hammered, rolled, and worked to the forms required.

Bessemer steel is much used for rails and for the tyres of wheels, also for large roofs and bridges, boiler-plates, etc.

**The Basic Process** is somewhat similar to Bessemer's, but that the con-

[1] From Kirkaldy's *Experiments on Iron and Steel.*

verters are lined with material which deprives the pig iron of some of its impurities, thus enabling iron from the less pure ores to be converted.

**The Siemens-Martin Process** consists in melting pig iron in a regenerative furnace and then adding various substances, so that the molten metal may contain the exact amount of carbon necessary to produce the description of steel required. Steel made by this process is much used for rails, tyres, bridges, roofs, boiler-plates, etc.

**Puddled Steel** is made by stopping the puddling process before all the carbon has been removed. It is a poor material, used chiefly for making inferior plates.

**Case-hardening** is a process by which the surface of wrought iron is turned into steel. This is effected by red-heating the article to be case-hardened when immersed in bone dust, which adds carbon to the surface and turns it into steel to the depth of from $\frac{1}{16}$ to $\frac{3}{8}$ inch. The parts required to be hardened are then quenched. The process is useful for keys, and other articles where a hard surface is required to be combined with toughness.

**Tests for Steel.**—The remarks made at pp. 34, 35, with regard to the tests for wrought iron, and the fractured surface, apply also to steel, except that in the case of steel the forge tests are much more important than for iron.

A recent specification for a large steel bridge requires that the bars and plates must have a tensile strength of not less than 28 tons or more than 31 tons per square inch, an elongation of not less than 20 per cent., and a limit of elasticity of 15 tons. Besides this there are tests as to welding and tempering, too elaborate to be described here.

**Working Stresses for Iron and Steel.**—The ultimate tensile stresses to which iron and steel are subjected when tested are the *breaking stresses*. When, however, they are used in structures it is so arranged that the members of iron and steel should be subjected only to safe *working stresses* such as certainly will not cause fracture.

### Table of Breaking and Working Stresses for Materials for a Dead Load.

| Material. | Breaking Stress in Tons per square inch. | | Working Stress in Tons per square inch. | |
|---|---|---|---|---|
| | Tension. | Compression. | Tension. | Compression. |
| Cast Iron | 9 | 48 | $1\frac{1}{2}$ | 8 |
| Wrought Iron | 23 | 18 | 5 | 4 |
| Steel | 32 | 32 | $6\frac{1}{2}$ | $6\frac{1}{2}$ |
| Timber, Fir | $4\frac{1}{2}$ | 3 | $\frac{1}{2}$ | $\frac{1}{4}$ |
| Oak | $6\frac{1}{2}$ | $4\frac{1}{2}$ | $\frac{3}{4}$ | $\frac{1}{2}$ |

**Copper** is found in the metallic state or is smelted from ores.

It is red in colour, not easily oxidized, very malleable, and has a greater tensile strength than any metal except wrought iron and steel.

It is used by the builder chiefly for slate nails, bell wires, and lightning conductors, also for dowels, bolts, and fastenings in positions where iron would be corroded or rusted, and sometimes for covering roofs.

**Lead** is reduced from ores. It is an extremely soft and plastic metal—very malleable, fusible, heavy, and very wanting in tenacity and elasticity.

It is used for covering flat roofs, for flashings, pipes, bedding girders, etc.

SHEET LEAD is to be purchased in two forms—*cast* or *milled;* both are described according to their superficial weight. Thus 7 lb. lead means lead weighing 7 lbs. per square foot.

*Cast Lead* is thicker, heavier, and with a harder surface than milled lead, but subject to flaws and sand-holes, and of irregular thickness. It is cast in sheets from 16 to 18 feet long and 6 feet wide.

*Milled Lead* is rolled out thinner than the other, is more uniform in thickness, bends easily and makes neater work, but is not so durable as cast lead.

The *Weights of Sheet Lead generally used for Roofs* are as follows:—

| | lbs. per square foot. | |
|---|---|---|
| Aprons and Flashings | 5 | Thicker if much exposed. |
| Roofs / Flats / Gutters | 6 to 8 | |
| Hips and Ridges | 6 or 7 | |

LEAD PIPES of very large diameter may be made out of sheet lead, but smaller ones should be *drawn.*

**Zinc** is obtained from ores of the metal. It is easily fusible, malleable when pure, soon destroyed by air containing acid.

It is used by the builder for roof coverings, gutters,

cisterns, chimney pots, slate nails, ornaments, and for covering iron (galvanizing) to keep it from rusting.

Good sheet zinc is of uniform colour, tough, easily bent backwards and forwards without cracking. The gauges used for roofs are mentioned at p. 111.

**Tin** is used for lining lead pipes and for small gas tubing. It is very soft, weak, and malleable, and more easily fusible than any other metal.

---

# CHAPTER III.

## *EXCAVATIONS, SHORING, SCAFFOLDING, PILE FOUNDATIONS.*

*Subjects required by Syllabus, and (in brackets) the pages at which they are treated upon.*

*The ordinary methods of timbering excavations, such as for foundations to walls or for laying down sewers* [p. 39]. *The erection of bricklayers' and masons' scaffolding* [p. 41]. *The use of piles in foundations* [p. 47].

### EXCAVATION.

In clearing and levelling the site for extensive buildings very large quantities of earth may have to be removed from one spot to another, for which special arrangements would be necessary. Such arrangements, however, are beyond the province of these Notes, in which it is proposed to consider only the excavations required for the foundations of buildings to be placed upon a site which requires no special preparation in the way of levelling.

In all excavations for foundations the solid ground at the bottom of the trenches should be left to the required levels—not made up with loose earth—and temporary drains should be cut to carry off the rain that may fall during the progress of the work.

In excavating trenches for brick or stone footings an extra width of about 6 inches on each side is generally allowed at the bottom of the trench to give the men room to build; but, when concrete is to be used, the excavations should be of the exact width required for the bed of concrete itself.

## SHORING AND STRUTTING.

When trenches have to be dug in loose ground it is necessary to support the sides of the excavation by timbering and shoring.

*In moderately firm ground*, after a depth of 3 or 4 feet has been excavated, a few rough planks or "*poling boards*" P P (Fig. 75) are placed at intervals varying with the nature

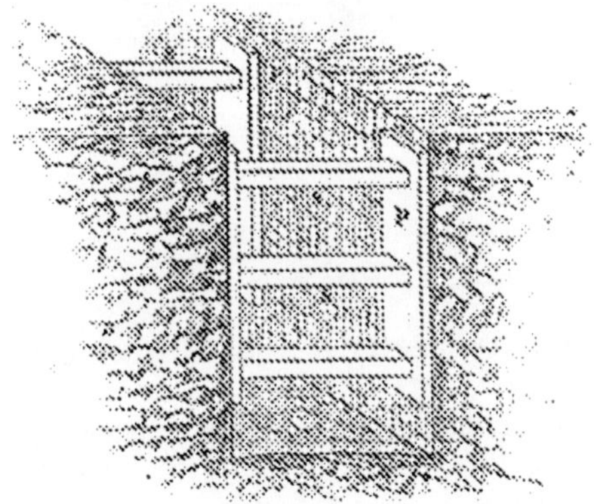

FIG. 75.

of the soil against the sides of the trench, and kept up by jamming or wedging in between them struts (S) of rough scantling from 4 to 6 inches square.

*In looser ground* it is necessary to place the poling boards closer together, and so support them (Fig. 76) by 3-inch planks W W called "walings." The struts must be made thick, in proportion to the width of the trench and the pressure upon them, and their distance apart will depend upon the strength of the walings and the nature of the soil.

The poling boards P P are often in short lengths of about 3 feet, so that no greater depth has to be excavated before they can be inserted.

*In very loose soils*, such as running sands or slipping clays, it is evident that the sides would fall in if an attempt was made

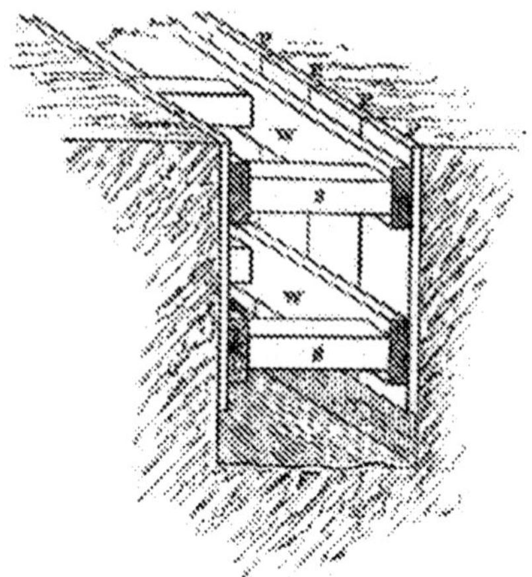

Fig. 76.

to excavate the trenches to a depth of 3 or 4 feet before supporting them (Fig. 77).

To prevent this the poling boards are sometimes put in horizontally—as "*sheeting*"—one at a time. A portion 9 inches or a foot deep is excavated, and at once supported by planks placed longitudinally on both sides and kept apart by struts, then another depth of 9 inches is taken out and another plank placed on each side below those already in position, and these last also strutted. When five or six planks have been thus inserted on

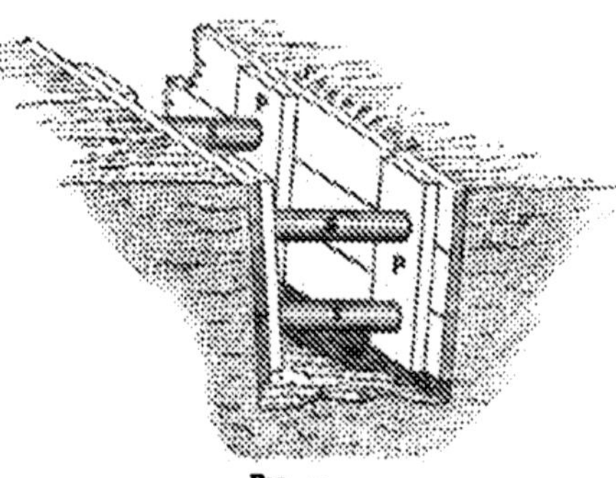

Fig. 77.

each side walings may be added, and some of the struts dispensed with.

*The timber used for shoring* important excavations should be hard and tough—seasoned,—barked before use—so placed as to receive the stress on its end grain, and as large a bearing surface as possible should be allowed, especially when the end of one timber bears upon the side of another.

All shores should be driven from above, not sideways or horizontally. The planks or walings at the sides of an excavation should be at a slight inclination, as in Fig. 77, the upper edge sloping toward the earth they support, so that when the shore, whose ends are cut to the proper angle, is driven down from above, it will take a fair bearing.[1]

Fig. 77 shows round shores, which are sometimes made by cutting up old fir scaffold-poles. Half-round walings are also often used.

Sometimes in very bad soil long planks called "runners," having sharp ends shod with iron, are substituted for the poling boards; these are driven in as the trench is dug, their points being kept a foot or so below the bottom of the portion excavated.

In very deep excavations platforms are required at vertical intervals of about 5 feet to receive the earth thrown up by the men from stage to stage.

In this case these stages may rest upon the struts of the timbering, which should be made particularly firm to ensure safety.

## SCAFFOLDING.

Scaffolds are temporary erections of timber supporting platforms close to the work, on which the workmen stand and deposit their materials.

**Bricklayers' Scaffolds.**—When a wall is built as high from the ground as the bricklayer can conveniently reach he commences a scaffold by planting a row of poles or "standards," S S, about 10 or 12 feet apart (Fig. 78).

Across these standards, at the level of the work already done, are poles, called "*ledgers,*" secured with lashings which are in many cases tightened up by wooden keys or wedges, and upon these are laid short transverse pieces, *p*, called "*putlogs,*" about 6 feet long and 3 inches thick, which form bearers to support the scaffold-boards, *b*.

The putlogs are from 4 to 6 feet apart, according to the strength of the scaffold-boards, which should be about 1½ inch thick; header bricks are temporarily left out, forming holes, *h h*, into which one end of each putlog is inserted, the other end resting upon the ledger.

[1] *Transactions*, Society of Engineers, 1875

Three or four scaffold-boards are laid across the put-logs; on these the bricklayer stands and his materials are deposited.

The materials are either carried up ladders in hods, or hoisted by means of a pulley or windlass and rope.

In many cases a platform for landing materials is erected in the same way as the scaffold, and close to it.

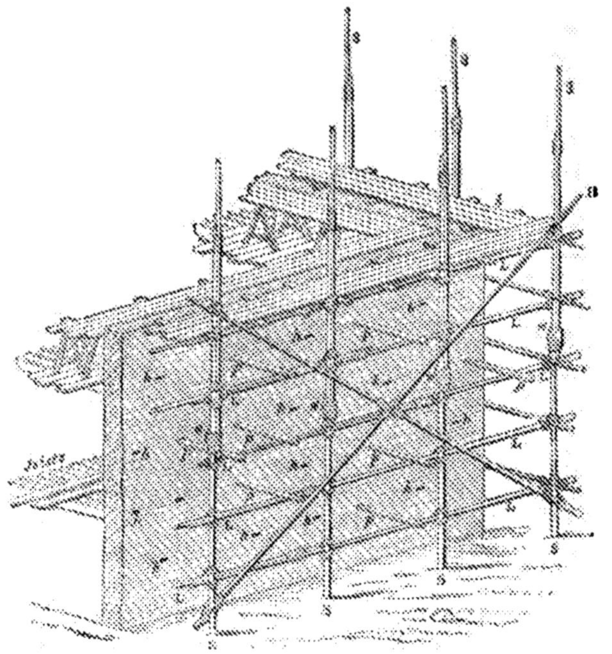

FIG. 78.—*Bricklayers' scaffolding.*

When the wall is so high that it can barely be reached from the scaffold-boards another row of ledgers is lashed to the standards, fresh putlogs laid, and the scaffold-boards are raised to the new level.

The ledgers and putlogs used at the lower levels are left in position to steady the scaffold, and if the building be very high and in an exposed situation the scaffolding must be stiffened by lashing long poles, called "braces," B B, diagonally across the outside of the standards and ledgers.

Care must be taken not to load a scaffold too heavily, otherwise the putlogs will injure the green work upon which they rest.

The scaffold for the inside of the brick or rubble walls of buildings sometimes consists merely of planks laid across the joists of the different floors, which are placed in position for the purpose; when the walling has risen more than 5 feet above a floor a fresh tier of planks is provided, supported on trestles, empty casks, or anything that may be available.

When there are no floors on the inside of the wall the scaffold then is constructed in the same way as for the outside.

**Masons' Scaffolds.**—Scaffolding for ashlar walls, of which the stones can be lifted without machinery, are formed with standards and ledgers; but as putlogs cannot conveniently be inserted in the face of the masonry, a row of standards is used on *both* sides of the wall, between which the putlogs are lashed, so that the scaffolding is entirely independent of the building.

*Building without Scaffolds.*—In some parts of the country houses many stories in height are erected without scaffolds at all, the work being all done from the inside, and the men supported only by temporary platforms formed on the different floors in succession.

**Special Scaffolds.**—*Scaffolds made from square scantling* have been used under the supposition that the timber might eventually be used in the building, that cords would be saved, and that the scaffolding could be more quickly erected and taken down.

Practically, however, these advantages have not been found to exist, and, where the scaffolding is high, iron sockets for uniting the lengths of scantling and other expensive and awkward contrivances have been found necessary, so that the system may be considered a failure.

*Gaber's Scaffolds*, made from pieces of flat timber or deals bolted together and well cross-braced, are sometimes used in Scotland. Their general construction will be understood from Figs. 79, 80, which are taken from an actual example.

**Gantries.**—When the stones to be lifted are very heavy, scaffolds of poles lashed with cords would not be safe, nor could they carry the necessary machinery for lifting the stones.

The standards or uprights at the end of the gantry should be strutted as shown, and so should every standard be supported by struts on the outside to prevent lateral movement.

In order to keep the timber as perfect as possible bolts should be avoided, and the balks united by straps or "dogs."

The latter are pieces of iron about $\frac{3}{4}$ inch square, the ends of which are turned down and pointed by being splayed on the *inside* so as to draw the timbers together when driven home.

It frequently happens that a line of railway can be brought from the stoneyard right under the gantry, as shown, in which case the stone can be lifted off the trucks by the traveller and set at once.

In some cases the gantry is omitted, and the traveller has high legs at its ends, with wheels at their feet which run upon rails laid upon the ground; sometimes the legs at one end of the traveller are shorter than those at the other to suit the levels of the ground.

**Derrick Cranes** of the form shown in Fig. 82 are some-

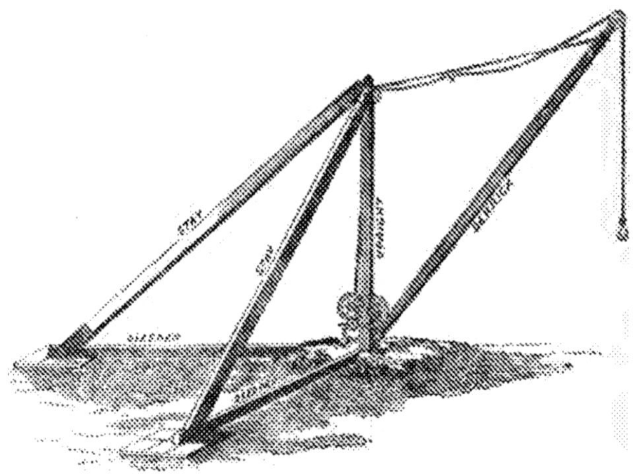

FIG. 82.

times used for lifting the materials required in building large houses, as well as other structures.

The crane is placed on a platform in a high and central position, so that it can reach the stones or other materials where they are deposited, and also, by revolving the jib or derrick, place them where they are required in the work. The derrick can be raised or lowered as well as revolved; this enables the length of its reach to be varied so that materials can be picked up or set down on any spot within its range.

## PILES AND PILE FOUNDATIONS.

**Timber Piles** may be made of elm, larch, fir, pitch pine, beech, oak, teak, or green-heart.

The straightest-grained timber should be selected, the bark removed, and any rough projections smoothed off; all large knots should be avoided, and diagonal knots especially are a source of danger, as a pile is very likely to be broken off at the point where they occur.

Piles should, if possible, be of whole timbers, and driven with the butt, or natural lower end, downwards, because that end is of the hardest wood containing closer annual rings than the other. Sometimes, however, when the pile tapers it may be driven with the narrow end downwards, so as to get a better grip of the ground.

The head of the pile should be bound round with a wrought-iron hoop to prevent it splitting when driven.

The lower end should be pointed, and, if it has to encounter stony or hard ground, should be shod with iron.

Fig. 83 shows an ordinary form of wrought-iron shoe, and Fig. 84 an improved form, in which the lower portion C is of cast-iron, forming a good wide abutment for the timber, which tends to prevent the danger of its being crushed as the pile is driven. The wrought-iron pins, *a a*, are cast into the portion C, and their heads hammered out like a rivet to secure the straps *s s*.

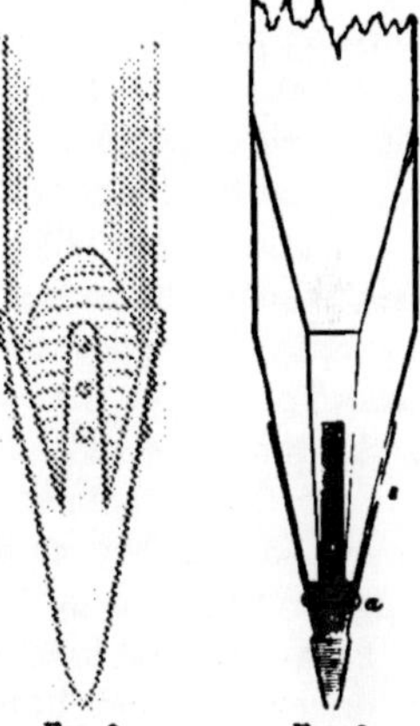

FIG. 83. FIG 84.

Piles are used for foundations in three diffeaent ways. They receive distinctive names, and their forms and dimensions are governed accordingly.

*Bearing Piles* are driven down either until they reach a hard stratum, or until the friction on their sides prevents them from sinking, upon which they are used as pillars to support a platform of timber.

Such piles, if of wood, should be whole timbers from 9 to 18 inches in diameter, and if they are in soft soil their length should never be more than about twenty times their diameter, or there will be danger of their bending when driven.

*Short Piles* are driven into soft soil to compress and consolidate it. Upon their heads may be placed a platform of timber or layer of clay or concrete.

These piles are only from 6 to 12 feet long—of round timber about 6 inches in diameter. They should be driven as close together as is possible without the driving of one pile causing the others to rise; to prevent this, it is found necessary to place them at intervals of about 2 feet 6 inches from centre to centre.

*Sheeting Piles* are used to enclose the areas of a foundation, and thus prevent the soil from spreading laterally, or to protect it from the action of water.

Sheet piles are flat planks, varying in width, and from 3 to 10 inches thick. They are sometimes grooved and tongued down their edges so as to form a tight joint, and sharpened to an edge at the lower end, which may be shod with iron.

In using sheet piling to enclose soft ground, long "guide piles," about 6 to 10 feet apart, are first driven in the direction required. On opposite sides of these are fixed beams ("string pieces" or "wales") at a horizontal distance apart just equal to the thickness of the sheet piles, which are driven down between them, commencing at the guide piles, and working inwards in each bay, so that the last sheet pile driven acts as a wedge and tightens up the whole.

PILE FOUNDATIONS.—*Platform on Piles.*—After the piles are driven, and their heads sawn off level, a timber platform is generally laid upon them.

This consists of heavy square balks, called string pieces and cross pieces, notched into one another so as to form a grating or "grillage." The string pieces are notched over the heads of the piles, and secured to them by trenails.

The ground between the piles is often taken out to a depth

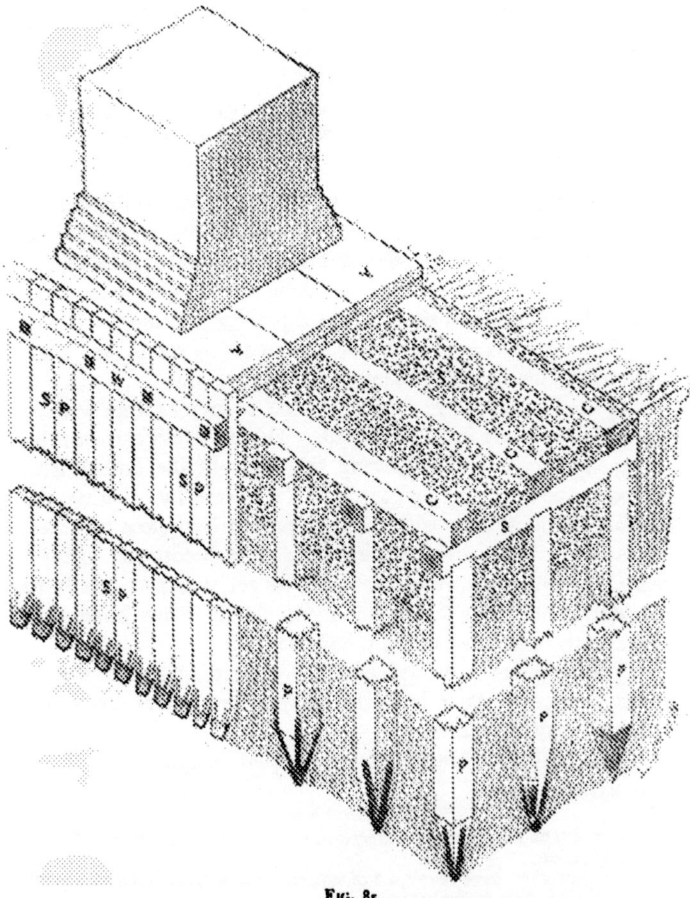

Fig. 85.

of 3 or 4 feet, and the space filled with concrete. The intervals between the timbers of the platform are sometimes similarly filled in, and in some cases a bed of concrete is substituted for the platform altogether.

Fig. 85 is an illustration of a portion of pile foundation for a thick wall. P P P are the piles (shod in different ways), S S the string pieces, and C C the cross pieces. The platform Y Y is composed of Yorkshire landings 6 inches thick.

A portion of the foundation is secured by sheet piling, S P, driven between the waling, W, and the outer cross piece of the grillage.

A disadvantage in the string pieces and cross pieces is that the heads of the piles, bearing upon their sides, bend and crush into the longitudinal fibres, indenting the timber, and causing it to sink down upon the pile heads. Where there is a really good strong bed of concrete the string and cross pieces can, with advantage, be omitted; in fact, in many cases a good broad and deep bed of solid concrete enables the use of the piles themselves to be dispensed with altogether.

Causes of Failure of Pile Foundations.—Pile foundations are liable to fail, from the softness of the ground being such that it does not offer sufficient resistance to a lateral movement, in consequence of which the piles lose their original position, and the wall has a tendency to upset.

Wooden piles are sure to be destroyed by rot in any position where they are alternately wet and dry.

If used in sea water they are liable to attacks from worms, by which they are soon destroyed. These attacks can best be delayed by completely charging the pores of the timber with creosote, or they may be prevented for a time by covering the surface of the timber with scupper nails driven close together, or, at a great cost, by sheathing the pile with copper. After a time, however, the worm manages to get under the nails or sheathing, and to eat the wood completely away, leaving an apparently sound but entirely hollowed pile.

Partial piling provided under a portion only of a wall is most dangerous, as it leads to unequal settlement, by which the wall may be fractured.

In a wall with buttresses the unequal weight on the piles has led to failure.

Iron Piles have been introduced to avoid the natural defects of those made of timber.

*Cast-iron Piles* have been used of various cross sections, such as square, round, hollow, and cross-shaped.

In driving them a block of wood or "dolly" must be interposed between them and the monkey, for fear of breaking the pile by the sudden shock.

They have a disadvantage for the foundations of buildings, inasmuch as they cannot be cut off to a level at the top.

Cast-iron sheet piling has been extensively used; it consists generally of flat plates, stiffened by vertical ribs, and furnished with overlapping edges. The guide piles may be of the same construction, square or semicircular in cross section.

*Screw Piles.*—In these the pile itself may be of timber, or a cylinder of cast or wrought iron.

It is furnished at the lower end with a short and broad cast-iron screw blade, which is twisted (Fig. 86) round under pressure so that it enters the ground, from which a great force would be required to withdraw it.

Fig. 86.

The best way of driving these piles is by attaching long radiating levers to the upper end, and turning them round by means of animals moving on a temporary platform.

Iron piles and tubes are more in use for the foundations of engineering works than for ordinary buildings; they need not, therefore, be further noticed in this course.

**Pile Engines** of various kinds are used for driving piles into the ground.

In all of them a heavy block of iron or wood called a "ram" or "monkey" is raised by a rope or chain over a pulley to the top of an upright frame and then allowed to fall suddenly upon the head of the pile, being guided in its descent by arrangements which vary considerably in different engines.

There is some difference of opinion as to whether piles are best driven by blows slowly delivered by a heavy monkey falling through a considerable height, or by a light monkey, with a short fall, delivering blows in quick succession. The latter plan is, however, in nearly every case by far the best, as the heavy blows crush the foot of the pile just above the shoe, and convert it into a large mass or ball of fibres, which prevents it from penetrating further.

*Ringing Engines.*—In these the chain or rope attached to the monkey, after passing over the pulley at the head of the frame, is connected with several short ropes, each of which is hauled on by a man until the monkey has been raised 3 or 4 feet, when upon a given signal the whole are let go at the same moment so as suddenly to release the monkey, which falls upon the pile.

Immediately after the blow is delivered, the men pull the rope so as to tighten it and take advantage of the rebound of the monkey from the head of the pile.

Fig. 87 shows a very simple form of ringing engine adapted for use by seven or eight men.

The frame consists merely of an upright pole or leader supported by two side braces, and steadied by guys secured to an iron strap at the head.

The monkey, M, here shown is of cast-iron, weighing from 250 to 300

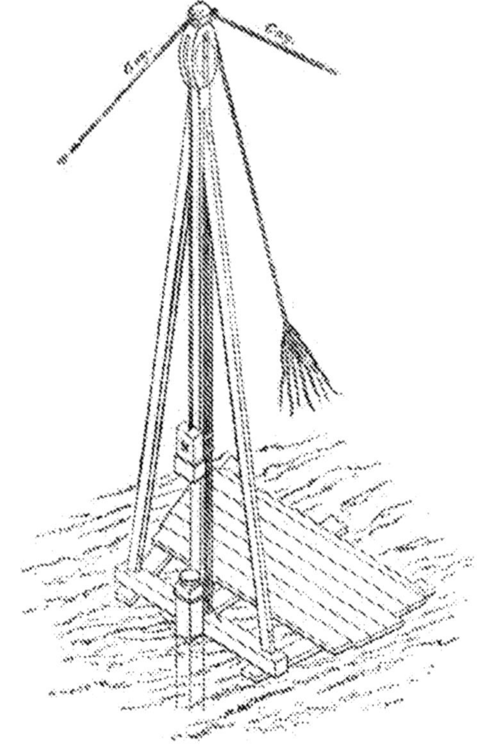

FIG. 87.

lbs., and is guided in its descent by wrought-iron straps fixed to its sides, which embrace the "leader," and are secured at the back by a transverse bar passing through slits formed in the ends of the straps.

The rope shown round the head of the pile is intended to keep it close up to the engine, so that it may not get out of place while it is being driven.

The engine is generally used for small piles; it delivers its blows with great rapidity, the monkey being raised only as far as the men can reach, some 3 or 4 feet each time, and the rope never being detached from it.

In some forms of this engine a monkey weighing from 600 to 800 lbs. is used.

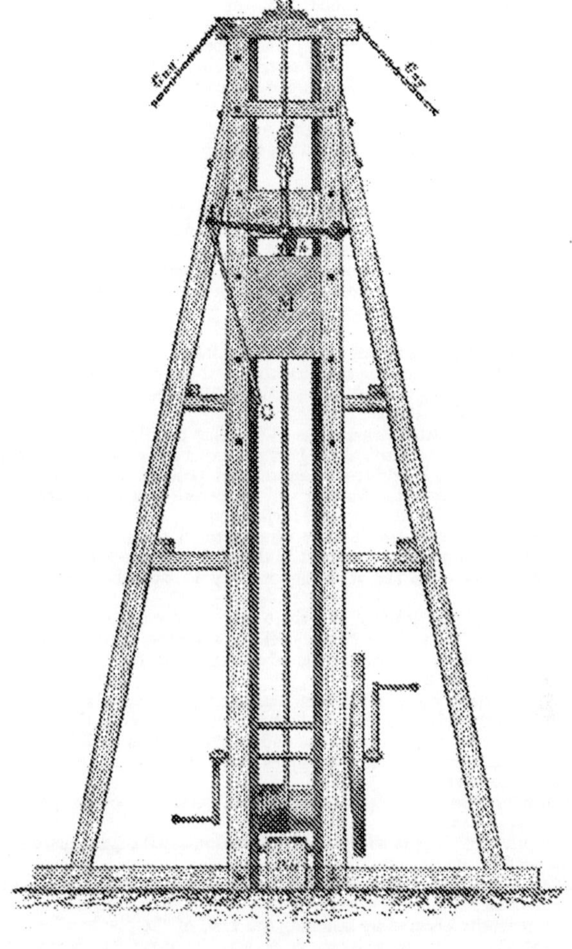

Fig. 88.

In these a stronger and more elaborate framing is required. Two parallel leaders, L L, are generally made use of, connected by a cross head, and further supported by framing.

In such engines the monkey may be provided with ears and projections cast on its sides, which travel in grooves formed on the inner sides of the leaders and thus guide the monkey during its fall.

Professor Rankine recommends that the men to work such an engine should be in the proportion of 1 to every 40 lbs. weight in the monkey, and states that they work most effectively when after every three or four minutes of exertion they have an interval of rest, and that under these circumstances they can give about 4000 or 5000 blows per day.

*Crab Engines* are similar to the last described in their general arrangements, but the framing is much higher and the monkey is lifted to a height of 10 or 12 feet by means of a windlass or crab worked by men, horses, or steam-power.

In the commonest form the monkey is raised upon a hook, *h* (Fig. 88), attached to a counter-weighted lever, *l*, to the long arm of which is attached a rope, by pulling which the hook is pulled out and the monkey is permitted to fall.

The monkey can be released at any height by pulling the trigger rope C.

It is generally desirable that the height of fall should be the same for each stroke; this may be ensured by attaching the trigger-rope to the head of the pile.

Sometimes the rope is tied below, to the framing of the pile-driver, so as to cause the release of the monkey always at the same point, but in this case the height through which the monkey falls of course increases as the pile is driven further down.

The monkey should always descend in a line parallel to the direction of the pile. When that is vertical the guides are in the uprights of the framing, but if the pile is to be driven in an inclined position the guides must be similarly inclined, or if the framing will not permit this, temporary guiding pieces must be fixed at the required inclination.

*Steam Pile-Drivers* are those in which a small steam engine takes the place of the manual power applied to the crab. There are several forms of steam pile-drivers, but it is unnecessary to describe them in these Notes.

A "*Punch*," or "*Dolly*," is a short post or block interposed between the head of the pile and the monkey, either when the former would otherwise be out of reach, or when it is advisable, as in the case of cast-iron piles, to deaden the blow.

"According to some of the best authorities, the test of a pile's having been sufficiently driven is that it shall not be driven more than ⅛ inch by 30 blows of a ram weighing 800 lbs. and falling 5 feet at each blow.

"It appears from practical examples that the limits of the safe load on piles are as follows :—

"In piles driven till they reach the firm ground, 1000 lbs. per square inch of area of head.

"In piles standing in soft ground by friction, 200 lbs. per square inch of area of head."—RANKINE.

DRAWING PILES.—This may be necessary when a pile breaks, or for other reasons.

It is generally effected by fastening the head of the pile to a long beam and using the latter as a lever, or it may be done by means of the hydraulic press.

A pile may also be drawn by means of a large screw, one end of which is fastened to the head of the pile while the other passes through a cross head temporarily but firmly supported above it.

# CHAPTER IV.

## *BRICKWORK AND MASONRY.*

THIS chapter will contain brief notes on a few points connected with Brickwork and Masonry, which by the Syllabus are excluded from the Elementary Course.

*Subjects required by Syllabus, and (in brackets) the pages at which they are treated upon.*

*Hoop-iron bond in brickwork* [p. 74]. *Diagonal and herring-bone courses in brickwork* [p. 69]. *Damp-proof courses* [p. 60]. *Bond timber in walls and the objections to it* [p. 74]. *How bricks are laid in hollow walls* [p. 61]. *Window or door openings with splayed jambs* [p. 70]. *Flues* [p. 77]. *Chimneys* [p. 77]. *Fire-places* [p. 82]. *Arches up to about twenty feet span* [p. 71]. *How mortar-joints are finished off, and the thickness usually allowed to them* [p. 65]. *Why bricks and stones should be wetted before being laid* [p. 66]. *Construction of brick ashlar walls* [p. 56]. *Rubble ashlar walls* [p. 57]. *Circular* [p. 75] *and egg-shaped drains* [p. 76].

### COMPOUND WALLS.

It has already been said that uniformity of construction in walling of any description is of the first importance.

All walls must be expected to consolidate and settle down when weight comes upon them, but so long as they settle equally no injury is done; *inequality* of settlement, however slight, is dangerous, and produces unsightly cracks in the masonry.

A want of uniformity in construction leads to such results, and other evils are involved, among which is instability when exposed to the action of fire. With regard to this, Captain Shaw, the Chief of the London Fire Brigade, says—

"The walls of a most pretentious and imposing building, of sufficient thickness, and apparently constructed of sound stones, are found to crack at an early stage of a fire, and perhaps to fall down altogether, and then it is discovered that they have been only a deception, having been constructed externally of stone and internally of brick."[1]

It will be as well to notice two or three forms of composite walls, in order that their structure and defects may be described.

In all compound walls the backing should have joints as nearly as possible equal in number and thickness to those in

[1] *Fire Surveys*, by Captain Shaw, C.B.

the face, so that the back and front may settle down under pressure to the same extent; if not, the joints should be in cement or quick-setting mortar, in order that they may become consolidated before any pressure comes upon them.

**Evils of Facing with Superior Bricks.**—It is a common practice, especially in using single Flemish bond, to build the face work with better bricks, and with thinner joints, than the backing. This leads to unsound work, and should not be allowed.

In such cases, on account of the joints of the backing being thicker than those of the face work, the courses will not be of the same depth in front and back. For example, it may require eight or nine courses of the face to gain the same height as six or seven in the backing (see Fig. 89), and it is only when they happen to come to a level, as at *aa* (once in every eight courses or so), that headers can be introduced. Even the few that can thus be used are liable to be broken off by inequality of settlement, caused by the difference in the thickness of the joints.

This may be partly remedied by using thinner bricks in the backing, so as to have the same number of joints in face and back; but even then the difference in thickness of the joints in facing and backing tends to cause unequal settlement, unless the work is built in very quick-setting mortar which will harden before any weight comes upon it.

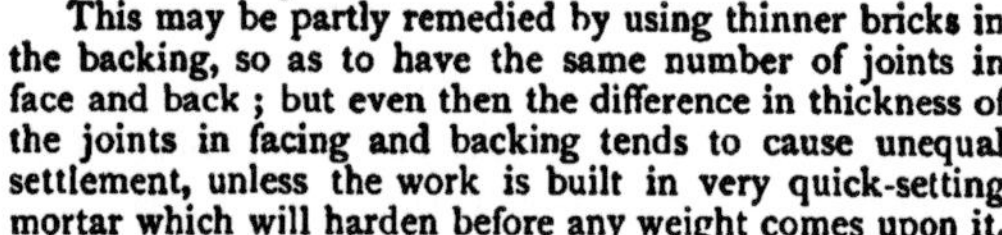

Fig. 89.

A further result of this practice is that, in order to economize the more expensive face bricks, dishonest bricklayers will cut nearly all the headers in half, and use "false headers" throughout the work, so that there is a detached slice, 4½ inches thick, on the face, having no bond whatever with the remainder of the wall.

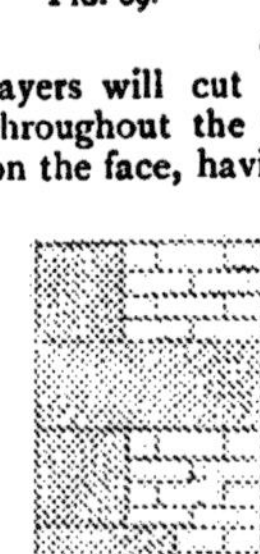

Fig. 90.

**Brick Ashlar.**—This is a name given to walls with ashlar facing, backed in with brickwork (Fig. 90).

Such constructions are liable in an aggravated degree to the evils pointed out as existing in walls built with different qualities of brick. The coarser and more numerous joints in the bricks backing are sure to consolidate to a greater extent than the few and fine joints of the ashlar, and thus tend to cause a separation of the face and backing; or, if this is prevented by bond stones, the facing will probably bulge outwards.

In building such work the ashlar stones should be of heights equal to an exact number of courses in the brickwork, in order that they may bond in with it; the stones should be properly square throughout, with the back joints vertical, so as to leave no vacuities between the facing and the brickwork, for these could not be properly filled in without the expense of cutting bricks to fit the irregularities.

**Rubble Ashlar** consists of an ashlar stone face with rubble backing (see Fig. 91), and is subject, even to a still greater extent than brick ashlar, to the evils caused by unequal settlement.

Fig. 91.

To avoid these evils, the stones and joints of the rubble backing should, as before mentioned, be made as nearly as possible of the same thickness as those in the ashlar facing, or, if the joints are necessarily thicker, there should be fewer of them, so that the total quantity of mortar in the backing and face may be about the same. This can seldom be economically arranged in practice, but it should be remembered that the more numerous and coarser the rubble joints, the worse the construction becomes.

The ashlar should be bonded in with "through-stones" or "headers," as previously described; their vertical joints should be carefully dressed for some distance in from the face, and their beds should be level throughout; the back joint and sides of the tails of the stones may, however, be left rough—the latter may even taper in plan with advantage—and they should extend into the wall for unequal distances, so as to make a good bond with the rubble, the headers from which should reach well in between the bond stones of the ashlar. Through stones may be omitted altogether, headers being inserted at intervals on each side extending about two-thirds across the thickness of the wall.

Care must be taken that the stones in the ashlar facing have a depth of bed at least equal to the height of the stone. In common work the facing often consists merely of slabs of stone having not more than from 4 to 6 inches bed, with a thin scale of rubble on the opposite side, the interval being filled in with small rubbish, or by a large quantity of mortar, which has been known to bulge the walls by its hydrostatic pressure.

The ashlar facing is in all respects, except those above mentioned, built as described in E.B.C.D., and the backing may be of random rubble done in courses from 10 to 14 inches high, according to the depth of the stones in the facing.

Fig. 91 is the section of a wall 3 feet thick, with an ashlar facing composed of good substantial stone.

## PREVENTION OF DAMP IN WALLS.

The importance of keeping moisture out of walls as far as possible need hardly be dilated upon.

In addition to the great importance of a dry building for sanitary reasons, it is also most necessary for good construction; dampness in the masonry communicates itself to the woodwork, and causes rot throughout the building, besides which, the masonry itself is not sound—the mortar, unless of good hydraulic lime or cement, does not set, and is always liable to the attacks of frost.

To give some idea of the quantity of water that the walls of an improperly protected building may contain, and of the evil effects caused by damp, the following remarks are quoted from an official report:—[1]

"In England the common bricks absorb as much as a pint or pound of water. Supposing the external walls of an ordinary cottage to be one brick thick, and to consist of 12,000 bricks, they will be capable of holding 1500 gallons or 6¾ tons of water when saturated. To evaporate this amount of water would require nearly a ton of coal, well applied. The softer and more workable stones are of various degrees of absorbency, and are often more retentive of moisture than common brick. Professor Ansted states that the facility with which sandstone absorbs water is illustrated by the quantity it contains both in its ordinary state and when saturated. He states that even granite always contains a certain percentage of water, and in the dry state is rarely without a pint and a half in every cubic foot. Sandstone, however, even that deemed fit for building purposes, may contain half a gallon per cubic foot, and loose sand at least two gallons. When water presents itself in any part of such material it readily diffuses itself by the power of capillary attraction, by which, it is observed on some walls in Paris, it ascends 32 feet from the foundations. Walls of such absorbent constructions are subject to rising wet by capillary attraction, as well as the driving wet of rain or storm. To guard against the driving wet on the coast, expensive external coverings, 'weather slates,' are used. But these do not

---

[1] *Report on Dwellings in the Paris Exhibition*, by Edwin Chadwick, Esq., C.B.

stay the interior rising wet. This wet having to be evaporated lowers temperature. Damp walls or houses cause rheumatism, lower strength, and expose the system to other passing causes of disease."

It is a wise precaution to cover the whole surface of the ground under a dwelling with a layer of concrete, or asphalte, in order to prevent the damp and bad air out of the ground from rising into the building.

This precaution is, however, generally omitted because it involves expense; but measures to keep the walls dry are or should be adopted in nearly all buildings intended for occupation by human beings.

The walls of a building are liable to be charged with moisture—

1. By wet rising in them from the damp earth.

2. By rain falling upon the exterior of the walls.

3. By water from the roofs or leaking gutters soaking into the tops of the walls.

Of these evils the first may be prevented by the construction of dry areas or "air-drains" and by the introduction of damp-proof courses; the second may be counteracted by impervious outer coatings or by the use of hollow walls; and the third avoided by the use of projecting eaves with proper gutters—or where parapet walls are used, by an upper damp course.

**Air-Drains** are narrow dry areas, 9 inches or more in width, formed around such parts of the walls of a building as are below the ground.

They prevent the earth from resting against the walls and imparting to the masonry its moisture, which, rising by capillary attraction, might cause the evils already referred to.

The outer wall of the area should rise slightly above the surrounding ground, so as to prevent the water from the surface from entering the air-drain. Arrangements should be made for keeping the area clear of vermin, for ventilating it, and also for draining off any moisture that may accumulate at the bottom.

In the section Fig. 141, p. 81, is shown an air-drain 12 inches wide, having a rubble retaining wall, and being covered by flag-stones built into the wall and weathered on the upper surface; of these, one here and there is removable in order to give access to the drain. The air-holes shown in the figure ensure the thorough ventilation of the drain and of the space below the floor of the building.

There are several forms of air-drains; the width of the area is often much less than that shown in the figure, and sometimes is so reduced that the arrangement simply amounts to providing a hollow wall. In other examples the outer remaining wall is curved in plan, between the piers, being concave on the inside, by which additional strength is gained and thinner walls may be used. The area is frequently covered by a small quadrant arch turned against the wall, instead of by paving.

In some cases, to avoid the expense of air-drains, the outer surface of the portion of wall below ground is rendered with cement, asphalted, or covered with a layer of slates attached to the wall.

Substitutes for properly built air-drains may be cheaply formed by placing a flagstone in an inclined position against the outside of the wall to be protected.

Wide and open areas are much more expensive, but allow a freer circulation of air, exclude damp more thoroughly, and are, on the whole, superior to air-drains.

**Horizontal Damp-Proof Course.**—Even where air-drains are provided, a damp-proof course should be inserted in all walls, to prevent the moisture out of the soil from rising in the masonry.

The damp-proof course should be 6 inches or more above the level of the external ground, but under the wall-plate carrying the floor-joists.

There are several forms in which a damp-proof course may be provided.

It may be of glazed pottery slabs built into the wall, as shown at D D in Fig. 93. The joints between the slabs must be left empty, or the damp will rise through them.

A layer of tough asphalte about $\frac{3}{8}$ inch thick is often used instead, as at AB in Fig. 94, and is frequently continued only through the inner thickness of the wall, as in Fig. 94.

In hollow walls, to prevent wet which comes into the hollow space, through the outer portion of the wall, from finding its way along the top of the damp-proof course to the interior of the wall, a cement fillet may be run along the angle at the bottom of the hollow space between the top of the damp-proof course and the inner portion of the wall, and an exit should be afforded—in any case temporarily—for the water at various points by leaving openings in the brickwork. If these are left permanently they should be protected by gratings.

In buildings finished with a parapet wall, a damp-proof course should be inserted just above the flashing of the gutter, so as to prevent the wet which falls upon the top of the parapet from soaking down into the woodwork of the roof and into the walls below.

In some localities damp-proof courses are formed of asphalted felt, or with slates set in cement; these latter are rather liable to crack, and thin impervious stones, or courses of Staffordshire bricks in cement, are better. Sheet lead has been used for the same purpose, and is most efficacious, but very expensive.

Arches over vaults, or cellars under footpaths, are frequently rendered all over the extrados with asphalte or cement to prevent the penetration of wet.

**Vertical Damp-Proof Course.**—In addition to the precautions adopted to prevent damp out of the ground from rising in walls, it is necessary (especially when using inferior bricks or porous stones) to prevent moisture falling upon the outer face from penetrating to the interior of the wall.

The wet may be kept out of the interior of the wall by rendering the exterior surface with cement, covering it with slates fixed on battens, or with glazed tiles set in cement. Taylor's pottery facing bricks answer the same purpose.

Another plan patented by Mr. Taylor consists of overlapping slates placed vertically in the middle of the wall—the two portions of which are united by peculiar iron ties.

*The Hygeian rock impervious wall-lining*, patented by Mr. White of Abergavenny, consists of a vertical sheet of waterproof composition introduced into the thickness of the wall.

**Hollow Walls** not only exclude the damp, but the layer of air they contain, being a non-conductor of heat, tends to keep the building warm. Such walls are formed in two separate portions, standing vertically parallel to one another, and divided by a space of about 2 or 3 inches, sometimes 4½ inches.

These two portions are generally united either by special bonding bricks or by iron cramps. There are several ways of arranging the thickness of the portions of the wall, and the consequent position of the air-space.

In some cases the two portions are of equal thickness, the air-space being in the centre.

Very frequently one of the portions is only 4½ inches thick, built in brickwork in stretching bond; the other is of such thickness as may be necessary to give the whole stability.

In such a case the thin 4½ portion is sometimes placed on the outer, and sometimes on the inner side of the wall.

*Hollow Walls with the Thin Portion inside.*—In some cases, such for instance as when the wall has a stone face, the 4½-inch portion is necessarily on the inside, but this arrangement has many disadvantages.

In the first place, the bulk of the wall is still exposed to damp, and the moisture soaks in to within 7 or 8 inches of the interior of the building.

Again, if the wall has to carry a roof, expense is caused, as the span should be increased so as to bring the wall-plates on to the outer or substantial part of the wall, clear of the 4½-inch lining.

This may be avoided by bridging over the air-space, so as to make the wall solid at the top, which, however, renders it liable to damp in that part.

There is an advantage in having the thick portion of the wall outside when deep reveals have to be formed for the door and window openings.

*Hollow Wall with the Thin Portion outside.*—If the 4½-inch portion is placed outside, the damp is at once intercepted by the air-space, kept out of the greater portion of the wall and at a considerable distance from the interior of the building.

The roof can be economically arranged so as to rest upon the interior thicker portion of the wall.

The stretching bond is, however, considered by some to be unsightly, unless made to appear like English or Flemish bond by using false headers, and, where the bricks are bad, the thin exterior portion, if liable to be attacked by frost, is in time destroyed.

Moreover, when the thin portion is outside, there is some difficulty in constructing deep reveals in a solid manner without their becoming a channel for damp across the opening. On the whole, however, the arrangement with the thin portion outside is the best.

*Hollow Walls with Bonding Bricks.*—Jenning's patent bonding bricks are made of vitrified pottery, and are of the shape shown in Fig. 92. These bricks are built in across the open-

FIG. 92

FIG. 93.
Scale, ¼ inch = 1 foot.

ing at horizontal intervals of about 2 feet 6 inches, and vertical intervals of about 9 inches to 12 inches. The bricks in the several courses are placed chequer-wise, so that each is over the interval between two below.

The peculiar shape of the brick enables it to be built into the wall so that the end in the front portion is a course lower than the end in the back portion of the wall. This prevents any moisture running along the surface of the bonding brick to the interior of the wall.

*Precautions.*—When building with these bricks, it is advisable to cover them temporarily with pipes swathed in hay-bands, or by a narrow strip of wood, in order to prevent the falling mortar from lodging upon them. As the wall rises, the strip is transferred in succession from each row of bonding bricks to cover the last built in.

*Sizes.*—The bent bonding bricks shown in Figs. 92 and 93 are made in four sizes from 7½ inches to 13½ inches horizontal length between their ends.

Their lengths and shape are arranged so as to afford either a 3-inch or a 4½-inch cavity, and to enter the wall either 2¼ inches at both ends—2¼ at one end and 4½ inches at the other—or 4½ inches at both ends.

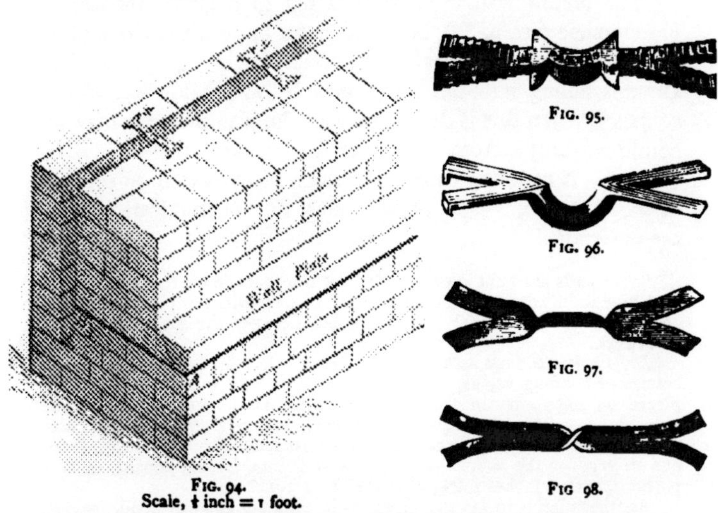


FIG. 94.
Scale, ¼ inch = 1 foot.

FIG. 95.

FIG. 96.

FIG. 97.

FIG. 98.

The bonding bricks may extend right through the thin portion of the wall, or, if this is objectionable on account of appearance, their ends may be covered by bats, as shown in the figure.

*Hollow Walls with Iron Ties and Cramps.*—Ties of cast iron, Figs 95, 96, or of wrought iron, Figs. 97, 98, and *x* and *y* Fig. 94, dipped when hot in tar, are frequently used instead of bonding bricks, and have the advantage of not being liable to be broken if the wall should settle unequally. On the other hand, they are subject to decay by rust, and to expansion from the same cause, which may injure the wall.

The ties are about 8 inches long, ¾ inch wide, by $\frac{1}{10}$ inch thick; they are placed about 3 feet apart, horizontally, and with 9-inch vertical intervals between the rows.

Each tie is either bent or twisted in the middle, so as to stop the passage of water along its surface, and hollow iron ties possessing great strength as struts have for some time been introduced.

Cast-iron cramps are made about ½ inch wide and $\frac{3}{16}$ thick, and somewhat similar in form to the above.

The hollow wall is often arranged to begin on the damp-proof course (see p. 60), but it is better to continue the hollow for two or three courses lower, as shown in Fig. 94, so that any wet falling into the cavity may be well below the damp course. When this is done the asphalte damp course may be continued only across the inner thickness of the wall, A B, Fig. 94. A covering course of brickwork is placed on the top of the air-space, which should have no communication with the outer air.

Some walls are built entirely of hollow bricks made for the purpose.

Stone walls are sometimes lined with 4½-inch brickwork on the inside, an air flue about 2 inches wide being left between the masonry and the brickwork.

*Hollow Walls built with Common Bricks only.*—In the absence of iron cramps or bonding bricks, hollow walls may be built with ordinary bricks placed on edge, after being dipped in boiling tar to make them as non-absorbent as possible. Every course is composed of alternate headers and stretchers, so arranged that each header comes immediately over the centre of a stretcher in the course below. The wall thus formed consists of two portions, each 3 inches thick, separated by a 3-inch space.

Another plan is to lay the bricks as in ordinary English bond, leaving a space of about 2½ inches between the stretchers in the front and back. This makes the wall (4½ + 2½ + 4½) = 11½ inches thick, and the headers are therefore too short to reach from face to back; the deficiency is made up by inserting bats at the ends of the headers.

These and other plans adopted for building hollow walls with ordinary

[1] Figs. 95 to 98 are from Messrs. Chambers, Monnery, and Co.'s advertisements.

bricks are defective in strength as compared with the walls constructed with special bonds or cramps, and, moreover, the common bricks, being porous, conduct moisture to the interior of the wall and defeat the object aimed at in making it hollow.

A better plan, in the absence of the special bonding bricks or ties, is to unite the portions of the wall by pieces of slate slab, or of dense impervious stone, used in the same way as the iron ties.

*Openings in Hollow Walls.*—Where the lintels of doors and windows occur in a hollow wall with a 4½-inch exterior portion, the following arrangement may be adopted to prevent the wet which may enter the air-space from dropping upon the window or door frame.

Just above the window or door head a piece of sheet lead is built in on the inner side of the 4½-inch exterior wall. This lead may be 4¾ inches wide, 2 inches being built into the 4½-inch wall, 1¾ inch projecting into the air-space, and the remaining inch turned up so as to form a sort of gutter, which should be carried about 2 inches farther than the ends of the lintel each way, so as to lead the water clear of the door or window frame

## JOINTS.[1]

Mortar is used to cement the parts of a wall together, and also to prevent the fracture of the bricks or stones by ensuring an even distribution of pressure, notwithstanding any irregularities in their beds.

The quantity and coarseness of the mortar that should be used will therefore decrease in proportion as the beds are more perfect; *e.g.* ashlar masonry has thinner joints than rubble, and good bricks can be set with closer joints than bad ones.

**Thickness of Joints.**—Excessively thick joints should be avoided when possible. They not only injure the appearance of the work, but, when the weight of the superincumbent walling comes upon them, the mortar is squeezed out, projects beyond the face of the wall, catches the rain, and leads it into the wall, rendering the work liable to injury by frost.

In good brickwork (not gauged) the joints should be about ¼ to ⅜ inch thick. For ashlar masonry or gauged brickwork

[1] Joints in Stonework are described in pp. 34-38 of E.B.C.

about $\frac{1}{8}$ to $\frac{1}{10}$ inch thick, while for rubble they vary in thickness according to the nature of the work.

The bricks or stones should be well wetted, especially in hot weather, so as to remove the dust, which would prevent the mortar from adhering to them, and also to prevent them from sucking the water out of the mortar. The mortar should be used stiff, and every joint well flushed, all interstices being filled with bits of brick or stone set in mortar.

*Larrying* is the method usually adopted for filling in the interior of very thick walls. After the bricks forming the exterior faces of a course are laid, a thick bed of soft mortar is spread between them, and the bricks for the inside of the wall are one by one pushed along in this bed until the mortar rises in the joints between them.

*Grouting* consists in pouring very liquid mortar over the course last laid, in order that it may run into all vacuities left by careless workmanship in not properly filling up all the internal joints with mortar. Grout is, however, a weak and objectionable form of mortar.

The joints, both of brick and of masonry, are finished so as to present a neat appearance on the face in several different ways, as in Pl. I., in which the joints are shown full size.

**Flat or Flush Joints.**—In these the mortar is pressed flat with the trowel, and the surface of the joint is flush with the face of the wall, as at *a*, Pl. I.

Such joints are not very ornamental, but are suitable for internal surfaces to be whitewashed.

*Flat Joints jointed*, *b*, Pl. I., are the same as those last described, except that an iron jointer is used to mark a narrow line along the centre of the joints, which improves their appearance. Sometimes both the upper and the lower edges of the joint are jointed as in *c*, Pl. I.

*Gauged work* has very thin joints (see *d*, Pl. I.) formed by dipping the bricks in white lime-putty before laying them.

**Struck Joints** should be formed by pressing or "striking" back the upper portion of the joint while the mortar is moist, so as to form a sloping surface which throws off the wet (see *e*, Pl. I.); the lower side of the joint is cut off with the trowel to a straight edge.[1] These joints are, however, usually struck along the *lower* edge as at *f*, Pl. I.; a ledge is thus formed above which catches the rain.

**Keyed Joints**, *g*, Pl. I., are formed by drawing a curved iron key or jointer along the centre of the flush joint, pressing

[1] Joints so struck are sometimes called *weather joints*.

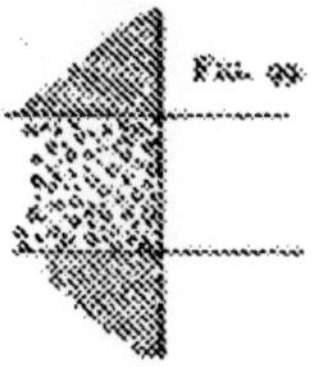

SECTIONS. ELEVATIONS. SECTIONS. ELEVATIONS. Plate L.

*a* *Flat joint* — Fig. 99. | Fig. 100. — *b* *Flat joint (jointed)*

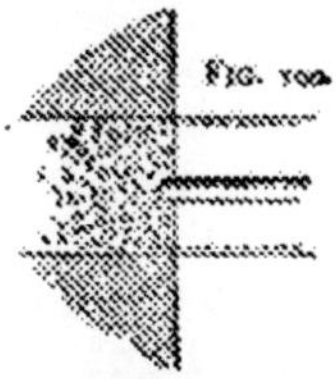

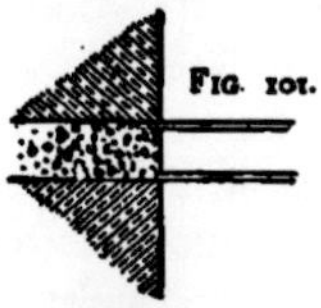

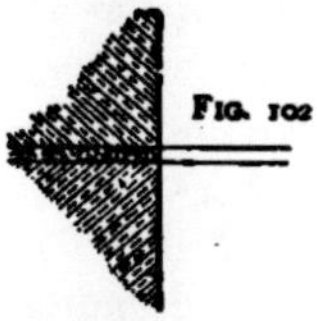

*c* *Flat joint jointed* — Fig. 101. | Fig. 102. — *d* *Gauged work*

*e* *Struck joint (proper form)* — Fig. 103. | Fig. 104. — *f* *Struck joint (common)*

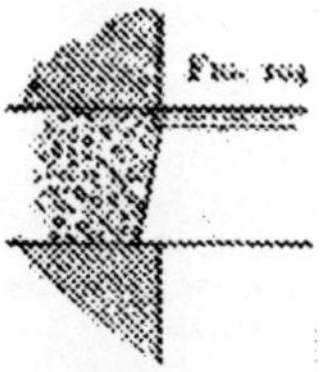

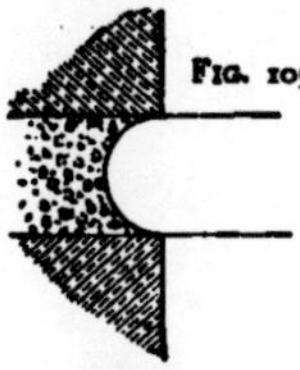

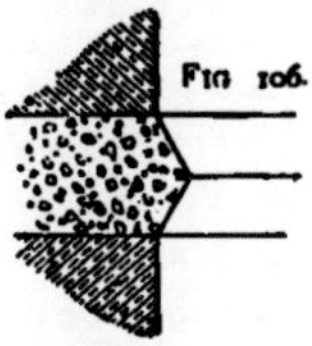

*g* *Key joint* — Fig. 105. | Fig. 106. — *h* *Masons V joint*

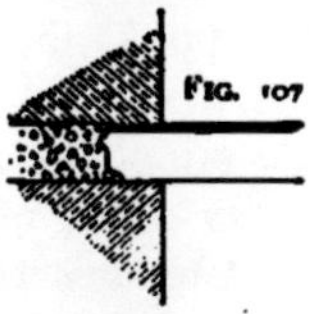

*i* *Raking* — Fig. 107. | Fig. 108. — *k* *Pointing (flat joint)*

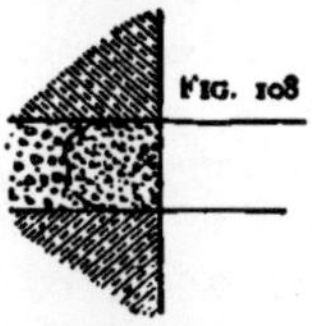

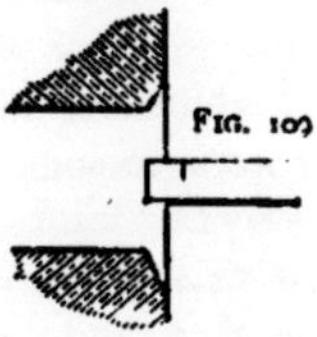

*l* *Tuck ptg.* — Fig. 109. | Fig. 110. — *m* *Bastard tuck*

it hard, so that the mortar is driven in beyond the face of the wall; a groove of curved section is thus formed, having its surface hardened by the pressure.

In some cases the moist key is dipped into ashes, which are thus rubbed into the surface of the joints.

**Mason's or V Joints,** *h* Pl. I., project from the face of the wall with an angular V section. With good mortar they throw off the wet, but when inferior lime is used they soon become saturated and destroyed by frost.

**Raking and Pointing** consists in removing the original mortar joints to a depth of about ¾ inch in from the face, *i* Pl. I., filling in with mortar, *k* Pl. I., and finishing the joints in one of the methods about to be described.

Pointing is not advisable for new work, when it can be avoided, as the joints thus formed are not so enduring as those which are finished at the time the masonry is built.

During severe frost, however, it would be useless to strike the joints at the time the work is built, for the mortar would be destroyed by the frost.

Pointing is, moreover, often resorted to when it is intended to give the work a superior appearance, and also to conceal the defects of inferior work.

In repairing old masonry or brickwork, the mortar of which has become decayed, raking out and pointing become necessary.

Both in old and new work, before pointing, the original mortar should be raked out with an iron hooked point, and the surface well wetted before the fresh mortar is applied.

**Flat Joint Pointing.**—The raked joints are filled in with fine mortar, and struck flat with the trowel or jointer, as at *k*, Pl. I. They may be jointed as at *b*, Pl. I.

**Tuck Pointing,** *l* Pl. I., is used chiefly for brickwork; the joints having been raked are "stopped," that is, filled up flush with mortar. This is coloured or rubbed over with a soft brick until the joints and bricks are of the same colour. A narrow groove is then cut along the centre of each joint, and the mortar is allowed to set. After this the groove is filled with pure white lime-putty, which is caused to project so as to form a narrow white ridge, the edges of which are cut off parallel so as to leave a raised white line about ⅛ inch wide. This process causes inferior work to look as if it had been executed with large bricks and very fine joints; in carrying it out any defects in the work, such as irregularity of joints, are corrected by smearing over the face and striking false joints, so that badly executed work is disguised and made to present a good appearance.

*Bastard Tuck Pointing*, *m* Pl. I., consists in forming a ridge from ¼ to ⅜ wide on the stopping itself, the edges being cut parallel and clean. There is no white line, the projecting part of the joint being of the same colour as the remainder.

**Blue or Black Pointing** is done with mortar mixed with ashes instead of sand.

**Keying for Plaster.**—When a wall is to be plastered, the joints are either raked as at *i*, Pl. I., or the mortar joints are left rough and projecting—in either case to form a key for the plaster.

**Vertical Joints** are similar to horizontal joints, but in many cases are much thinner.

## VARIOUS BONDS NOT MENTIONED IN E.B.C.

The principal bonds used in brickwork were described in E.B.C., but there are one or two varieties not so commonly used which remain to be noticed.

**Raking Bond** is of two kinds, *Diagonal* and *Herring-bone*. In both the bricks in the interior of the wall are placed in directions oblique to the face. A course or two of raking bond is sometimes introduced at intervals in thick walls built in English bond.

The proportion of stretchers in a brick wall diminishes according to its thickness. The raking courses are therefore useful in giving longitudinal strength to thick walls which are deficient in stretchers.

In both kinds of raking bond alternate courses rake in opposite directions.

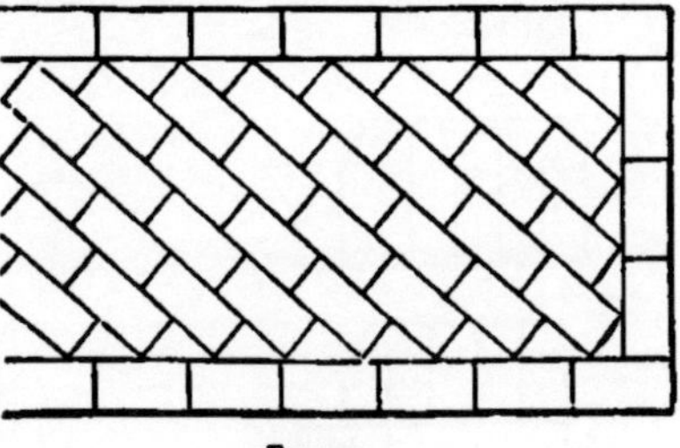

Fig. III.
*Diagonal Bond.*

Diagonal Bond.—In this the bricks (except those in the face of the wall) are laid diagonally, at such an angle with the face that the bricks will just fit in without being cut.

A two-brick wall is the thinnest in which this can be done, and then only in the stretching courses. In thicker walls diagonal bond may be inserted in any course.

The triangular spaces at the back of the facing bricks are objectionable; it takes some trouble to cut a piece to fit them, and they are therefore frequently left empty.

HERRING-BONE BOND consists of bricks laid raking from the sides toward the centre line of the wall, as shown in Fig. 112.

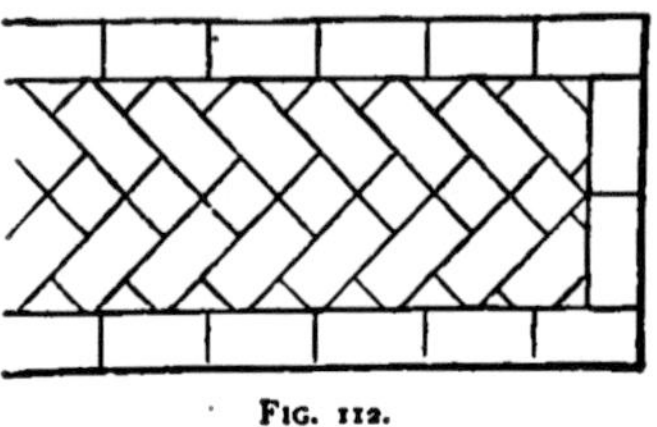

FIG. 112.

This is a defective bond, for, in addition to the triangular spaces at the back of the facing bricks, there are likely to be voids, each larger than half a brick, left in the centre of the wall, unless great care be taken to have them properly filled in.

Herring-bone courses cannot be introduced at all in walls less than three bricks thick, and only in the stretching courses of such a wall; in thicker walls, however, this bond may be introduced in any course.

In practice this bond is rarely, if ever, adopted for walls.

**Reveals with Splayed Jambs.**[1]—Splayed jambs in brickwork are weaker than square jambs, and should only be used where there is a good interval between the windows.

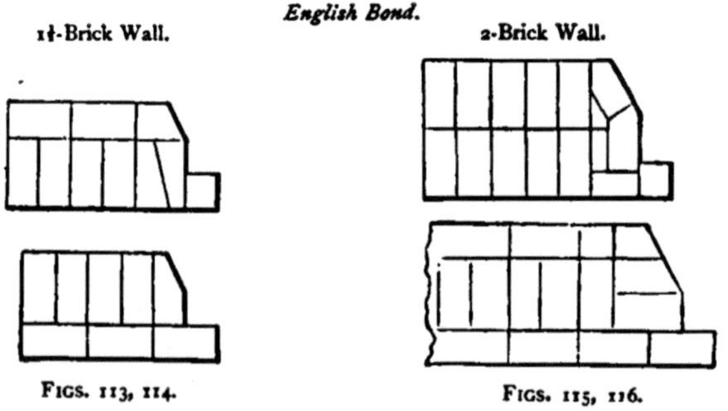


FIGS. 113, 114. FIGS. 115, 116.

Figs. 113, 114, are plans of the alternate courses of a reveal

[1] Reveals with square jambs belong to the Elementary Course.

with splayed jambs for a 14-inch (1½-brick) wall in English bond. Figs. 115, 116, are plans of the same in an 18-inch (2-brick) wall.

Figs. 117–120 give the same information for 14-inch and 18-inch walls in Flemish bond. There is a peculiarity in

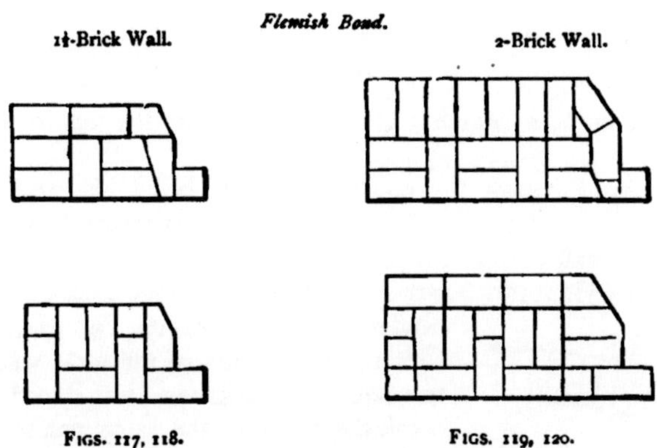


Figs. 117, 118. Figs. 119, 120.

the bond of these walls which may be noticed. It will be seen that there are no false headers in the face. Every header is a whole brick: this makes stronger work, and causes fewer splits in the wall than the ordinary single Flemish bond.

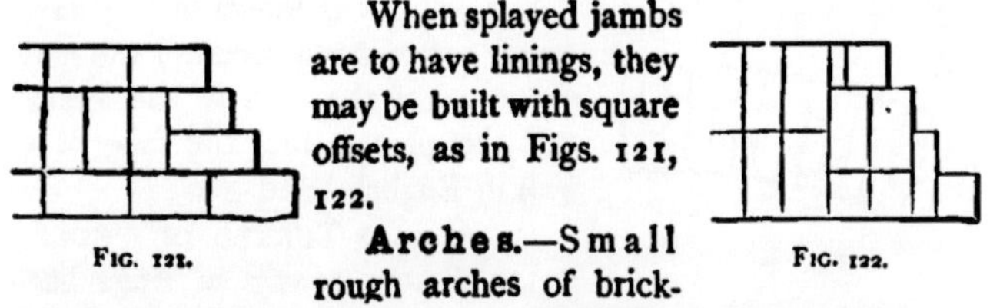

Fig. 121. Fig. 122.

When splayed jambs are to have linings, they may be built with square offsets, as in Figs. 121, 122.

**Arches.**—Small rough arches of brickwork are generally turned in half-brick rings, and this is especially necessary when the arch is of a quick curve, in order to avoid large joints upon the extrados.

Some authorities, however, recommend that flatter arches, especially those of larger span, should be built in 9-inch rings. This may be done in two or three different ways.

1. In English Bond.—Fig. 123 being the section, and the plan consisting of alternate courses of headers and stretchers,

Fig. 123.

presenting the appearance of English bond on the soffit of the arch.

2. In Flemish Bond.—The section being like that in Fig. 123, and the soffit showing the same arrangement as the face of a wall built in Flemish bond.

3. In Heading Bond.—The ring throughout consisting of headers as in the section, Fig. 124, excepting at the ends of the arch, where three-quarter bricks are introduced to break the bond, in the same manner as is done in the face of a wall built in heading bond.

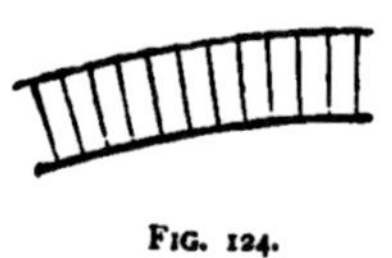

Fig. 124.

Of the above varieties the heading bond is the strongest, as the voussoirs are each in one piece and no bats are required; but it is very difficult to make neat work with such a bond, and it is therefore very seldom adopted.

Arches 1½ Brick thick may be built as shown in Fig. 125, which represents a section; the end elevation of the arch is the same, and the plan is like the face of a wall in English bond.

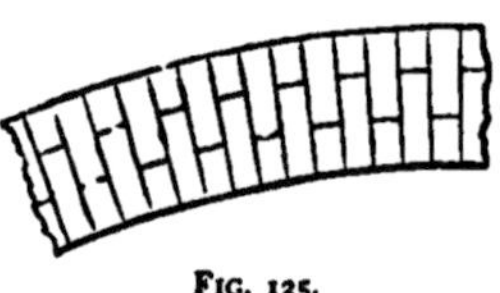

Fig. 125.

1. Arches Turned in Whole-Brick Rings consist of rings like that in Fig. 124 superposed one over the other.

2. Arches in Half-Brick Rings (see Fig. 126) are very commonly used, and are easily built; they should not, however, be adopted for spans exceeding 30 feet. The rings have a tendency to settle unequally; in such a case the whole weight may be thrown for a moment upon a single ring: if this is

crushed, the pressure comes upon the next ring, and so on, resulting in the failure of the whole arch.

In building arches with half-brick rings it is advisable to build the undermost ring with thin joints and gradually to thicken the mortar joints as the extrados is approached; this prevents the lowest ring from settling while those above remain in position, which would cause an ugly fissure.

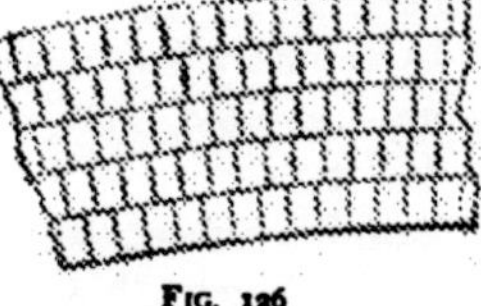

FIG. 126

*Arches with Bond Blocks.*—To avoid the disadvantages above mentioned, arches have been built with blocks, B B, set in cement, running through their thickness at intervals, so as to form a bond right through the thickness of the arch.[1] Stone bonds may be used instead, cut to the shape of a voussoir. These bond blocks should be placed at the points where the joints of the various rings coincide: those points will be determined by the radius of curvature of the arch, the thickness of the bricks, and of the joints.

FIG. 127.

*Bonding Rings in Pairs.*—Another

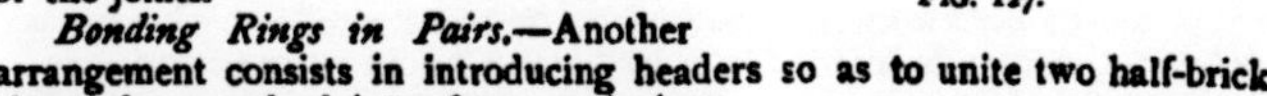

arrangement consists in introducing headers so as to unite two half-brick rings wherever the joints of two such rings happen to coincide. The rings are sometimes thus united in consecutive pairs right through the thickness of the arch.

THICK ARCHES BONDED THROUGHOUT THEIR DEPTH, as shown in Fig. 128, have sometimes been used for large spans.

The joints in the extrados are necessarily very wide, but the evil effects of this may be guarded against by using cement or quick-setting mortar, or by wedging up the joints of the outer portion with pieces of slate. In this latter case, however, the inner rings are apt to be relieved of pressure, and the stretches are liable to drop out.

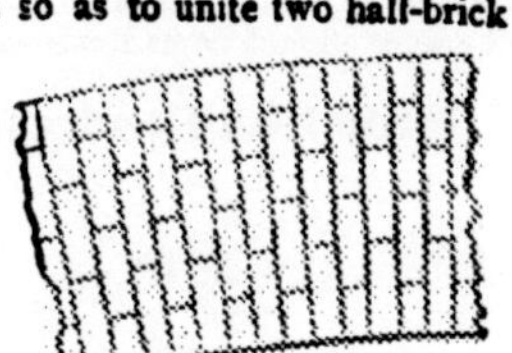

FIG. 128.

ARCHES OF LARGE SPAN, in whatever way they are bonded, should be built in good hydraulic mortar, setting moderately quickly, so that when the centres are struck the joints may be soft enough to adapt themselves to the inequalities of the

[1] The block B is drawn in thicker lines to make it distinct, but its joints are of the same thickness as those of the rest of the arch.

bricks, and thus enable them to obtain a firm bearing. Hoop-iron bond is sometimes introduced between the rings parallel to the soffit.

In ordinary buildings, however, arches of large span are seldom required, and they need not, therefore, be further alluded to.

**Bond Timbers** were at one time extensively used to give longitudinal strength to walls, but they are injurious in many ways.

In process of time they shrink, they rot, and, in case of fire, they burn away; in either instance the whole superincumbent weight of the wall is thrown upon a small portion of it; or, again, they may absorb moisture, swell, and overthrow the masonry.

RANGING BOND consists of narrow horizontal pieces built into the joints of walling parallel to one another at intervals of about 18 inches, to form grounds for battening, etc., etc. The face of the pieces projects slightly from the wall, so that the battens may be clear of the masonry.

Dry wood plugs[1] may be used instead, let into holes cut in the stones or bricks, not in the beds or joints, otherwise they may swell and disturb the wall.

It has already been stated that timber in every shape and form should be kept out of brickwork and masonry as much as possible; where it is absolutely necessary to insert it in order to form a hold for woodwork, etc., the pieces should be as small as practicable.

**Hoop-iron Bond,** consisting of strips of hoop-iron (about 1½ inch broad and $\frac{1}{18}$ to $\frac{1}{20}$ inch thick), tarred and sanded, and inserted in the joints as shown in Fig. 129, is far preferable to bond timbers, and is frequently used, especially in half-brick walls.[2]

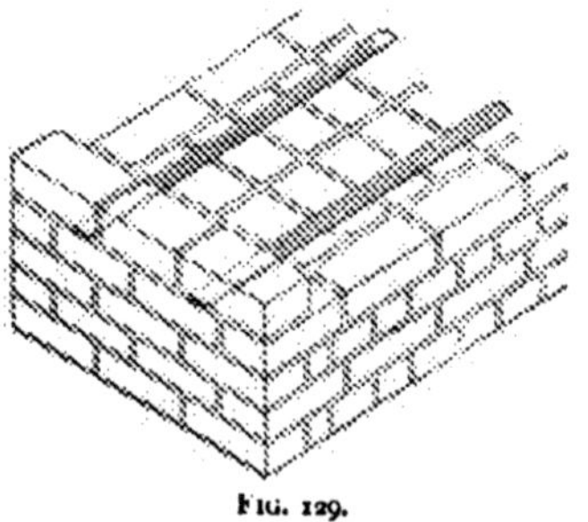

FIG. 129.

The hoop-iron should in every case be thoroughly protected from the action of

[1] Breeze-bricks may be substituted for these.

[2] Sometimes one or two strips are used for each brick in the thickness of the wall. Seddon's *Builders' Work.*

the atmosphere, or it will oxidize and destroy the masonry; if used in thin walls, they should be built in cement.

The ends of the hoop-iron should be bent so as to hook one another at the joints in the length, and at corners where two walls meet, forming an angle.

Pieces of hoop-iron are often used to make a junction where the bond of the brickwork is defective.

## BRICK DRAINS AND SEWERS.

Brickwork is evidently not adapted for drains of very small diameter, as there are, necessarily, very wide joints on the extrados of rings turned to a quick curve.

Earthenware pipes, being cheaper and preferable in every way have in most cases long since superseded brickwork for drains of less than 18 inches or 2 feet in diameter.

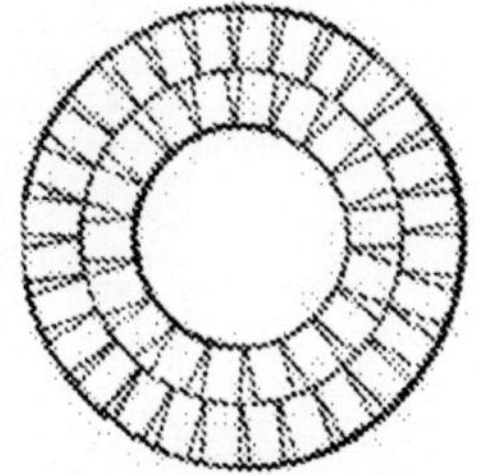

Fig. 130.

**Circular Drains.**—When pipes are not procurable, circular drains may be constructed with bricks as shown in section Fig. 130.

This figure shows an 18-inch drain constructed with two half-brick rings, but as a rule the thickness of the brickwork need not be more than one ring (or 4½ inches), in sewers of less than 3 feet diameter.

**Covered Drain.**—Another form of brick drain consists of a semicircular inverted arch covered with a flat stone, S, the removal of which gives easy access to the drain for examination.

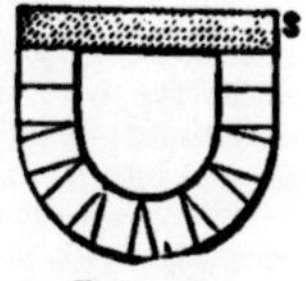


Fig. 131.

**Egg-shaped Sewers** may be constructed of the section shown in Fig. 132. The proportions of such sewers vary according to circumstances; but in all cases the invert, *i*, should have a quick curve (of radius not exceeding 9 inches), and the crown should be a semicircle.

The usual method of construction is to make the diameter of the invert half that of the crown, and the height of the sewer equal to 3 times the diameter of the invert.

Thus in Fig. 132—

$$hi = cf = 1. \quad gh = \tfrac{1}{2}. \quad ai = df = dk = 3.$$

The invert may be formed either of brickwork in cement, with a terra-cotta invert block, or with an invert block bedded in concrete, as shown at B in Fig. 132.

*Bricks and Inverts.*—Bricks for sewers should be of the hardest possible description, and laid in hydraulic morter. Even the best bricks will be gradually destroyed by the sewage.

The inverts especially require to be of hard lasting material with a smooth surface, so as to resist as little as possible the passage of the sewage matter passing over them. They should, therefore, be formed with a smooth terra-cotta or fireclay invert block, as shown in Fig. 132, or built with

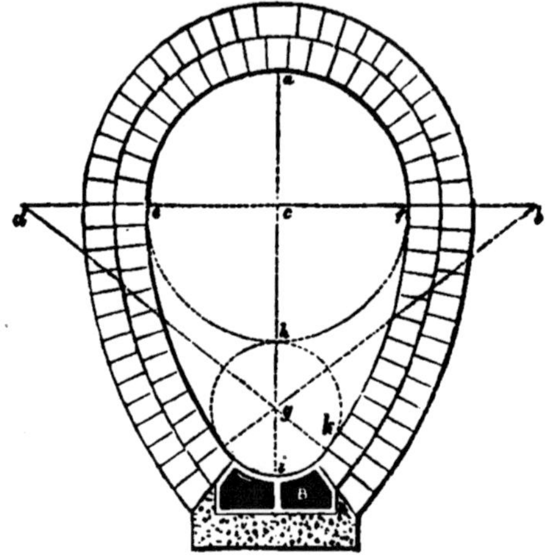


Fig. 132.

glazed or very smooth bricks. Bricks "purpose-moulded" to the radii make the best sewers; but where they cannot be obtained, blocks are sometimes formed with common bricks placed in frames, grouted and formed into a solid mass with cement.

When sewers are constructed in a porous soil, the invert should be very carefully built, and a lining of puddle clay placed outside the sewer, so as to render it water-tight to half its vertical depth.

Great care should be taken in filling in over sewers, so that large clods or masses of earth may not be allowed to fall upon the brickwork and injure it.

The construction of drains with stoneware pipes, and of sewers in concrete, or in segment blocks, need not be noticed, as the subject does not fall within the limits of this Course.

## CHIMNEYS.

The fireplaces in a house frequently stand one immediately over the other, and each chimney flue [1] from the lower rooms has in consequence to be carried to one side or the other to avoid the fireplaces above it.

**Arrangement of Flues.**—Flues from the lower stories are therefore necessarily curved, but not those from the attics; a curve is, however, considered advisable in all flues, to prevent rain or sleet from beating vertically on to the fire, and to stop down-draughts of cold air. This curve should be sufficient to prevent daylight from being seen when looking up the flue.

The funnel, or opening above the fireplace, is gathered over (see p. 82), so as to be contracted to the size of the flue required.

Fireplaces generally require more depth than can be provided in the thickness of the wall; this necessitates a projection to contain the fireplace and flues called the *chimney breast*. Sometimes this projection is on the back of the wall, in which case it gives more space and a more convenient shape to the room. When on the outer wall of a house it may be made an ornamental feature.

Every fireplace should have a distinct flue to itself; if the flues of two fireplaces communicate, and only one fire be lighted, it will draw air from the other fireplace, and smoke; moreover, its own smoke may enter any other room the fireplace of which is connected with the same flue.

The air heated by the fire is rarefied, rendered lighter, and ascends the flue, drawing the smoke with it, whilst cold air rushes into its place from below.

Hence the throat or lower opening of the flue should be small, so that no air may pass through it without first coming into contact with the fire and being thoroughly warmed.

The flue should not be larger than is necessary for conveying the smoke and heated air; if too large, it will smoke in certain winds.

With regard to the proper size for flues there are great differences of opinion. The size should vary according to the circumstances of different cases; but generally speaking a flue 9 inches square is sufficient to carry off the smoke from very small grates, a flue 14 inches × 9 inches for ordinary fireplaces, and a flue 14 inches × 14 inches for large kitchen ranges.

The smaller the flue, and the greater the height, the more rapid the draught and the less likely the chimney to smoke, provided that sufficient air is supplied and that the flue is large enough to carry off the smoke.

The flue should change its direction by gradual curves and contain no

---

[1] Sc. *Vents.*

sharp angles, otherwise soot accumulates and makes it smoke. The Building Act requires that if any angle is necessarily less than 130° an iron soot-door should be provided at the bend, so that the soot may be removed (see S, Fig. 141).

Much depends upon the height of a flue, the shortest, *i.e.* those from upper rooms, or in low buildings, being most liable to smoke.

The air should pass through or very near the fire.

Thus a high opening above the fire is bad, as it admits cold air, which gets up the flue without being heated, and cools the rising warm air.

The fireplace should, therefore, be not much higher than the grate.

All walls about chimneys should be well built, and so should the "withes" or partitions between flues, as cold air may penetrate badly built walls from the outside, or from an unused flue cold air may get into one in use, thus cooling the heated air and causing the chimney to smoke.

If openings are left in the withes, the smoke from a flue in use may penetrate another, and from it enter a room in which the fire is not burning.

**Arrangement of Flues.**—The width of the chimney breast for each room of a high building must be arrived at by drawing the plan of the fireplace of each room, including the flues from the fireplaces of the rooms below; they can be arranged in plan in such a form as may be most convenient for the chimney stack.

A very common practice is to build the fireplaces of adjacent rooms or houses back to back, in which case the arrangement on each side of the wall is exactly the same.

The plan of bringing a number of flues into a "stack" is economical and tends to preserve an equal temperature in them.

*First Illustration of Arrangement of Flues.*—Figs. 133, 134 are respectively longitudinal and cross-sections of the fireplaces and flues in the wall between two 5-storied buildings.

The dotted lines in Fig. 134 show the direction of the flues of the fireplaces on the other side of the wall.

The remaining figures on p. 79 show the plan of the chimney breasts on the level of each floor.

The weight upon the chimney breasts should be spread over a greater area by introducing footings,[1] as shown in Figs. 133, 134.

In some cases the same object is attained by turning an invert arch between the chimney breasts under the fireplace.

In order to economize the brickwork, and to leave as much interior

[1] Sc. *Coddings.*

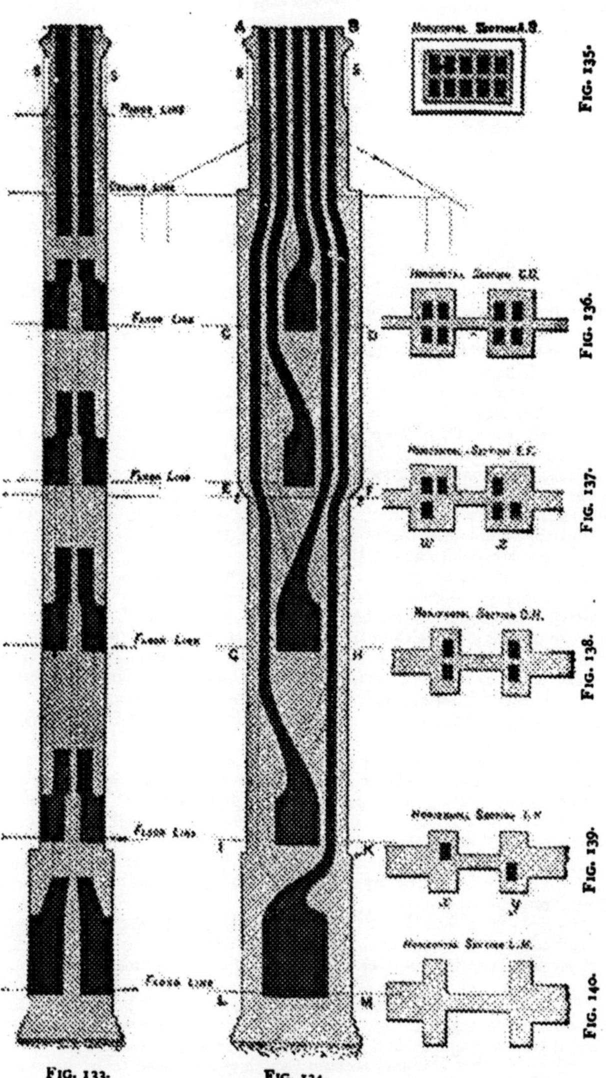

Fig. 133.

Fig. 134.
Scale, $\frac{1}{16}$ inch = 1 foot.

Fig. 135.

Fig. 136.

Fig. 137.

Fig. 138.

Fig. 139.

Fig. 140.

space in the building as possible, the part of the chimney breast in each room is generally made of the minimum width that is absolutely necessary to contain the flues at that point.

Thus it will be seen that the chimney breasts on floors I K and G H are made narrower than those above them, because they contain fewer flues. The extra width required for the flues in the chimney breast on the other floors is gained by corbelling out as shown at *t t*. The projections in the brickwork are concealed under the floor and by the cornice of the ceiling below.

Sometimes one side of the chimney breast is made narrower than the other; thus the side *x* (Fig. 139) might be made narrower than *y*, and *w* narrower than *z* (Fig. 137), for in each case the chimney breast on the left contains one flue less than that on the right. This causes an unsymmetrical appearance, but is often done even in superior buildings.

The whole of the external walls, both of chimney breasts and shafts, are generally made half a brick or only 4½ inches thick.

It is safer, however, to make the front and outside wall of the chimney breasts 9 inches thick, especially when they are in contact with woodwork, such as skirtings, roof-timbers, etc.

Again, even when this is done, the outside wall of the chimney shaft itself is often reduced to half a brick directly it has passed through the roof. It is better, however, to keep the external walls of the shaft 9 inches thick throughout (as dotted at S S in Fig. 133), for the reasons stated at p. 78.

*Second Illustration of Arrangement of Flues.*—It is frequently necessary, for the sake of appearance, to place the chimney in a symmetrical position, such as the centre of the roof. To this end, and also in order to avoid a multiplicity of chimney shafts, the flues have to be collected from opposite sides of the house into a central stack.

Fig. 141 shows an example of this. The flues from the rooms A, B, C, and E, converge towards a central stack, the space between the chimney breasts of the upper rooms being bridged by an arch W, over which the flues are carried; the brickwork forming the upper wall of the flue is racked back as shown, leaving only thickness sufficient for safety above the flues.

The chimney breast of the room C cannot be carried down to the foundation, as it would interfere with the folding-doors in the room below. It is therefore supported by courses corbelled out into the room from the wall, as shown in dotted lines.

It will be noticed that the chimney breast of the room A is nearer the outer wall than that of the room below; in order to avoid widening the chimney breast below, the upper and outer chimney breast *p* is supported by courses corbelled over to one side as dotted. The corbelling is concealed by being carried out within the floor.

The projecting part of the upper chimney breast might be supported by turning an arch, as shown by the dotted line X, and this is a construction often adopted.

It will be seen that the flue from the room E is carried vertically up in the thickness of the outer wall as high nearly as the ceiling of room C, then over an arch covering the recess between the chimney breast and the outer wall.

The portion of flue in the thickness of the outer wall is rather apt to be cold and to check the draught, and the construction might in this case be avoided by carrying the flue across the corner of the party wall of room D, and up the left chimney breast *s* (which would have to be widened to receive it) of the room C, above.

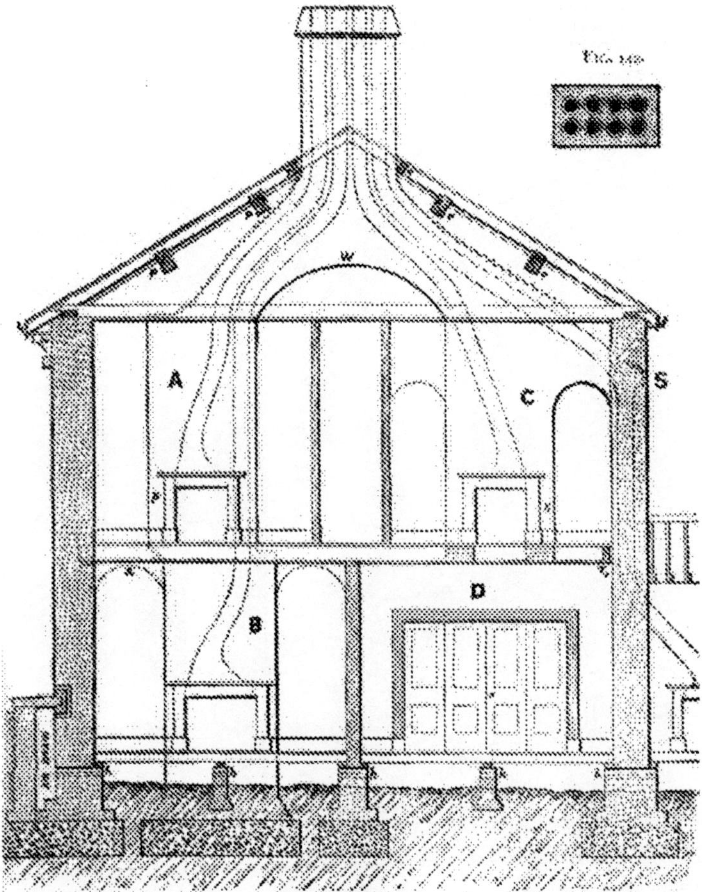


FIG. 141.
Scale, $\frac{1}{10}$ inch = 1 foot.

This Figure is the section of an ordinary dwelling-house taken on this side of the flue from E, and is intended to show two or three different arrangements of flues. The whole surface of the ground may, with advantage, be covered by a layer of concrete.

The flues in this illustration are supposed to be formed with circular earthenware pipes[1] of 9 inches diameter, shown in plan in Fig. 142.

The external walls are here shown only 4½ inches thick, because the thickness of the flue-pipe itself affords a great protection and renders it unnecessary to make the brickwork so thick as it should be round pargetted flues.

**Chimney Shafts.**[2]—At the ceiling of the highest room the chimney breast is reduced in size to the chimney shaft of

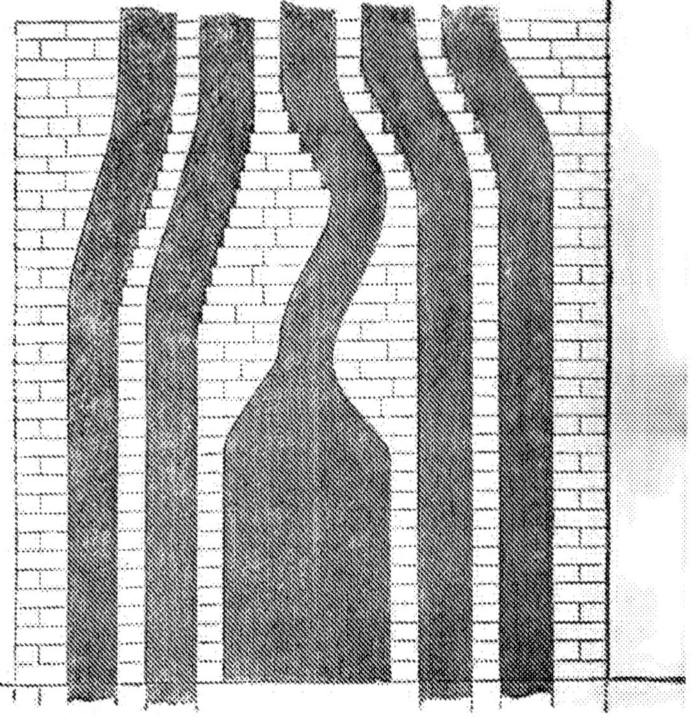

Fig. 143.

a width just sufficient to contain the flues. This shaft should be carried well above the roof, higher if possible than adjacent roofs or buildings, which are apt to cause eddies or down-draughts and make the chimney smoke.

[1] Sc. *Vent linings.*

[2] Sc. *Stalks.*

**Chimney Caps.**—A few of the upper courses of high chimney shafts are generally made to project, and should be built in cement to serve as a protection from the weather.

The cap is frequently made ornamental by bricks, placed anglewise, etc. Stone caps are also used for brick as well as for stone chimneys.

**Fireplaces.**—Jambs of fireplaces are built in the same manner as brick walls. The chimney breasts should be carefully founded, resting upon footings, or supported by corbels where necessary.

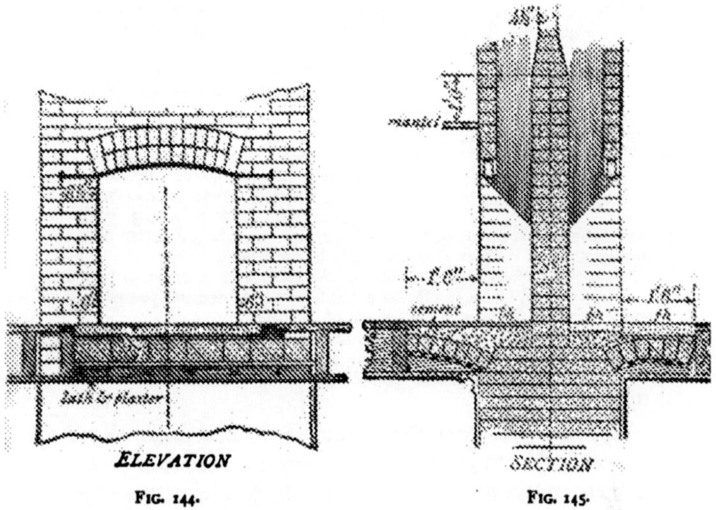


Fig. 144. Fig. 145.

In order to form the throat of the chimney, the courses are "gathered" over, each projecting $1\frac{1}{8}$ inch or so over the last, until the opening is narrowed to the required dimensions. The exact projection depends of course upon the curve required. The narrowest part or throat should be immediately over the centre of the fireplace. Above the throat, the flue ascends vertically for a short distance, then gathers again to the right or left, as shown in Fig. 143.

The projecting corners of the offsets are cut off, and where the flue recedes the re-entering angles are sometimes filled up with bits of brick, or by the rendering of the flue.

In consequence of the number of bats necessary in such work, the bond cannot be laid down beforehand, but must be left a good deal to the bricklayer.

Fig. 143 is an enlarged section of the flues contained in the chimney breast just above the floor, C D, in Fig. 134. It shows the method of gathering over for the flue of a small fireplace, and also the arrangement of the bricks in forming the withes, etc., for the flues from the stories below.

Fig. 144 is an elevation, and Fig. 145 a section, of a fireplace, showing the rough arch supported by a "*turning bar*,"[1] T T, of which a sketch is given in Fig. 146. The bricks next to the skew-backs are often laid as headers.

This bar is from ½ to ⅝ inch thick, and about 3 inches wide. It has a bearing of 4½ inches on each jamb, and beyond the bearing portions, ends about 3 inches long. These ends are sometimes split longitudinally, and *corked*;[2] *i.e.* turned in opposite directions, up and down, as shown in Fig. 146. Very frequently the ends are turned either up or down without being split, and this is a better plan than that shown, for it renders it unnecessary to cut bricks.

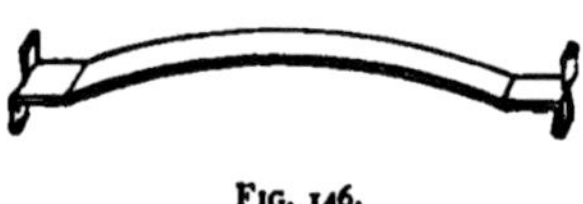

Fig. 146.

The bar is curved to fit the soffit of the arch, and in order to prevent it from straightening under the thrust a small bolt is sometimes passed through it and secured to a plate on the crown of the arch.

Flat turning bars have been advocated as tending to draw the jambs together instead of thrusting them out, but they are seldom if ever adopted.

The interior of the jambs of chimney breasts should always be filled in solid.

**Hearths** are stone flags about 2½ inches thick, placed so as to catch the droppings from the grate. The *back hearth*, *bh* Fig. 145, covers the space between the jambs of the chimney breast.[3] The *front hearth*, *fh*, rests upon the trimmer arch described in E.B.C.

**Bond of Chimney Shafts.**—It has already been mentioned that the external walls of chimneys should be 9 inches thick, at least until the shaft has passed through the roof; they are better if built in cement.

Such a thickness is almost necessary for safety within the building, where the woodwork of the roof and skirtings is frequently brought up against the chimney.

---

[1] Or chimney-bar. [2] Or caulked.

[3] Solid concrete hearths are frequently used instead of stone hearths on brick trimmer arches.

It is, moreover, an advantage to have a thick wall round the chimney shaft, even in the open air, as it tends to keep the flue warm. A thin wall is soon partially destroyed by the weather, and admits cold air to the flue, causing it to smoke.

WHOLE-BRICK EXTERNAL WALLS, ENGLISH BOND.—

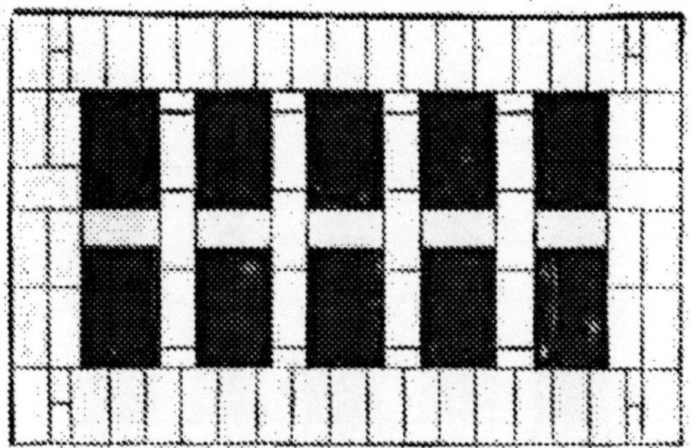

FIG. 147.

FIG. 148.—*Chimney. Whole-brick external walls. English Bond.*

Figs. 147, 148, give horizontal sections of two courses of the chimney in Fig. 134, just before it emerges from the roof. It has an exterior wall 9 inches thick built in English bond.

It will be seen that the cross withes are well bonded into the external walls in alternate courses, and the longitudinal withe may also be bonded in either by cutting bricks as at A, or by mitreing as at B.

HALF-BRICK EXTERNAL WALLS, ENGLISH BOND.—In ordinary buildings the external walls of chimneys and chimney breasts are, for economy, made only half a brick thick throughout, both inside the building and above the roof. Examples of the necessary bond are therefore shown in Figs. 149, 150, though such thin external walls are objectionable for the reasons already stated.

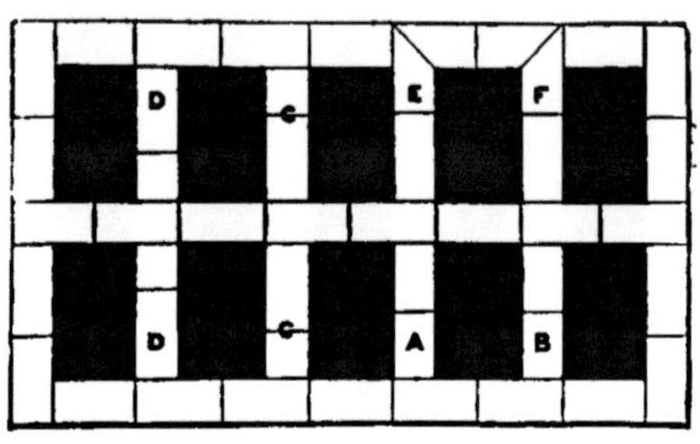


FIG. 149.

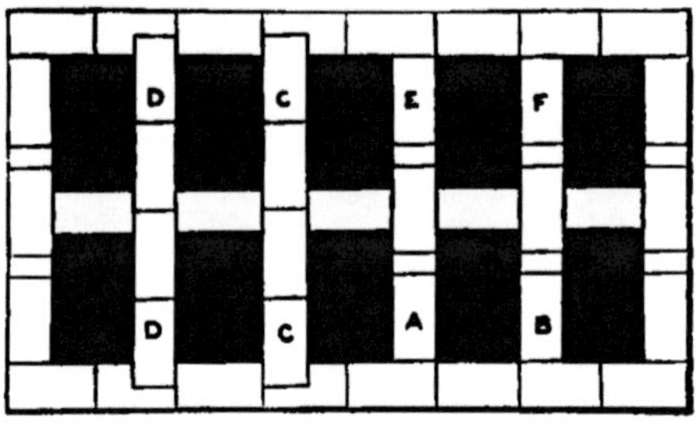


FIG. 150.—*Chimney. Half-brick external walls. Stretching Bond.*

STRETCHING BOND—These 4½-inch external walls are generally built in stretching bond; such a bond, however, carried out in the ordinary manner, leaves the cross withes quite detached from the side walls, as are the withes A B in Fig. 150.

This may, however, be avoided by causing the withes in alternate causes to penetrate the side walls to the depth of ½ brick or 2¼ inches, as shown in withes C C, D D, Fig. 150, or by cutting the bricks forming the ends of the withes to a mitre, as at E F, Fig. 149, so as to fit the adjacent bricks in the external walls, which are similarly cut.

In both these arrangements the bricks are not allowed to show on the face of the external wall, as headers would interfere with the appearance of the stretching bond.

**Half-Brick External Walls, Flemish Bond.**—The external walls of chimneys may very conveniently be built in Flemish bond, as shown in Figs. 151, 152. It will be noticed that there is no elaborate cutting of bricks, the bond is perfectly symmetrical, and the withes are admirably united with the external walls.

Fig. 151.

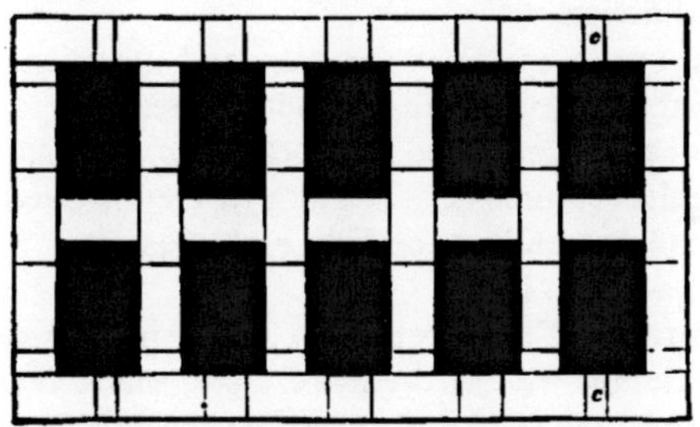


Fig. 152.—*Chimney. Half-brick external walls. Flemish Bond.*

If the flues at one end were required to be 14 inches square, as for a very large kitchen chimney, ¾ bricks would be used instead of *c c*, and half bricks or false headers inserted at *h h*.

The exact arrangement of bond in a chimney must depend upon the size, shape, diameter, and arrangement of the flues, the thickness of the outer walls, the bond adopted in the building, and other particulars depending upon circumstances.

It would of course be impossible to illustrate even a very

small portion of the various arrangements required by different combinations of the above particulars.

Further examples cannot here be given, but it will be good practice to the student to draw for himself the bonds best adapted for chimneys of different forms and arrangements, in doing which it is hoped that he will find the above illustrations a useful guide.

**Stone Chimneys.**—Chimney breasts in stone buildings are very often built with bricks, which are better adapted than stone for forming the thin withes and walls required, and generally less expensive than sound masonry.

The chimney breasts and flues are, however, frequently built in rubble.

When the chimney passes above the roof it is of course necessary that, for the sake of appearance, it should be of the same material as the walls of the building generally.

Chimneys in rubble are built in a very similar way to those in brickwork; those of cut stone or ashlar are very varied in form and design.

Figs. 153 to 155 show the plan and elevations of a chimney in cut stone, of a form frequently used.

The cap is supported by blocks, *d*, *d*, and surmounted by semicircular "terminals," T, T, which are intended to prevent down-draughts, and to protect each flue from the action of those adjacent to it.

**Chimney Flues**, especially those in masonry, are frequently formed with earthenware pipes, which afford but little resistance to the smoke, are free from the objectionable corners of brick flues, do not collect the soot, and are easily kept of uniform section throughout; on the other hand, if the internal surface is too smooth, the soot is apt to collect and fall in lumps.

RENDERING.—The flues may be rendered inside with Portland cement.

PARGETTING.—The ordinary method is, however, to plaster the inside of the flue over with a mixture of one part of lime with three of cow-dung; this forms a tough lining with a smooth surface, and not so liable to crack as ordinary mortar.

Coring.—While a chimney flue is being built, it is advisable to keep within it a bundle of rags or shavings called a "sweep," in order to prevent mortar from falling upon its sides; and after the flue is finished, a wire brush or core should be passed through it to clear away small irregularities, and to detect any obstruction that there may be in the flue.

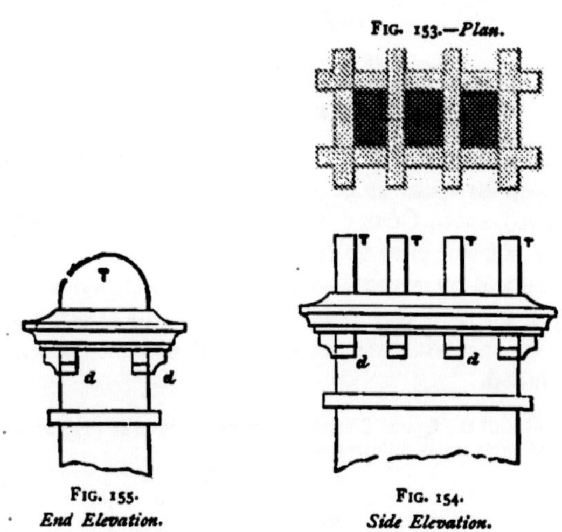


Fig. 153.—*Plan.*

Fig. 155. *End Elevation.*

Fig. 154. *Side Elevation.*

Chimney Pots[1] are frequently placed over flues, to prevent the eddy of wind that would be caused by a flat surface at the top of the chimney.

[1] Sc. *Chimney cans.*

# CHAPTER V.

## *TIMBER ROOFS.*

### *Subjects required by Syllabus.*

"*Roofs of . . . wood for spans up to 60 feet.*"

THE king-post roof and simpler forms described in E.B.C.D. are adapted for spans up to 30 feet.

This Advanced Course includes the trusses ordinarily used for spans of from 30 to 60 feet.

Gothic and other roofs adapted for special styles of architecture, or for particular situations, will not be referred to.

Trusses involving the use of curved or built-up beams are also excluded.

*N.B.*—In all the figures illustrating timber roofs, the distinctive letters for different parts are as follows:—

|  |  |  |  |
|---|---|---|---|
| Angle Tie | *a* | Pole Plate | *pp* |
| Battens | *b* | Princess Post | *PP* |
| Binders | *Bi* | Purlin | *P* |
| Blocking Course | *Bc* | Rafters, Principal | *PR* |
| Boarding | *B* | ,, Common | *CR* |
| Ceiling Joists | *Cj* | ,, Jack | *JR* |
| Cleats | *C* | Ridge | *r* |
| Collar Tie | *CT* | Soffit | *fs* |
| Cornice | *c* | Struts | *S* |
| Fascia | *F* | Slates | *s* |
| Gutter | *G* | Straining Beam | *SB* |
| Gutter-bearer | *gb* | ,, Sill | *SS* |
| Gutter-plate | *gp* | Templates (wall) | *wt* |
| King Bolt | *KB* | Tie Beam | *T* |
| ,, Post | *KP* | Tilting Fillet | *tf* |
| Queen Bolt | *QB* | ,, Batten | *tb* |
| ,, Post | *QP* | Truss (Principal) | *TP* |
| Parapet Wall | *PW* | Wall Plates | *wp* |

**King and Queen Post Roofs.**—King-post trusses will do very well for roofs up to about 30 feet span, but for wider roofs it is found that the tie beam requires support at more than the one central point; additional vertical ties, called queen posts, have therefore to be introduced, as at QP, QP, Fig. 156.

The common rafters being longer, require support at more than one point; two purlins are therefore introduced on each side of the roof.

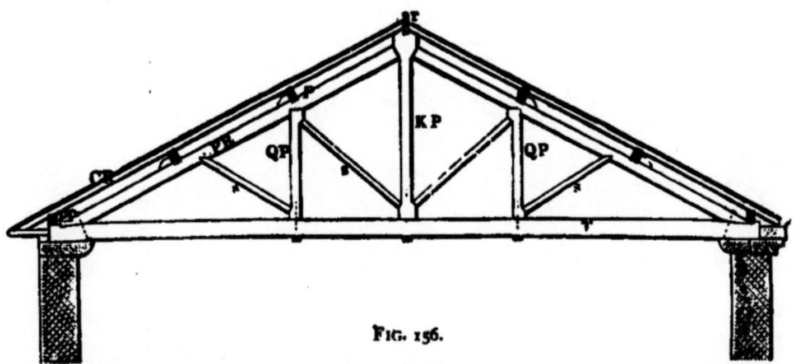


Fig. 156.

**Queen-Post Roof with King Bolts.**—This excellent construction is shown in Fig. 167, p. 98.

When a flat top is not required, purlins with common rafters running down the slope of the roof are adopted, as in Fig. 156, and the apex of the roof finished as there shown.

## QUEEN-POST ROOFS.

When rooms have to be formed in the roof, and frequently besides, the king post is omitted, in which case, to prevent the heads of the queen posts from being forced inwards, a straining beam is placed between them, as shown at SB in Fig. 157, and their feet are kept apart by a straining sill, SS.

This form of roof is well adapted for spans of from 30 to 45 feet.

**Parts of a Queen-post Roof.**—The parts common to all ordinary roofs, such as tie beams, rafters, wall plates, purlins, ridges, gutters, etc., have already been considered in E.B.C.D., and it remains only to give a description of those peculiar to queen-post roofs.

**Queen Posts.**—These have, between them, to carry about $\frac{2}{3}$ the weight of the tie beam, together with that of the ceiling, if any, suspended therefrom, and they frequently have to support additional loads brought upon the tie beam by the occupation of the space between the queen posts as a garret.

The heads of the queen posts are kept apart by a "straining beam," SB (Figs. 157, 159), and the feet are tenoned into the tie beam and prevented from moving inwards by a "straining sill," SS.

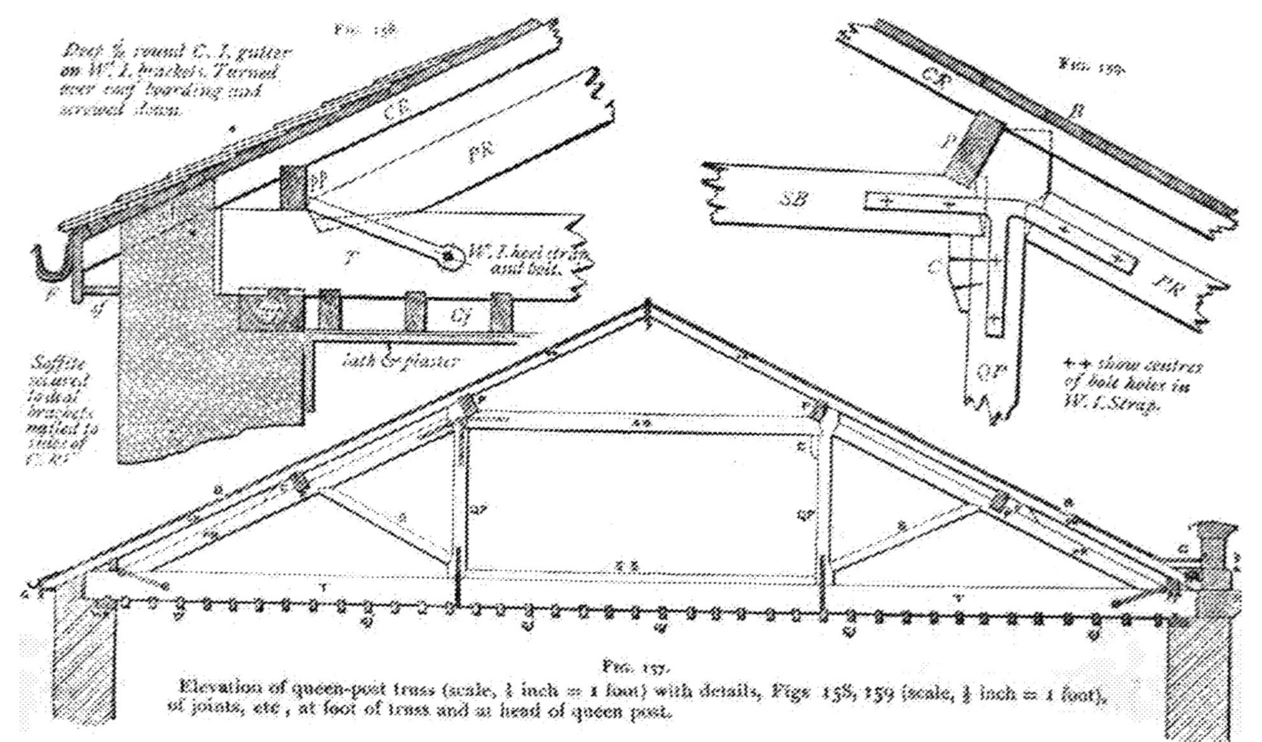


Fig. 157.

Elevation of queen-post truss (scale, ⅛ inch = 1 foot) with details, Figs 158, 159 (scale, ½ inch = 1 foot), of joints, etc , at foot of truss and at head of queen post.

The feet of the queen posts are sometimes secured by being housed on their inner sides into the tie beam, in which case the straining sill may be dispensed with.

**Straining Beam.**—The object of this beam has just been mentioned—its ends are supported by being housed and tenoned into the heads of the queen posts, additional security being generally afforded by cleats, C, nailed to the posts as shown.

The strap above C is omitted in Fig. 157, in order to show the joint.

When the straining beam is of considerable length it is sometimes supported in the centre by struts inclining inwards from the feet of the queen posts, as in Fig. 167, p. 98.

In that figure it is shown as supporting a lead flat, in which case it may with advantage be made thicker in the centre than at the ends, so as to strengthen the beam, and to give the lead a slight slope outwards.

**Straining Sill.**—This is generally merely a piece of scantling lying on the tie beam, and butting against the feet of the queen posts (Fig. 157).

The straining sill is sometimes bolted and keyed to the tie beam, or arranged so as to form a truss and give support to the centre part of the tie beam.

In the roof with princess posts, straining sills may advantageously be introduced between the feet of the queens and princesses.

*Binders*, marked *Bi*, are shown in Fig. 166 framed in between the tie beams. This is sometimes a convenient arrangement for stiffening the roof. It may also be adopted when the principals are widely spaced, in order to afford a shorter bearing for the ceiling joists.

**Details of the joints** at the foot of the principal rafter and at the head of the queen post are given in Figs. 158, 159; another detail for the joint at the head and one for that at the foot of the queen post is given in E.B.C.D., p. 131.

**Roof with Queen Posts and Princesses.**—In roofs of

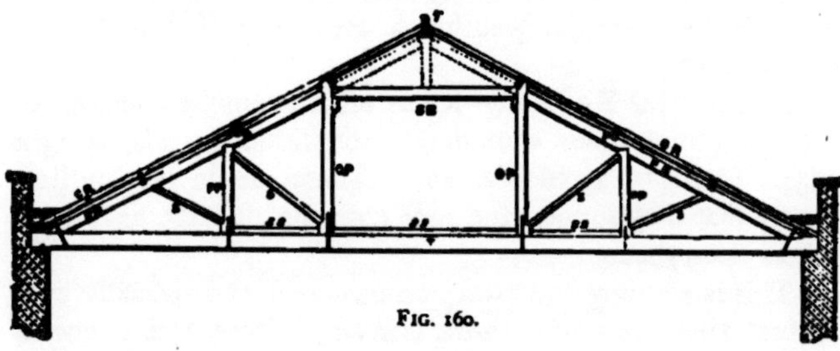

FIG. 160.

a greater span than 45 feet, the tie beam requires to be upheld at more than two intermediate points.

The extra support necessary is furnished by the introduction of additional suspending posts, PP, known as *Princesses.*

Such a construction as that shown in Fig. 160 may be used for spans between 45 and 60 feet.

In roofs of above 50 feet span the straining beam between the heads of the queen posts is so long that it would sag without support, and this may be afforded by means of a small king tie, suspended from the junction of the principal rafters, which are prolonged above the straining beam, as dotted in the figure.

In a roof of this kind the space between the queen posts affords convenient accommodation.

**Roofs of Spans greater than 60 Feet.**—The consideration of such roofs does not fall within the limits of this course, and in these days they would generally be constructed of iron.

**Roofs composed of Wood and Iron for Spans of more than 40 Feet.**—The chief use of wrought iron in composite roofs is as a substitute for the wooden posts or suspending pieces which uphold the tie beam.

Cast iron is also used, in the form of shoes, heads, etc., for receiving and connecting the members of the truss.

It is not considered worth while to give any illustrations of composite roofs of wide span; they are not included in the Syllabus, and have not been much used since the introduction of iron roofs.

**Horizontal Rafters.**—Roofs are sometimes constructed with horizontal rafters extending across the principals, at right angles to them, as in Fig. 167. These are in fact purlins, except that they support the roof covering directly, having no rafters upon them.

This is a strong and cheap arrangement, and specially convenient when the roof covering is in large pieces, such as sheets of corrugated iron, which can be laid on the rafters without boarding.

When boards are required, they of course extend lengthways down the slope of the roof, and their edges are thus not so liable to be soaked with wet, in case of a leak, as they are when laid parallel to the ridge.

**Roofs of Various Shapes and their Parts** are described at p. 110, E.B.C.D.

**A Hipped Roof**[1] is sloped back at the ends as in Fig. 161. These terminating slopes are called the "hipped ends."

**Hips**[2] are the salient angles formed by the intersection of the sides and ends.

**Valleys** are the intersections similarly formed in re-entering angles (see VR VR, Fig. 162).

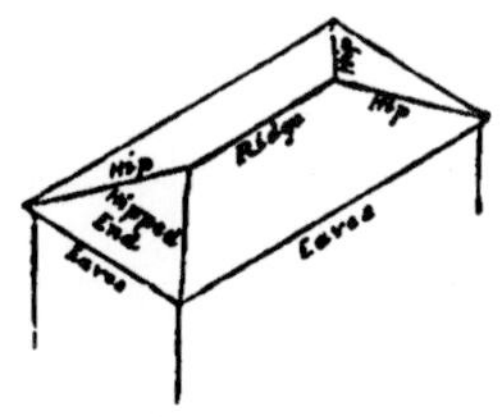

FIG. 161.

**A Pavilion Roof** is hipped uniformly at both ends, as shown in Fig. 161.

**Construction of Hipped Roofs.**—If a roof terminates in gables, only ordinary principals are required in its construction, but if it is cut into by another roof or is hipped back at the ends, special arrangements have to be made for the valleys and hips.

When a simple couple roof is "hipped," deep and narrow "*hip rafters*"[3] HR, Fig. 162, are carried from the end of the ridge to the angles of the end of the building, and short rafters, called "*jack rafters*," JR, are cut to fit in between the hip rafters and the wall plates.

The same course is followed in the valley caused by the intersection of two roofs, "*valley rafters*" or *valley pieces* being introduced, as at VR VR in Fig. 162.

In framed roofs the jack rafters fit in between the hip rafters and the wall plates, or between the valley pieces and the ridges.

Fig. 162 is the plan, and Fig. 163 a sectional elevation, of a collar-tie roof covering a building of irregular form.

In the former figures, HR HR are the hip rafters, VR VR the valley rafters, DD the dragon pieces in the angles (see p. 97), TT the trimmers carrying the rafters round openings left in the roof for chimneys, skylights, etc.

Fig. 163 shows in section the collar-tie roof trimmed to

[1] Sc. *Piend roof.* [2] Sc. *Piends.* [3] Sc. *Piend rafters.*

clear the chimney, and in elevation the gable end G, and the end hipped back at F.

FIG. 162.—Scale, $\frac{1}{16}$ inch = 1 foot.

*Plan.*

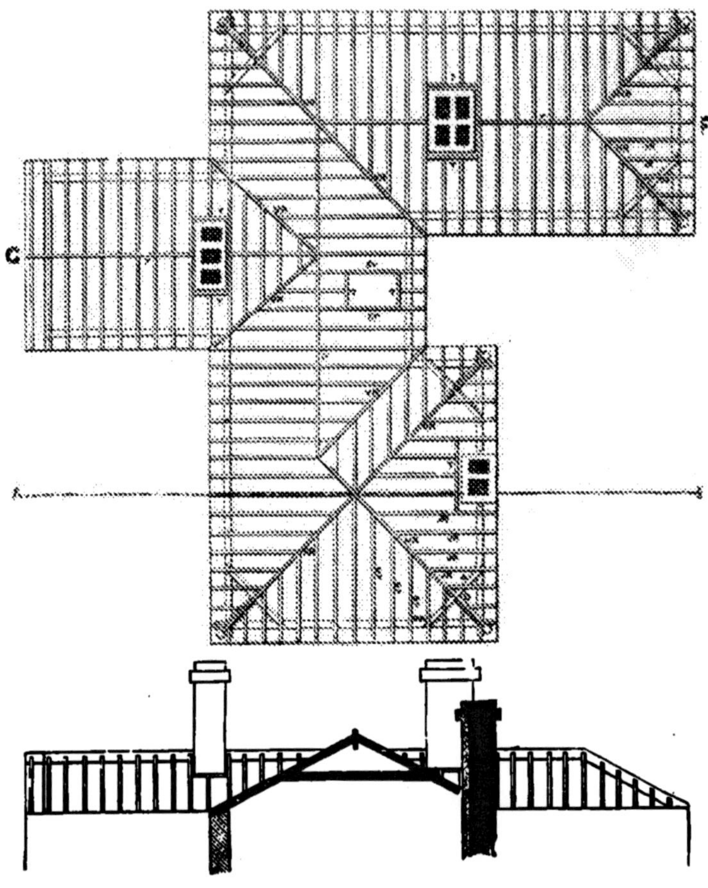


FIG. 163.

*Sectional E evation on A B.*

In a larger roof, such for instance as requires king-post trusses with purlins, as in Fig. 164, the length of the purlin, PP, on the hipped end would be too great to be left without support; in such a case a half king-post truss may be introduced at KT.

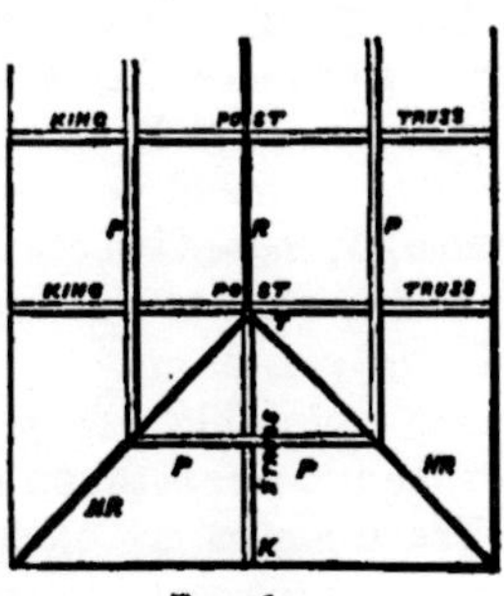


Fig. 164.

Similarly in a queen-post roof half principals are placed abutting against the queen posts of the first main truss, and at right angles to it.

In larger roofs flat-topped trusses must be introduced at intervals in the hipped ends to carry the rafters.

Framed Angle.—In a construction such as that described above, the hip rafter, being very long and heavy, requires to be well supported at its lower end, or it would thrust out the corner of the building; moreover, the angle requires to be tied together.

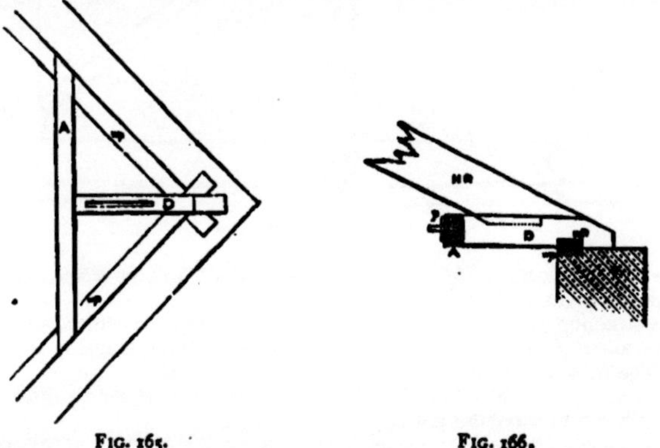


Fig. 165. Fig. 166.

These objects are fulfilled by the arrangements shown in Figs. 165, 166. The foot of the hip rafter is tenoned into a mortise in the *dragon beam*[1] D, one end of which is notched into the wall plate *wp*, while the other is furnished with a strong tusk tenon which passes through a hole in the *angle brace* A.

[1] Or dragging-tie.

After the hip rafter is fixed it is tightened up by driving a pin into the hole, *h*.

**Trimming.**[1]—Wherever rafters come across any obstacle, such as a chimney, they must be trimmed in the same way as described in Part I. for floor joists. Thus in Fig. 162 the rafters *tr tr* would be made thicker than the others, and a trimmer, T, framed in between them. The rafters are similarly trimmed in order to leave openings for skylights, etc., as shown at T, Fig. 221, p. 136.

The roof in Fig. 141, p. 81, is trimmed to clear the chimney; the trimmer is shown in section at T.

The trimmers are often placed vertically, and sometimes supported in the centre by corbels protruding from the chimney.

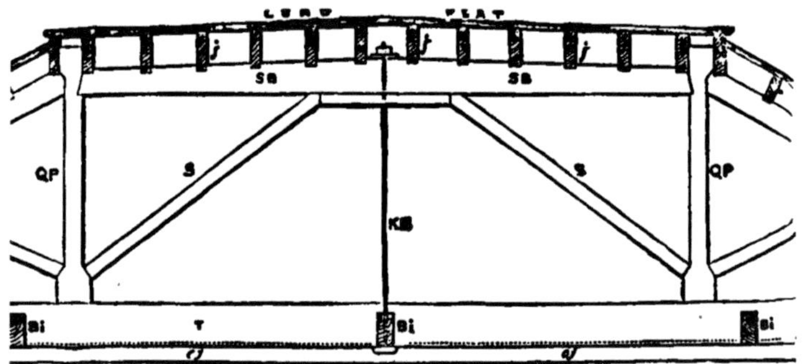


FIG. 167.—Scale, ⅛ inch = 1 foot.

**Flat-topped Roofs.**—Fig. 167 shows a method of forming a very nearly flat top to a queen-post roof.

The straining beam, SB, is made slightly thicker in the centre, so as to raise the joists, *j j j*, supporting the lead flat, sufficiently to throw off the wet. The rolls for the lead are not shown (see E.B.C.D.).

Sometimes rafters at a very flat slope are introduced above an ordinary straining beam to carry the joists.

As a considerable weight comes upon the straining beam, it receives additional support from two struts branching inwards from the feet of the queen posts, and kept asunder by a small straining piece. Fig. 167 shows also binders framed in between the tie beams.

**Tredgold's Tables of Scantling for Roofs 30 to 60 feet span.**—The following tables give the sizes of timbers for roofs of from 30 to 60 feet span.

[1] *Bridling.*

QUEEN-POST ROOFS, such as in Fig. 157.—TABLES of SCANTLINGS of TIMBER for different spans, from 30 to 46 feet.

| Span. | Tie Beam, T. | Queen Post, QP. | Principal Ra'ters, PR. | Straining Beam, SB. | Struts, S. | Purlins, P. | Common Rafters, CR. |
|---|---|---|---|---|---|---|---|
| 32 ft. | 10 by 4½ | 4½ by 4 | 5 by 4½ | 6¾ by 4½ | 3¾ by 2½ | 8 by 4¾ | 3½ by 2 |
| 34 ,, | 10 ,, 5 | 5 ,, 3½ | 5 ,, 5 | 6¾ ,, 5 | 4 ,, 2½ | 8½ ,, 5 | 3¾ ,, 2 |
| 36 ,, | 10½ ,, 5 | 5 ,, 4 | 5 ,, 5¾ | 7 ,, 5 | 4½ ,, 2½ | 8½ ,, 5 | 4 ,, 2 |
| 38 ,, | 10 ,, 6 | 6 ,, 3¾ | 6 ,, 6 | 7½ ,, 6 | 4¾ ,, 2½ | 8½ ,, 5 | 4 ,, 2 |
| 40 ,, | 11 ,, 6 | 6 ,, 4 | 6 ,, 6 | 8 ,, 6 | 4½ ,, 2½ | 8¾ ,, 5 | 4½ ,, 2 |
| 42 ,, | 11½ ,, 6 | 6 ,, 4½ | 6½ ,, 6 | 8½ ,, 6 | 4 ,, 2¾ | 8¾ ,, 5½ | 4½ ,, 2 |
| 44 ,, | 12 ,, 6 | 6 ,, 5 | 6½ ,, 6 | 8½ ,, 6 | 4½ ,, 3 | 9 ,, 5 | 4¾ ,, 2 |
| 46 ,, | 12½ ,, 6 | 6 ,, 5½ | 7 ,, 6 | 9 ,, 6 | 4¾ ,, 3 | 9 ,, 5½ | 5 ,, 2 |

QUEEN AND PRINCESSES ROOFS, such as in Fig. 160.—TABLE of SCANTLINGS of TIMBER for different Spans from 46 to 60 feet.

| Span. | Tie beam, T. | Queen Post, QP. | Princesses, PP. | Principal Rafters, PR. | Straining Beam, SB. | Struts, S. | Purlins, P. | Common Rafters, CR. |
|---|---|---|---|---|---|---|---|---|
| 48 ft. | 11½ by 6 | 6 by 5¾ | 6 by 2½ | 7½ by 6 | 8¾ by 6 | 4½ by 2¾ | 8½ by 5 | 4 by 2 |
| 50 ,, | 12 ,, 6 | 6 ,, 6½ | 6 ,, 2½ | 8½ ,, 6 | 8½ ,, 6 | 4½ ,, 2½ | 8¾ ,, 5 | 4½ ,, 2 |
| 52 ,, | 12 ,, 6½ | 6 ,, 6¾ | 6 ,, 2¾ | 9½ ,, 6 | 8¾ ,, 6 | 4¾ ,, 2½ | 8¾ ,, 5½ | 4½ ,, 2 |
| 54 ,, | 12 ,, 7 | 7 ,, 6¼ | 7 ,, 2½ | 6½ ,, 7 | 9 ,, 6 | 4¾ ,, 2¾ | 8¾ ,, 5½ | 4½ ,, 2 |
| 56 ,, | 12 ,, 8 | 7 ,, 6¾ | 7 ,, 2 | 7½ ,, 7 | 9½ ,, 6 | 5 ,, 2¾ | 8¾ ,, 5½ | 4½ ,, 2 |
| 58 ,, | 12 ,, 8½ | 7 ,, 7½ | 7 ,, 2½ | 8½ ,, 7 | 9½ ,, 7 | 5 ,, 2¾ | 9 ,, 5½ | 4¾ ,, 2 |
| 60 ,, | 12 ,, 9 | 7½ ,, 7 | 7 ,, 3 | 9 ,, 7 | 10 ,, 7 | 5 ,, 3 | 9 ,, 5½ | 4¾ ,, 2 |

*N.B.*—In these Tables the pitch of the roof is supposed to be about 27°; the trusses 10 feet apart. The covering slates and the timber to be good Memel or Riga fir. Inferior timber will require to be of larger dimensions. The scantlings for the tie beams may be considerably reduced when they do not carry ceiling joints.

## BEST FORMS OF ROOF FOR DIFFERENT SPANS.

The best form of roof truss or principal to be used for a given span is determined by the following considerations :—

1. The parts of the truss between the points of support should not be so long as to have any tendency to bend under the thrust; therefore the length of the parts under compression should not exceed twenty times their smallest dimension. This is explained in Part IV., N.B.C.

2. The distance apart of the purlins should not be so great as to necessitate the use of either purlins or rafters too large for convenience or economy.

3. The tie beam should be supported at such small intervals that it need not be too large for economy or convenience.

It has been found by experience that these objects can be attained by limiting the distance between the points of support on the principal rafter to 8 feet.

In determining the form of truss for any given span, it is therefore necessary first to decide the pitch, then roughly to draw the principal rafters in position, ascertain their length, divide them into portions 8 feet long, and place a strut under each point of division.

By this it will be seen that a king-post truss is adapted for roofs with principal rafters 16 feet long, *i.e.* those having a span of 30 feet A queen-post truss would be adapted to a roof with principal rafters 24 feet long, that is of about 45 feet span.

For greater spans with longer principal rafters, roofs such as that in Fig. 160.

---

# CHAPTER VI.

## *ROOF COVERINGS.*

*Subjects required by Syllabus, and (in brackets) the pages at which they are treated upon.*

*Roof coverings of tiles* [p. 102] *and zinc* [p. 107]. *Slate ridges and hips* [p. 112].

**General Remarks.**—Roofs are covered with different materials according to the locality, the climate, and the nature and importance of the building.

As a rule, the smaller the pieces in which the covering is put on, the heavier will it be, and the more difficult to keep water-tight, as it will contain a greater number of openings or of joints.

Substances which conduct heat very slowly, such as slate, make better coverings than the metals; the former preserve an equable temperature, while the latter conduct the heat in summer, and the cold in winter, to the interior of the building.

**Pitch of Roofs.**—The pitch, or inclination of the sides of a roof, is determined chiefly by the nature of the covering.

Thus thatch, which would easily allow wet to penetrate it, must be laid at a steep angle, so as to throw the water off at once; whilst, on the other hand, hard and impervious slates may be laid at a much smaller angle, and sheets of metal may be nearly flat.

The pitch is, moreover, varied greatly to suit different styles of architecture, and also according to climate. Some writers have gone so far as to prescribe an exact pitch for every variation in latitude.

The following remarks by the late Professor Robison are of a more practical character :—

"A high-pitched roof will undoubtedly shoot off the rains and snows better than one of lower pitch ; the wind will not so easily blow the dripping rain in between the slates, nor will it have so much power to strip them off ;" and further—"A high-pitched roof will exert a smaller strain upon the walls, both because its strain is less horizontal, and because it will admit of lighter covering ; but it is more expensive, because there is more of it—it requires a greater size of timbers to make it equally strong, and it exposes a greater surface to the wind."

The pitch of a roof is expressed either by the angle which its sides make with the horizon, or by the proportion which its height in the centre bears to the span.

Thus the roof shown in Fig. 157, p. 93, may be said to have a pitch of 26½ degrees, or ¼.

The subjoined table, taken chiefly from Tredgold, gives the inclination for roofs covered in different ways. The weights of various coverings are also given, but these will vary considerably according to the quality and thickness of the material used.

TABLE.

| Kind of Covering. | Inclination of sides of Roof to Horizon. | Height of Roof in parts of Span. | Weight on a square (*i.e* 100 square feet of roofing) in lbs. |
|---|---|---|---|
| Asphalted Felt . . | 3° 50′ | 1/30 | 30 to 40 |
| Copper . . . . . | 3° 50′ | 1/30 | 80 to 120 |
| Corrugated Iron, 16 BWG[1] | 4° 0′ | 1/20 | 350 |
| Sheet Iron, 16 BWG . | 18° to 20° | 1/8 | 250 |
| Lead . . . . . | 3° 50′ | 1/30 | 550 to 850 |
| Slates (large) . . . | 22° 0′ | 1/5 | 900 to 1100 |
| ,, (ordinary) . . | 26° 30′ | 1/4 | 550 to 800 |
| ,, (small) . . . | 30° 0′ | 1/3 | 450 to 650 |
| Slabs of Stone . . | 39° 0′ | 2/5 | 2380 |
| Thatch (Straw) . . | 45° 0′ | 1/2 | 650 |
| Tiles (Plain)[2] . . . | 52½° | 2/3 | 1800 |
| ,, (Pan) . . . | 24° 0′ | 2/9 | 1200 |
| ,, (Taylor's Patent) . | 30° 0′ | 1/3 | 830 |
| Zinc (1/16 in. thick) . . | 4° 0′ | 1/26 | 150 |
| Boarding (¾ thick) . . | 26° 30′ | 1/4 | 250 |
| ,, 1 ,, . . . | 26° 30′ | 1/4 | 350 |

[1] BWG stands for Birmingham wire-gauge—a measure of thickness.
[2] Plain tiles are used on roofs of any pitch from 30° to 60°.

*N.B.*—The additional pressures to be taken into account in practice are the following :—

Pressure of wind . . . 2500 to 5000 lbs. per square of 100 feet.
do. of snow, in this country 500 lbs. per square.

**Slating.**—The particulars connected with the different methods of laying slates have been entered upon in E.B.C.D., and need not here be repeated. The only roof coverings included in the advanced course are tiles and zinc; slate ridges and hips are, however, mentioned in the Syllabus, and are described at p. 112.

**Tiles** of burnt clay are made in several different forms, a few of the more important of which will be described.

They are heavy and rather apt to absorb moisture, and to communicate it to the laths and rafters of the roof, thus rendering the latter liable to decay.

PLAIN TILES are slabs of burnt clay, either rectangular or in various patterns, as at *p*, *p*, Fig. 168, Pl. II., generally about 10½ inches long, 6½ inches wide, and about ½ inch thick. They are slightly curved in their length to make them lie close.

They are laid on battens 1½ inch × ½ inch, or on laths of oak or fir, being hung from them by wooden pins driven through holes near the upper edge of the tiles. Sometimes the tiles are hung by projecting nibs, of which there are generally two or three upon their upper edges. Sometimes only every third or even only every tenth course is nailed.

The arrangement of the tiles is similar to that of slates—the tail of each rests upon the tile below for a length of about 6 inches, the gauge being 4 inches (often 3½ inches) and the lap over the head of the tile next but one below about 3 inches.

WEATHER TILING.[1]—Plain tiles are often used vertically to protect walling. Battens are nailed upon the wall, and the tiles hung upon them in somewhat the same manner as for roofs,—each tile being bedded in mortar so as to make the covering warm and weather-tight.

**Plate II.** shows in Figs. 168, 169, part of a plain tiled roof and of a wall with hanging tiles. Figs. 170 to 172, and 174 to 176 show various forms of tiles which are necessary to make good work, as shown in Fig. 168.

[1] Or *Hanging tiling*.

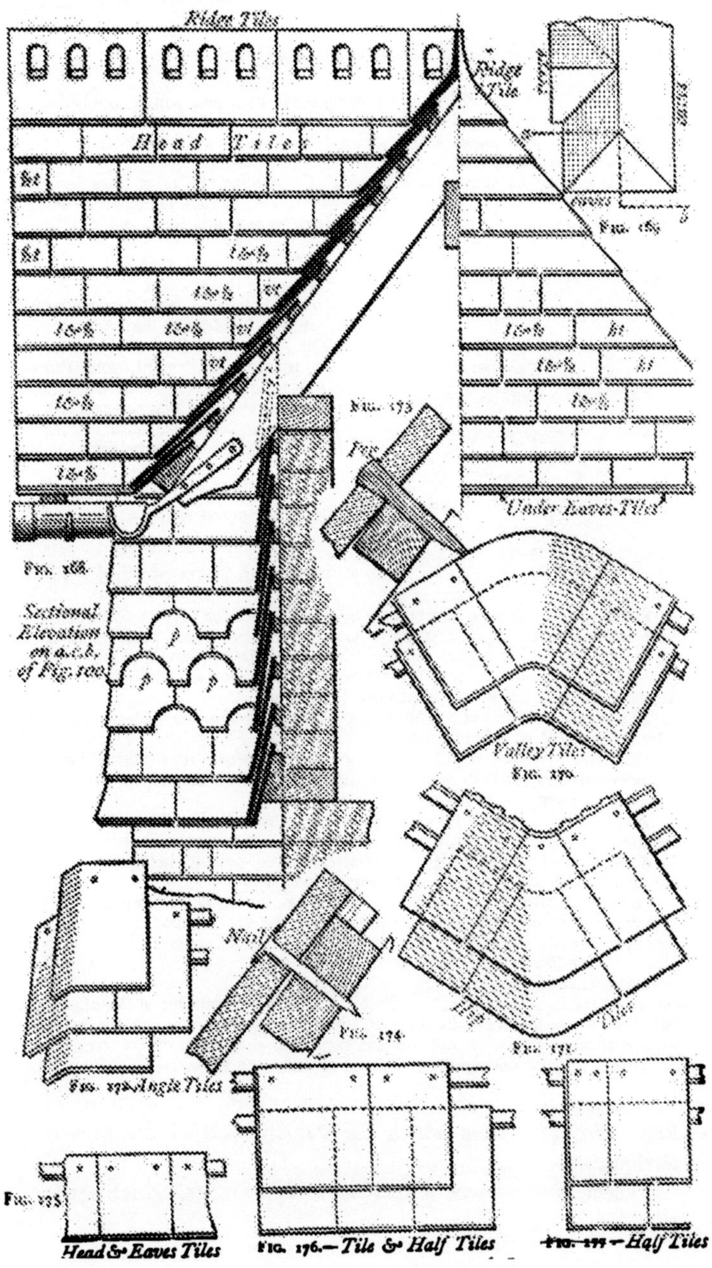
Ridge Tiles
Ridge Tile
Head Tile
Under Eaves-Tiles
Sectional Elevation on a.c.b. of Fig. 100
Valley Tiles
Nail
Angle Tiles
Head & Eaves Tiles
Tile & Half Tiles
Half Tiles

Fig. 172 shows the method of securing a tile by a pin, which should be preferably of oak or otherwise of heart of Memel, cut with a knife out of any dry stuff. Fig. 173 shows a tile secured by a nail, which should be of copper or of malleable iron.

*Ridges* may be as shown in Fig. 168. Sometimes the ridge tiles have longitudinal grooves along their upper edges, into which detached ornamental "fleurs" are fitted. Sometimes they have ventilating openings in them.

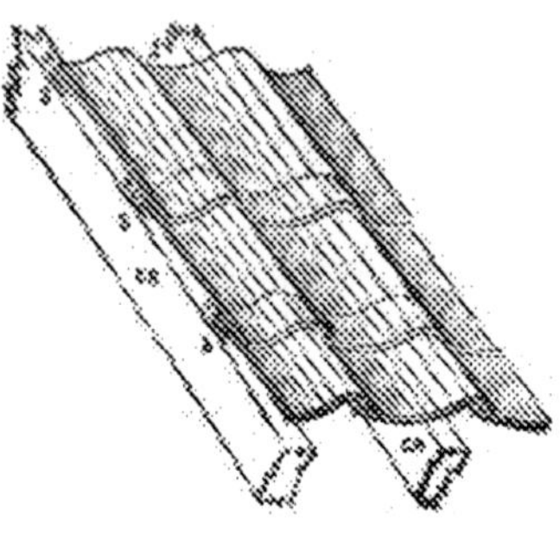

Fig. 178.

*Torching and Pointing.*—The tiles after being laid should be *torched* or *tiered*, that is pointed from the inside with hair mortar. The *Verges* (see Fig. 169) should be pointed in cement, and the ridges, finials, etc., set in cement. In very exposed places each tile may be bedded in hydraulic mortar or cement upon those below it.

Pan Tiles form a covering not so warm as one of plain tiles, and liable to injury from gusts of wind.

The tiles are about 14 inches long by 9 inches straight across the width. Each is hung on to the laths or battens, *b b*, by a nib which projects from the upper edge of the back of the tile—shown in section at *x x x*. It should be remarked that this projection is not continuous throughout the width of the tile, but is only about one inch wide.

The tiles have a lap of 3 inches to 4 inches, and the joints on the under sides are pointed with hair mortar.

Pan tiles are well adapted for roofing over workshops where large furnaces are used, as they withstand the heat, and the interstices between them afford plenty of ventilation.

*Half round* or concave tiles set in mortar, and nailed to the woodwork, are used for the ridges, hips, and valleys. For common work sometimes the tiles themselves are used—the smaller curved portion being cut off—but special tiles are generally made for the purpose.

In exposed situations, and where much ventilation is not required, the tiles are bedded on each other in mortar, and the space between the ridge tiles and those in the ridge courses at the top of the slopes are filled in with pieces of flat tiles bedded in mortar.

*Glass Tiles* of this form are made, and may be introduced among the others where light is required. *Double Roll Tiles* are similar to the above, but have a double wave in their width. *Corrugated Tiles* are similar in general form to pan tiles, but they are bent into several narrow, curved, or sometimes angular corrugations, instead of only two broad ones.

Italian Tiles are shown in elevation and section in Figs. 179, 180, from which the construction of the tiles is obvious.

These tiles present a handsome appearance, which leads

to their use in some cases; but they are not well adapted to the British climate, as they cause the snow to lodge, and, when it thaws, the water frequently gets through the roof.

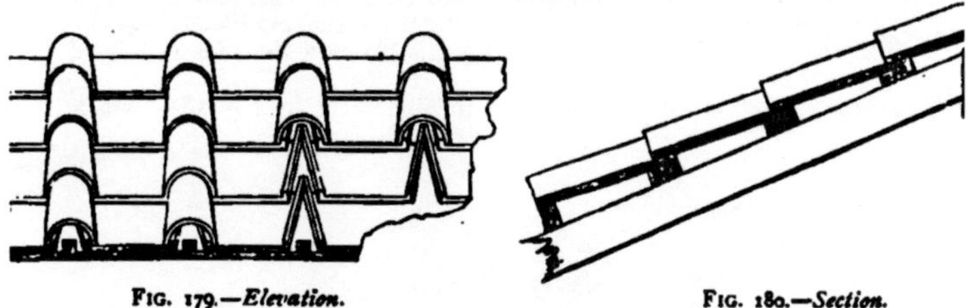

Fig. 179.—*Elevation.* Fig. 180.—*Section.*

Taylor's Patent Tiling is somewhat similar in principle to the Italian tiling just described.

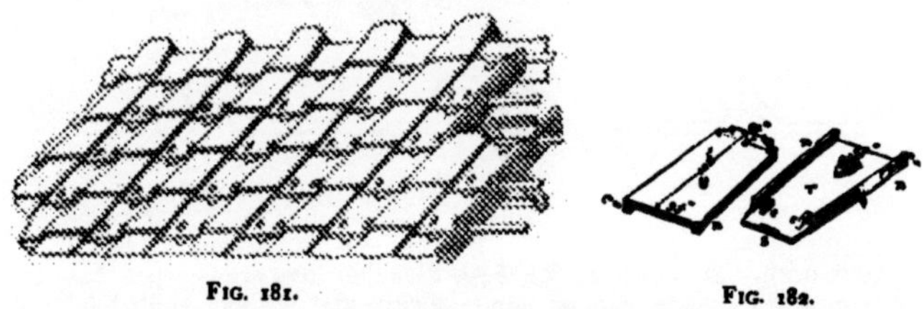

Fig. 181. Fig. 182.

In this case, however, the upper or *capping tiles* are exactly like the lower or *channel tiles*, so that every tile can be used in either position.

Fig. 181 shows the general appearance of this kind of tiling, which is very picturesque.

Fig. 182 gives an upper and lower view of the tiles.

Fig. 183 shows a few channel tiles, T T, with one capping tile, U, in position.

Fig. 183.

The tiles are hung on battens 2¼ inches wide and 1 inch thick, laid to about a 10-inch gauge. The channel tiles are first laid in rows along the slope of the roof from eaves to ridge; the narrow end of each tile is pushed into the wide end of the one below until the splay, *s*, fits firmly into the undercut in the shield, A, of the lower tile.

There are notches in the sides of the tiles, as shown at *n n*, Fig. 182;

each channel tile is secured by wedge-shaped nails[1] driven in alongside, so as to hold the tile down by these notches as at *x x*.

After the channel tiles are all fixed, the capping tiles are put on. These tiles are turned over, and so placed as to cover the intervals between the channel tiles. They are pushed downwards until the little blocks or cogs, *c c*, rest upon the nail-heads, *x x*, which secure the channel tiles below.

The under side of the corners of the joints between the tiles is pointed with cement mortar.

**Foster's Lock Wing Roofing Tiles** are illustrated in Fig. 184,[2] which

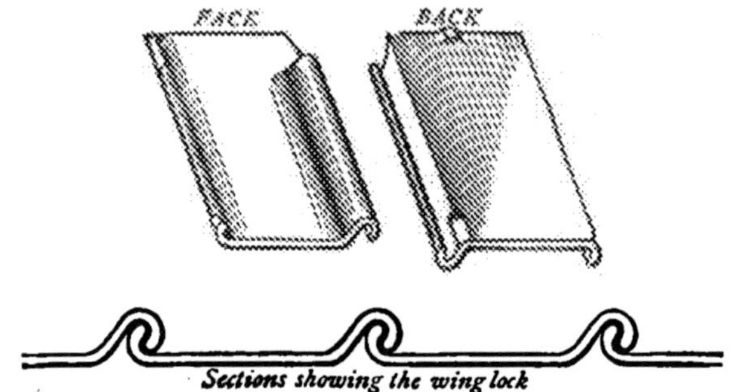


Fig. 184.

explains itself. It is claimed for these tiles that they are cheaper than the commonest tiles made, can be hung quickly and without skilled labour, require no pointing, and cannot be blown off the roof, as the stronger the pressure is underneath, the tighter the lock.

**Poole's Patent Bonding Roll Roofing Tiles** are shown in Fig. 185[3], which requires no description.

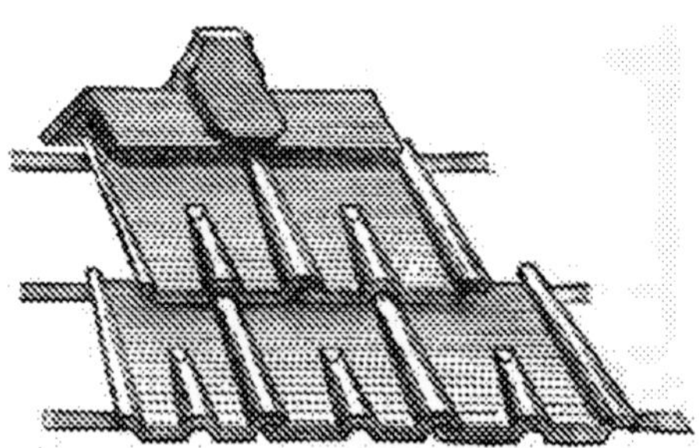

Fig. 185.

[1] Or side keys.

[2] From the Patentee's Circulars.

[3] Ibid.

**Zinc** is laid as a roof covering in several different ways. Its lightness, as compared with slates, tiles, or lead, enables

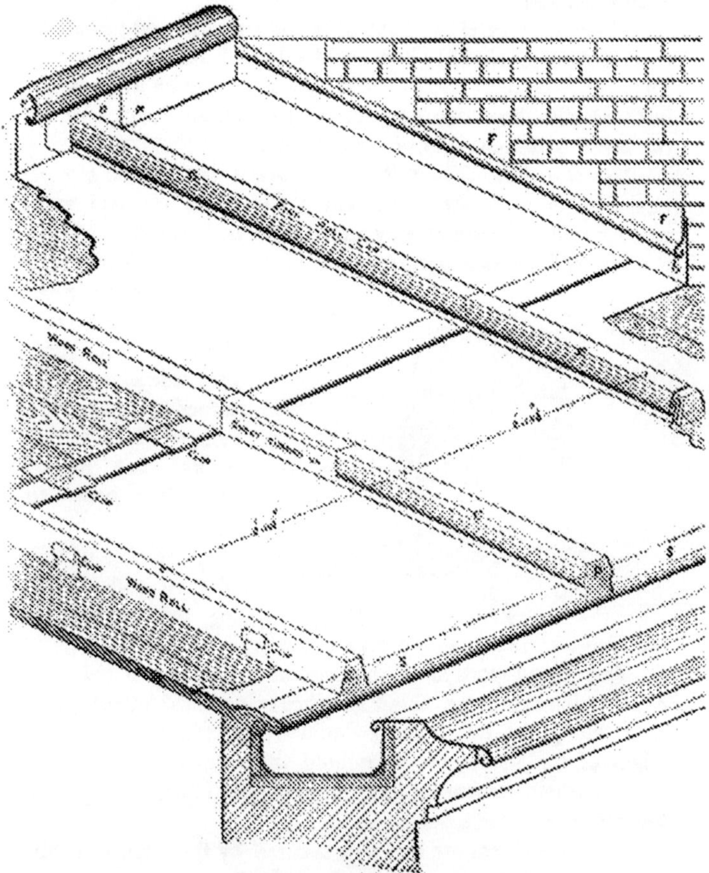

FIG. 186.—Scale, ½ inch = 1 foot.

it to be laid on roof-timbers of much smaller scantlings than those required for the coverings just mentioned.

The method of laying zinc in this country has been greatly improved through the exertions of the Vielle Montagne Zinc

Company, from whose beautifully illustrated pamphlet[1] on the subject the figures and most of the information here given have been extracted.

There are several methods of laying zinc on roofs; in all of them the object should be to avoid soldered and rigid connection, and to arrange the joints so that they may be water-tight, but may still allow free play for contraction and expansion of the metal under changes of temperature.

*Zinc laid with Plain Roll Caps on Boarding.*—Flat sheets of zinc from 7 to 10 feet long and 3 feet wide, are laid with wooden rolls on boarding very much in the same manner as lead.

Fig. 186 shows a portion of a roof covered in this manner. The sheets run lengthways down the slope of the roof, their side edges being turned up against the rolls, which are placed 2 feet 10½ inches apart from centre to centre.

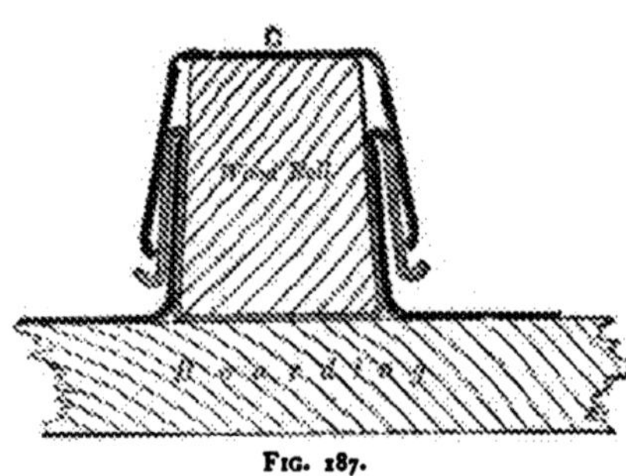


Fig. 187.

A section of one of these rolls, showing the method of securing the zinc, is shown on a larger scale in Fig. 187.

The scored portion of the section shows one of the zinc clips, which are strips about 2 inches wide, fixed about 3 feet apart along the roll. Being doubled over the upturned side edges of the sheets, the clips hold them down, without preventing their expansion and contraction under changes of temperature.

After the sheets are laid and secured by the clips, the rolls are covered by the cap C, also formed of sheet zinc, doubled down as shown. In very exposed situations these clips may be continued so as to turn up again over the sides of the cap C, and be secured at the top.

[1] Published by their manufacturing agents, Messrs. F. Braby and Company.

The cap is secured by "fork connections." These consist of pointed pieces of zinc 2 or 3 inches long by about an inch wide, one end of which is soldered to the inner surface of the cap on each side, the point being free. As the cap slides on to the roll, the points of these forks slip in under the hooked portion of the clip. They thus prevent the clip from flying off, without impeding its expansion and contraction in direction of its length.

*Braby's Patent Saddle-piece and Stop-end.*—The extreme ends of the roll caps may be covered with a piece soldered on, as shown at O and P; but this plan has been improved upon by merely spreading out the roll cap itself at O, forming what is called a saddle-piece, and dressing it up against the side of the ridge; and at the end, P, by turning the end of the cap over the end of the roll, and doubling the corners of the sides of the cap under the end—thus, in both cases, doing away with soldered joints, and allowing perfect play under expansion and contraction. There are other patented methods of effecting the same object, which cannot here be described.

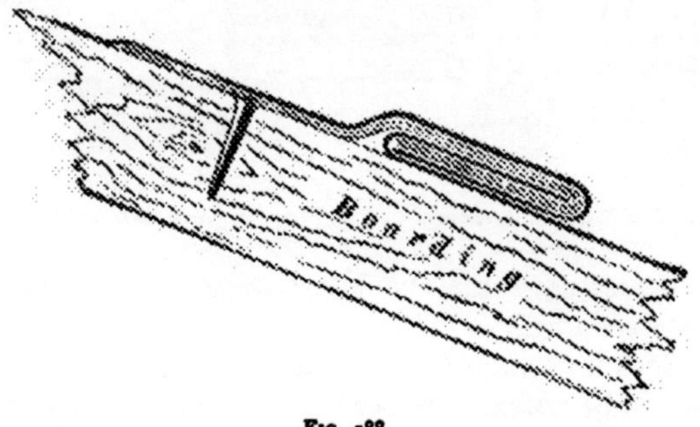


FIG. 188.

WELTED JOINTS.—The sheets having been fastened at the sides by means of the rolls as above described, it next becomes necessary to make a connection between the lower edge of each sheet and the upper edge of the sheet next below it on the slope of the roof (Fig. 186).

This is done by means of the joint shown in section in Fig. 188 and called a *Welt* or *Fold* joint.

In this figure the hatched section is that of a "clip," or strip of zinc about 2 inches wide nailed to the boarding, and doubled in between the edges of the two sheets to be connected, which are shown in section by the black lines, so as to make a secure joint, and yet to give them plenty of play for expansion and contraction.

Welted joints are used only when the roof has a sloop of $\frac{1}{4}$ or more; for flatter roofs drips are introduced.

The lower edges of the sheets nearest the eaves are strengthened where they project over the gutter, by being doubled back so as to form a bead; and further, by a strip of stout zinc (S in Fig. 186), nailed along the edge of the boarding over which the bead is formed.

The ridge is covered by a zinc roll cap turned over it, which latter is strengthened on the lower edges by their being bent round to form beads.

DRIPS.—Zinc may be fixed with rolls on boarding laid upon roofs of any pitch not less than about 1 in 15.

When, however, the slope of the roof is flatter than $\frac{1}{7}$, drips should be formed similar to that shown in Figs. 189, 190, at intervals of from 7 to 8 feet—that is, at the end of each sheet.

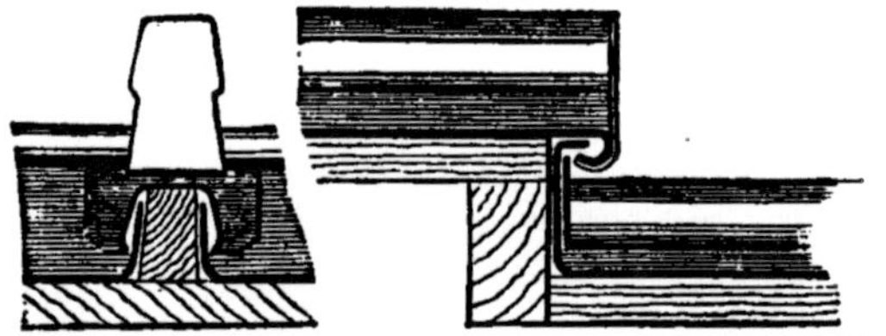

FIG. 189.—*End Sectional Elevation.* FIG. 190.—*Side Sectional Elevation.*

The figures show the end elevation and the section of a drip joint over a roll.

The thick lines show the sections of the sheets, the ends of which, it will be noticed, are bent inwards, so that they may be able to expand and contract without danger of any water getting in behind the joint.

The stopped end of the roll cap on the upper level is bent over with the edge of the sheet.

Drips in flats should be $2\frac{1}{2}$ inches deep, and in gutters $1\frac{1}{2}$ inch deep.

*Zinc laid with patent drawn Roll Cap.*—Another form of roll patented by the Vielle Montagne Zinc Company is recommended as lasting longer than the simple form just described, and as being peculiarly suitable "for terraces or flats of warehouses where weights are stored, or where there is much walking about;" and, as regards appearance, for Mansard or high-pitched roofs.

The method of laying zinc with these rolls is somewhat similar to that with the ordinary rolls; but the loose zinc roll cap is done away with, the zinc being drawn tight over the roll by machinery.

CORRUGATED ZINC ROOF.—When the zinc is required to be laid without boarding—which is, of course, a great saving—it must be strengthened by corrugations, *i.e.* by curved indentations or flutes formed along the sheet.

The ordinary corrugated zinc consists of flutes about 3½ inches wide, lying close together, and it is laid upon purlins placed about 2 feet 6 inches apart.

*Italian Corrugated Zinc Roof.*—In this form of zinc the corrugations are spaced more widely, being 1 foot 3 inches apart.

In Fig. 191 one sheet is shown in section by the thick black line, the ends of the adjacent sheets being scored in section.

FIG. 191.

The zinc may be laid upon rafters, so spaced and shaped as to fit into the corrugations (Fig. 191), but for the sake of durability it is better to lay it upon boarding.

The sheets are secured to them, either by patent holding-down clips shaped so as to allow of the expansion and contraction of the sheets, or by patent sliding studs. Both methods are fully described in Messrs. Braby's pamphlet.

Fig. 191 shows in section a portion of a roof covered with Italian corrugated zinc. The zinc rolls or rafters are 1 foot 3 inches apart, and are supported upon purlins, which in large roofs may be 10 feet apart.

The depth of the rolls when they act as rafters, and are laid upon purlins about 7 feet apart, is about 3 inches; but when laid upon boarding they are only 2 inches deep.

*Thickness of Zinc for roofing.*—The gauges recommended by the Vielle Montagne Company are Nos. 14, 15, and 16 zinc gauge (see Part III., N.B.C.) for the roof covering.

"No. 14 to be used only where it is necessary to exercise the greatest possible saving in the first cost."

No. 15 or 16 for gutters.

Nos. 13 and 14 are frequently used for roofing where economy is an object.

It must be noted that these are numbers of the Vielle Montagne Company's *zinc* gauge, not of the ordinary Birmingham wire gauge.

*Zinc Flashings* are very similar to those of lead described in E.B.C.D. An illustration of one is shown at F in Fig. 186.

The edge of the sheet is generally turned up about six inches against the wall, and the apron over it is finished and stiffened by being bent round to form a bead *b* as shown.

The ridge roll is covered with zinc in nearly the same manner as with lead, except that the zinc is not worked so much into the angles under the roll. It is secured by forks, similar to those described in p. 109.

ZINC GUTTERS.—*Valley Gutters* are formed in somewhat the same manner as those of lead.

For roofs laid with wood rolls the wooden trough is lined with sheet zinc,—the sides of which are turned up, and the upper edges bent inwards under the bead formed by the lower edge of the sheet at the eaves.

Where Italian corrugated zinc is used the sides of the zinc lining to the gutters are turned up, and the edges bent over the thickness of the wood sides of the trough.

The minimum fall for such gutters should be $\frac{1}{40}$.

*Zinc Tiles*, generally of diamond or shield shape, are sometimes used for roof coverings, each being hung from a hook fixed upon battens or boardings, and passed through a hole near the top of the tile.

*Zinc Eaves Gutters*[1] are made of various forms, very similar to those of cast-iron, and are fixed in the same positions.

They soon perish, and are hardly strong enough to bear the weight of snow or even the pressure of a ladder.

Zinc gutters, not being so strong as those of iron, require stays about one foot six inches apart. These are simply hollow cylinders of zinc—placed across the gutter—through which is passed the screw fixing the gutter to the woodwork. The stay keeps the upper part of the gutter from bending inwards as the screw is driven home.

The various gauges for zinc and other metals are given in Part III., whence the following remarks are taken.

Zinc should not be allowed to be in contact with iron, copper, or lead. In either case voltaic action is set up, which soon destroys the zinc. This occurs especially and more rapidly when moisture is present.

Zinc should also be kept clear of lime or calcareous water, and of any wood, such as oak, which contains acid. Zinc laid on flats or roofs where cats can gain access is very soon corroded.

An objection to zinc for roofs is that it catches fire at a red heat, and blazes furiously.[2]

**Slate Ridges and Hips** have been illustrated in E.B.C.D., p. 140.

They are much used to save the expense of lead. A common form in which the roll and one wing are in one piece is given in Fig. 192[3]; another form having the roll and wings

[1] Sc. *Rhones*. [2] Bloxam. [3] From N.B.C.

in three separate pieces, the two latter being screwed together

Fig. 192. Fig. 193.

by copper screws, is shown in Fig. 193 from E.B.C.D. There are several other forms of slate ridging, and nearly all are made to suit different pitches of roof.

---

## CHAPTER VII.

### *JOINERY.*

*Subjects required by Syllabus, and (in brackets) the pages at which they are treated upon.*

*The fixing* [p. 113] *of architraves* [p. 116], *skirting to walls* [p. 117], *shutters to windows* [p. 127], *skylights* [p. 136].

### FIXING JOINERS' WORK.

ALL joiners' work that is not framed should be fixed so as to be free to expand or contract.

In boarding generally, this may be effected by fixing one edge, and forming the other with a groove and tongue; or the board may be fixed in the centre, with both edges free.

For example, the upper part of the skirting in Fig. 210 is fixed to the "ground," but the lower edge is free to move, the joint between it and the floor, which would open as the skirting shrinks, being covered by the tongue along the bottom of the skirting which enters the groove formed in the floor. If the skirting board were not thus free to move it would split as it became seasoned.

Again, it will be seen that the frame of the window back (Fig. 210) is free at the lower edge.

The dado in Fig. 197 is also fixed at the upper edge only.

*N.B.*—In the figures illustrating this section the parts are marked with the following distinctive letters :—

*A* . Architrave.
*B* . Bracket.
*b* . Batten.
*ba* . Backing.
*bl* . Back lining of sash frame.
*bk* . Blocks or blockings.
*br* . Bottom rail of sash.
*bw* . Weight to balance bottom sash.
*C* . Capping.
*c* . Cradling.
*D* . Dado.
*f* . Fillet.
*g* . Ground.
*H* . Head of sash frame.
*h* . Hinges.
*SS* . Stone sill.
*SL* . Stone lintel.
*SF* . Solid frame.
*sb* . Sash bar.
*sk* . Skirting.
*t* . Throating.
*tl* . Top lining.
*tr* . Top rail of sash.
*ib* . Inside bead.
*il* . Inside lining of sash frame.
*l.* . Laths.
*mr* . Meeting rails.
*ol* . Outside lining of sash frame.
*os* . Oak sill.
*P* . Plaster.
*Pp* . Pocket piece.
*p* . Pulley.
*pb* . Parting bead.
*ps* . Pulley style.
*psl* . Parting slip.
*RA* . Relieving arch.
*s* . Styles.
*SB* . Surbase.
*tw* . Weight to balance top sash.
*WB* Wood bricks.
*wb* . Water bar.
*wp* . Wood plug.
*WL* Wood lintel.
*WiBd* Window board.
*x* . Wedge.
*y* . Do.
*zps* . Zinc parting slip.

**Grounds** are pieces of wood nailed to plugs, wood bricks, breeze fixing blocks, or slips,[1] in the wall, so as to form a firm basis to which the more ornamental portions, such as architraves, linings, etc., may be fixed.

Grounds are used round the margins of openings not only to receive the linings and architraves, but to form a solid finish to the plastering.

*Mitred or Splayed Grounds* have the side next to the plastering splayed or bevelled as shown in Fig. 194, so as to form a key for the plaster and secure the joint. This term is often used for grounds which are of a splayed form in plan, such as that in Fig. 213.

*Grooved Grounds* are those which have the inner edge grooved instead of splayed, to answer the same purpose, *i.e.* that of affording a key for the edge of the plaster.

Examples are given in Fig. 195, and several other figures.

When the joint between the ground and the plaster is covered by an architrave, the splay or groove on the edge of

[1] Wood bricks, slips, plugs, etc., have been described in E.B.C.D.

the ground is often omitted, as in Fig. 204. It is, however, better to have it, to form a key for and to secure the plaster firmly until the architrave is fixed.

*Finished or Wrought Grounds.*—In most cases the ground is rough, its surface being flush with that of the plaster on the walls, and concealed by the architrave fixed to it: sometimes, however, either the whole or part of the surface of the ground is exposed to view; it is then said to be "finished," and is wrought, beaded, or otherwise ornamented.

Fig. 208 shows an example in which the whole of the ground is visible. In Fig. 212 only part of the ground is seen, which forms the fascia of an architrave, and is embellished by mouldings attached to it.

*Framed Grounds* are used as margins for openings in superior work.

They form a sort of rough frame, generally concealed from view, and consisting of two upright sides or posts mortised to receive a head terminating in haunched tenons.

*Backing.*—In order to form a firm support to the lining between the grounds, cross pieces are dovetailed in between the uprights of the adjacent frames, as shown in elevation in Fig. 203 and in plan in Fig. 204 and several other figures; these are firmly attached to wood bricks, whose edges may be seen in elevation behind them (see Fig. 203), or to slips.

*Common Grounds.*—In very common work the grounds consist only of the upright posts or styles, and are not framed into a head at all; in other cases a head is provided, but the styles, instead of being framed, are merely halved or notched into it.

*Fixing Grounds.*—The grounds should be fixed before the plastering is commenced; they form a "screed" or guide, to which the surface of the second coat is floated (see p. 214).

It is therefore important that the grounds should be solidly and accurately fixed, their surfaces and edges should be perfectly true, and so firm that they will not be easily disturbed by the plasterers.

In fixing grounds the face of the ground should project about ¾ inch from the naked wall, if it is to be rendered or plastered; or the same distance from the battens, if it is to be battened, lathed, and plastered.

The inner edges of grounds for door and window openings should be kept perfectly plumb, and equidistant from the centre line of the opening, the face of the ground being parallel to that of the door or sash-frame.

The width of such grounds will depend upon their finish; also upon the nature of the opening.

If there are linings, the grounds may be from 3 to 6 inches wide, the linings being attached to them (Fig. 209). If the grounds are wrought, the architrave or fillet covering the junction of the plaster with the ground may lap over about half the width of the ground (Fig. 209). When boxings are used the grounds will be of sufficient width to contain the shutter and back-flaps required, and may be wrought (Fig. 212) or covered with a double-faced architrave (Fig. 213).

Several examples of grounds are given in pages 117–133, and there described, so that it will be unnecessary to enter upon them further in detail at present.

## ARCHITRAVES

Are borders fixed round the openings of doorways or windows for ornament, and also to conceal the joint between the frame and the plastering.

These borders may be of almost any pattern or dimensions to suit the character of the room.

They are sometimes covered with elaborate mouldings, or made in the form of a pilaster.

The mouldings of the architrave may extend down to the floor as in Fig. 198, or they may rest upon blocks or plinths as in Fig. 202.

The architrave should never be fixed until the plastering is completed and quite dry. It should then be placed so as well to cover the joint (see Fig. 205).

Grounds fixed to the wall are generally provided to form a support to the architrave, and are covered by it (see Fig. 205). But in some cases, as already mentioned, the ground itself forms the face of the architrave, as in Fig. 206, or in inferior work it may serve all purposes, as shown in Fig. 208.

In order to save labour, and to avoid large pieces of timber, architraves are generally built up in parts glued together. Examples of this will be seen in Figs. 205, 216.

These parts generally consist of a flat portion or base, which is merely a board, beaded, or otherwise ornamented, on edge, and called the face. This is surmounted by mouldings according to taste.

Larger architraves are formed of pieces of different thicknesses tongued together, as in Fig. 200. Those made by machinery may, however, be procured all in one piece.

*Double-faced Architrave.*—When the base of the architrave is not of equal thickness throughout, but stepped back in the centre, as shown in Fig. 213, it is said to be "*double-faced.*"

## SKIRTINGS.

The *Skirting*[1] is a board from 6 inches to 18 inches wide running round the base of the wall of a room. It is intended to cover the junction of the floor with the walls, and also for ornament.

The skirting board may be square or plain, ornamented by a bead or moulding *stuck* upon it (Fig. 194), or by a detached moulding (Fig. 197). Again, it may be sunk to form a double plinth similar to that in Fig. 195. The skirting may be plugged close up to the wall, or fixed to grounds.

These grounds are rough battens nailed to plugs in the wall, and they should be dovetailed at the angles. A narrow horizontal ground, plugged to the wall, runs close behind the top of the skirting; and, if the latter is wide, blocks, placed about 9 inches apart, extend from the floor to this horizontal ground. Such a skirting is seen in Fig. 194, and another in Fig. 196, where it forms the base of a "dado;" a portion of the skirting is stripped off in order to show two of the blocks supporting it.

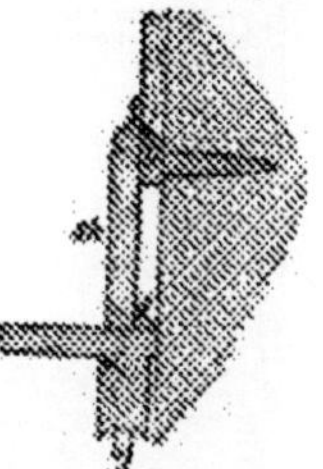

Fig. 194.
Scale, 1 inch = 1 foot.

The lower edge of the skirting is sometimes housed into the floor, as in Fig. 195, or tongued, as shown in Fig. 197; or it may rest upon it, as in Fig. 194; in either case a fillet, *f*, may be added to cover the joint at the back, though this is not absolutely necessary when it is let into the floor. To save material

[1] Sc. *Base*, if mouldings are run upon it.
,, *Base plate*, ,, ,, separate.

the fillet may be splayed, *i.e.* made of triangular section (Fig. 194).

When the floor is uneven the lower edge of the skirting must be "*scribed*" to fit it—that is, a line is drawn upon it parallel to all the irregularities of the surface of the floor, and the lower side of the skirting is cut to this line.

FIG. 195.
Scale, 1 inch = 1 foot.

The skirting boards should be tongued (or dovetailed) at the internal angles of rooms and mitred (see E.B.C.D.) at external angles; in either case the top edge of the joint is mitred right through. The skirting boards should also be tongued wherever they are pieced in length.

The hollow behind the skirting harbours vermin, and the plastering should always be continued down to the floor so as to fill it up (Fig. 196).

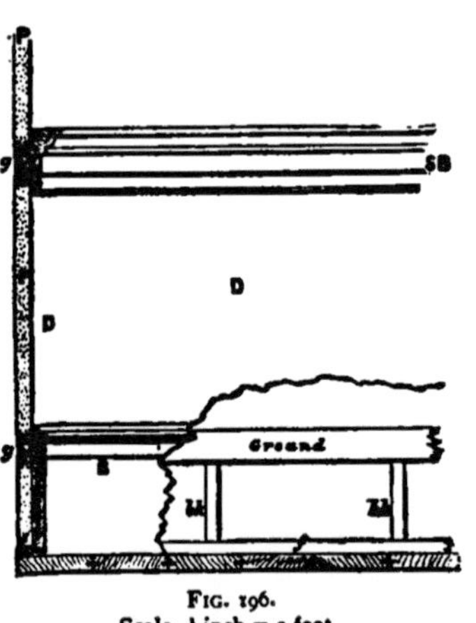


FIG. 196.
Scale, ½ inch = 1 foot.

The boards of skirtings, as in all joiners' work, should be fixed so as to allow of contraction and expansion without splitting. This may be done by fixing one side of the board, and tonguing and grooving the joint on the other edge.

Several examples of ordinary skirtings may be seen in the figures illustrating other parts of joiners' work, some of which have just been referred to.

*A Double Skirting* consists of two skirtings, one above the other, as in Fig. 195. The width of both skirtings may be equal, as in the illustration given. The lower one is sometimes wider than the other, or it may be narrower, according to taste.

Skirtings are often formed in cement and moulded, but such constructions do not come within the province of the joiner.

**Dado and Surbase.**—For the sake of ornament, and to prevent the wall from being injured by chairs knocked up against it, a moulded bar, called a "chair rail," is sometimes fixed at a height of about 3 feet from the floor, and parallel to the skirting.

This rail should be fixed to a narrow horizontal ground, and should be wide enough to cover the grounds and their junctions with the plastering.

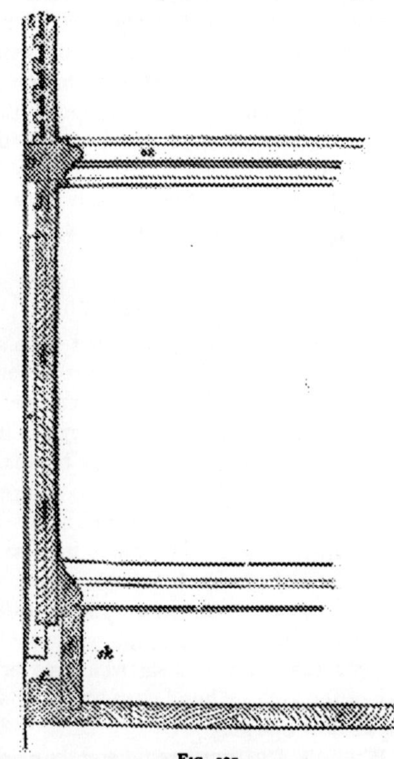

FIG 197.
Scale, 1 inch = 1 foot.

The interval between the rail and the skirting is called the *Dado*, D in Fig. 196, and the chair rail, SB, is called the "*surbase*" of the dado—the skirting forming the "*base*" B, or, as it is sometimes called, the *plinth*.

The dado may be either panelled, simply boarded, or formed only by the surface of the plastered wall, as in Fig. 196.

Fig. 196 shows a chair rail or surbase, SB, and plastered dado, D, with wooden "base" or "skirting," B.

The chair rail and the upper moulding of the skirting are nailed to narrow grounds, *g g*, Fig. 196, fixed to plugs inserted in the wall.

A portion of the skirting is broken away to show the blockings, *bk*, supporting it as described at p. 117.

The dado illustrated in Fig. 197 is entirely of wood, being formed of wide boards, grooved and feathered, and hung by thin tongues of hard wood, *j*, at intervals of about 3 feet, to the narrow ground, *g*, which supports the surbase, SB. The boarding is strengthened and kept together by taper keys, *k*, about 3 feet apart.

The boarding of the dado is thus suspended from the upper "ground," and is free to expand and contract without opening the joints.

## LININGS.

*Linings* are coverings of wood so placed as to conceal or ornament portions of the interior of buildings. There are several varieties of linings, distinguished by technical names denoting the position in which they are fixed.

All linings should be of narrow boards, ploughed or grooved and tongued, or rebated; free to expand and contract, and nailed to battens fixed to the wall about 2 feet apart.

In superior rooms the linings may be framed and panelled as described at p. 165, E.B.C.D.

LININGS TO DOORWAYS.—*Jamb Linings* cover the sides of the jambs or openings through walls, such as doorways.

*Soffit Linings* are those which cover the soffit or under sides of the arch or lintel spanning over a door, or the interior of a window opening.

WINDOW LININGS are differently named according to their position.

*Breast Linings* are those that cover the portion of the wall between the inside ledge or window board and the skirting. These are more commonly called "*window backs.*"

*Elbow Linings* cover the splays of the wall between the

inside ledge or window-board and the skirting when there are no shutters (see Fig. 209).

*Back Linings* are those at the back of the recesses for shutters (Fig. 212). This name is also given to that side of the boxing in a cased sash frame which is opposite the pulley stile (see p. 185, E.B.C.D.).

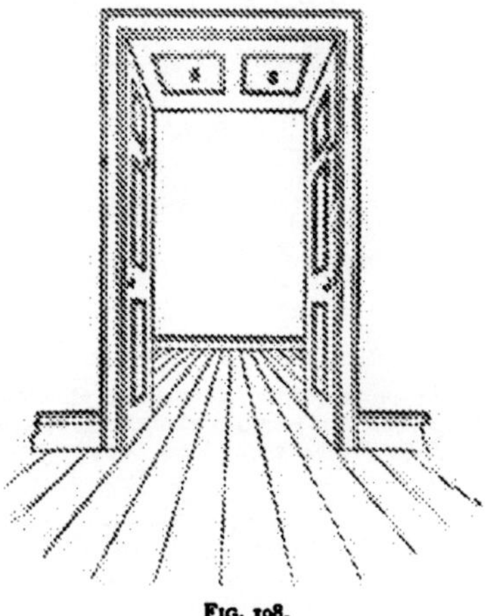

Fig. 198.

*The Outside and Inside Linings* are those forming the outer and inner sides respectively, of the boxings in cased sash frames.

*Wall Linings* are of the same nature as the above, but cover the whole surface of the walls.

**Jamb and Soffit Linings.**—In doorways the sides or "*jambs,*" J J, and the "*soffit,*"[1] S S, of the opening are generally boarded over or lined for the sake of appearance.

This boarding is called the jamb and soffit linings. These linings serve to conceal the rough sides and soffit of the opening beyond the recess containing the frame. If more than 9 or 10 inches wide they should be panelled, moulded, or otherwise made to correspond in appearance with the face of the door.

*Jamb Linings to external Doorway.*—It has been mentioned that external doors are nearly always hung in solid frames. If the doorway is in a thick wall, and for any reason it is required to keep the door near the front of the wall, there remains a considerable depth of the opening behind it which may be lined.

Such cases are shown in Figs. 199, 200. The lining in these examples is very simple, consisting merely of a 1-inch framed, moulded, and square

[1] Sometimes called *jamb-head.*

panelled lining, flush at back, tongued into the door frame at one end, and

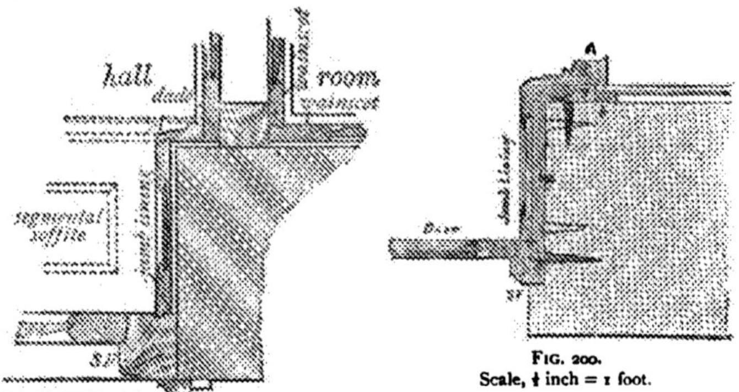


Fig. 199.

Fig. 200.
Scale, ½ inch = 1 foot.

at the other butting against the architrave A. The lining in Fig. 200 is supported by a rough backing fixed to plugs in the wall.

*Solid Frames with Jamb Linings for Internal Doorways.*—In this case the jamb lining is kept back from the edge of the frame a space equal to the thickness of the door, thus forming a deep rebate into which the latter may shut.

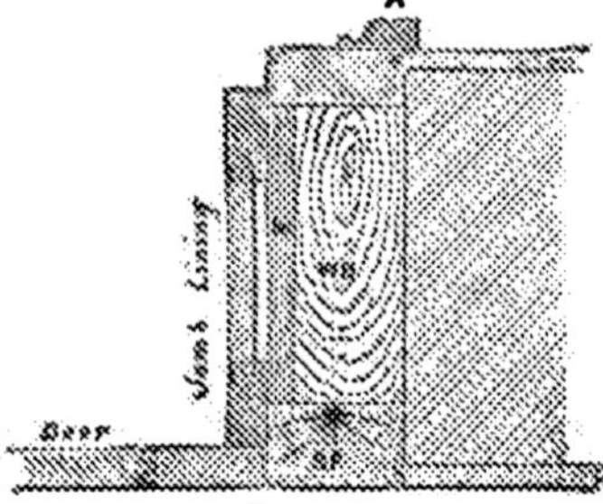


Fig. 201.
Scale, 1 inch = 1 foot.

The lining is fixed as before to a rough backing, *ba*, which is secured to wood bricks or slips in the wall.

This is a very strong way of hanging a door, but is expensive and seldom adopted for interior doors, unless very heavy and substantial work is required.

The solid frame may be beaded or chamfered on both edges and itself form the finish of the doorway, as at SF Fig. 201, or the joint between it and the plaster may be covered by an architrave, as at A on the opposite side.

The lower ends of the frame may be tenoned into the floor, which keeps it very firm.

*Jamb Linings with framed Grounds.*—This is the most usual way of hanging a door in ordinary work.

Figs. 202, 203, 204 give an elevation, cross-sectional elevation, and plan respectively, of a four-panelled interior door, with jamb and soffit lining of this kind. Fig. 205 shows a portion of the plan enlarged.

In this case it will be seen that the door is hung to the

FIG. 202.—*Elevation.*

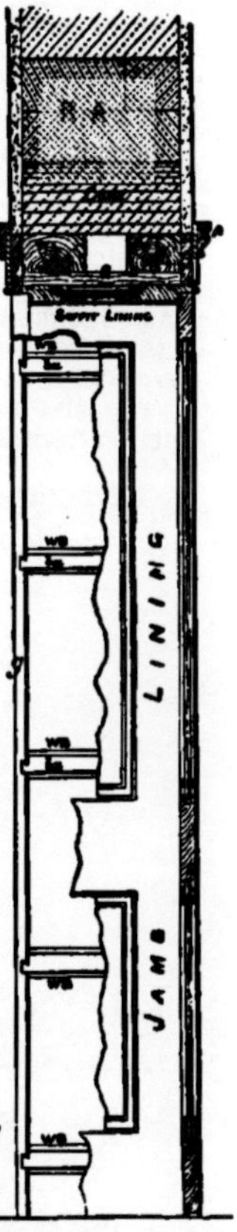

FIG. 203.—*Sectional Elevat*

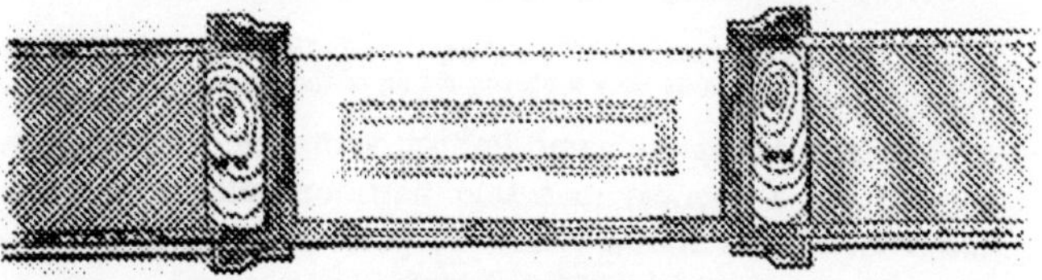

FIG. 204.—*Plan.*

FIGS. 202–204.—Scale, ½ inch = 1 foot.

jamb lining itself; the latter is attached to a backing, *ba*, dovetailed in between the framed grounds, and secured to wood bricks in the wall, the edges of which may be seen in elevation in Fig. 203.

In some cases the grounds are tongued into the jamb linings, but this is very seldom done.

The jamb linings go right through the depth of the opening, and on one side of the wall have their edges rebated to receive the door; the edges on the other side of the wall being (in superior work) similarly rebated to correspond.

The soffit lining is secured to cradling or backing, *c*, consisting of rough battens attached to the under side of the lintels over the opening.

Of course the doorway might be spanned by a rough axed arch, or by a concrete beam, without wood lintels, in which

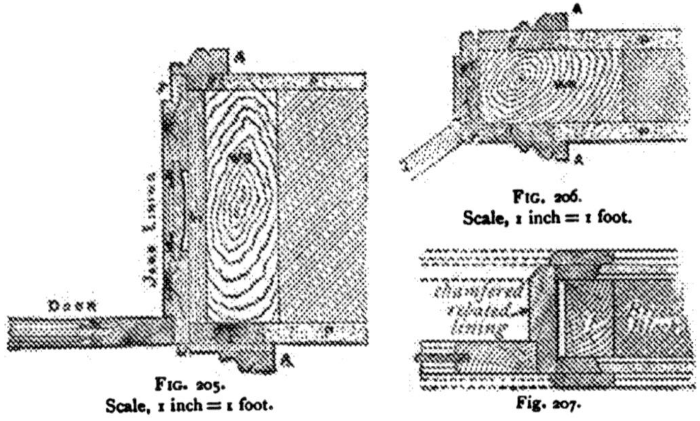

Fig. 205.
Scale, 1 inch = 1 foot.

Fig. 206.
Scale, 1 inch = 1 foot.

Fig. 207.

case the cradling would be secured to plugs let into the arch or beam, unless the beam were made of coke breeze concrete, which will admit and hold nails.

The enlarged plan in Fig. 204 differs slightly from Fig. 205, inasmuch as a smaller architrave is shown on the inside of the doorway.

Fig. 206 shows the jamb linings, with framed and finished grounds for a doorway in a thin partition wall. In practice, however, a solid frame would be preferable as in Fig. 207. It would run up and be secured to the joists above.

*Jamb Lining with Finished Grounds.*—In common work—

to save the expense of architraves—the grounds may be wrought so as to present a finished appearance, and themselves form an ornamented margin to the opening.

In Fig. 208, *g* is a wrought and chamfered ground secured to the backing *ba*, which is plugged to the wall. It will be seen that *g* acts both as a ground and as an architrave. This is taken from an actual case, but has little to recommend it, as the ground really forms only a feeble sort of door frame.

*Single and Double rebated Linings.*—Single-rebated linings are those having a rebate formed to receive the door, but none on the other side of the wall. In superior work there is a similar rebate formed on the opposite side, as at *r* in Fig. 205, and the lining is said to be *double-rebated.*

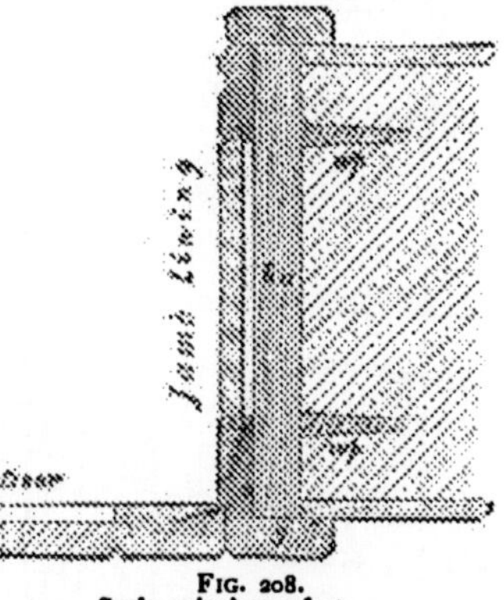


Fig. 208.
Scale, 1 inch = 1 foot.

**Window Linings.**—Figs. 209, 210 give a half-plan and

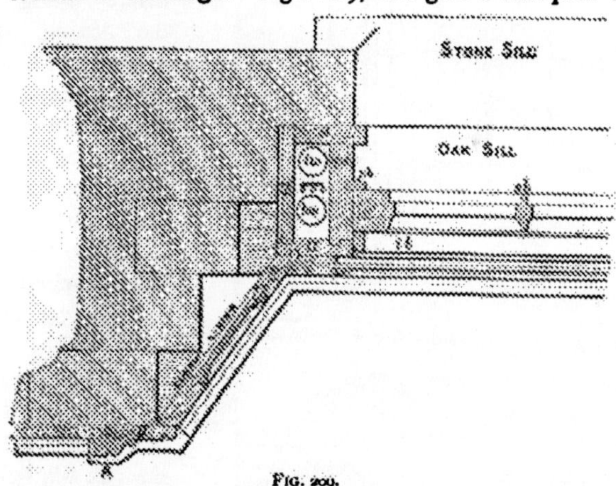


Fig. 209.
Scale, 1 inch = 1 foot.

a section of a window with cased frame and double-hung sashes, furnished with panelled and moulded linings.

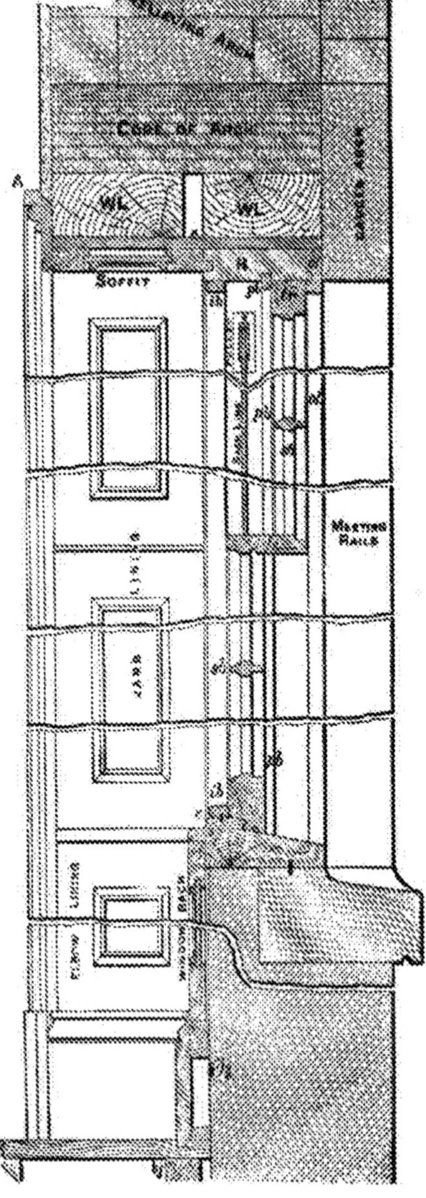


Fig. 210.—Scale, 1 inch = 1 foot.

It will be noticed that the head of this window is solid, being secured to the cradling *c* attached to the under side of the lintels, WL, its inner end being grooved to receive the tongued extremity of the soffit lining, the other end of which is nailed to the ground.

The jamb lining is grooved at one end into the inside lining of the boxing, and at the other nailed to the projecting framed and finished ground which forms the face of the architrave. It is supported by being nailed to the splayed wood brick, WB.

The upper rail of the window back is secured to the oak sill, being surmounted by a capping *c*. The lower rail rests upon the ground *g*, the joint being covered by the moulding of the skirting,[1] so that the expansion and contraction of the window back are not prevented.

The jamb lining is here shown as finished to look like shutters, sometimes described as "*sham shutters.*" When the lining is narrow it is often merely a plain board, tongued if the width requires it, wrought on face, but not framed; when moulded it is made to correspond in appearance with the doors or other panelled work of the room.

The wood brick, $WB_1$, is inserted in this case, so that the boxed frame may be nailed to it obliquely through the inside lining, *il*, but it is generally considered sufficient to drive a wedge in between the back lining and the wall.

## SHUTTERS.

Windows, especially those of ground-floors, are frequently fitted with shutters for security and warmth at night.

*Inside Shutters* are fixed on the inner side of the wall of a building.

*Outside Shutters* are fixed on the outer side of the wall.

**Inside Shutters** are hung in several different ways, which may be generally arranged under two heads.

1. *Folding.*—In leaves, hinged together and folding back into recesses or "*boxings*" prepared for them.

2. *Sliding.*—In leaves, sliding up and down, and counterbalanced by weights in the same way as sliding sashes; or sliding *laterally* upon rollers in and out of recesses formed for them at the sides of the window.

Folding Shutters.—A recess or boxing for these is formed in the space between the inside lining of the sash frame and the framed ground at the back of the architrave.

The back of this recess is plastered in common work, but in better work it is covered by a lining, called the "back lining."

This back lining has one end tongued into the inside

[1] In practice it is more usual to frame the window back and elbows with flush beaded skirting: (1) To avoid the difficulty of stopping the projecting skirting against the architrave; (2) in order to make the framing from floor upwards in one piece. The flush bead ranges with the top of the ordinary skirting.

lining of the sash frame, and the other housed or tongued into the ground behind the architrave.

In Fig. 212 the architrave is fixed to a finished ground, into which the back lining is grooved.

As the interior of the boxing is exposed to view when the shutters are closed, the back of the ground is sometimes covered, for the sake of appearance, by a return lining such as that marked *l* in Fig. 213.

The leaf which is exposed to view during the day may be framed and panelled like the doors of the room, and is called the *shutter*, the remaining leaves are called the *back flaps.*[1]

The back flaps, if they exceed 6 or 7 inches in width, are framed, but may be of a plainer description of panelling, or sometimes not panelled at all.

In most of the accompanying illustrations the shutter and flaps are shown as framed square on the outer side and bead flush on the inner side. The inner side is often finished bead butt for the sake of economy; or the flaps are often framed square on both sides, or moulded on one or both sides according to the class of work.

In the very best work, however, the shutters and flaps are all made the same on both sides, so that when closed they will all appear alike, whether seen from the interior of the room or through the glass from the outside.

In hanging shutters the knuckle of the hinges of the front leaf should be about half an inch from the inner angle of the inside lining—so that the whole width from one extremity of the shutters to the other, when they are open, is an inch more than the width of the window opening.

The flaps are connected by small "back-flap" hinges fixed as shown, or by butt-hinges attached to the edges of the flaps. In the former case the shutters, when folded back, are kept apart by nearly the thickness of the hinge, and there is room for an iron bar or other fastening to hang between them.

*Shutter and One Flap.*—When the opening is narrow, or the wall of considerable thickness, the shutter may be hung in two leaves, as in Figs. 211, 212.

[1] Sc. *Backfolds—closers.*

Fig. 211 is an interior elevation of a window with sliding sashes fitted with shutters hung in two leaves. The shutter and flap to the right of the elevation are closed, the other shutter and flap being folded back into the boxings, as shown in the half-plan Fig. 212.

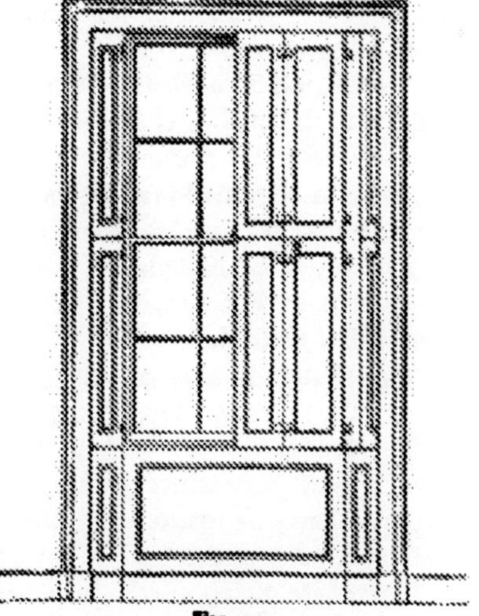

FIG. 211.
Scale, ½ inch = 1 foot.

The shutter is moulded on the side exposed to view during the day; the back of this shutter and that of the back flap (which are seen together on the inside of the room when the shutters are closed) are bead flush, while the front or outer side of the back flap is framed square.

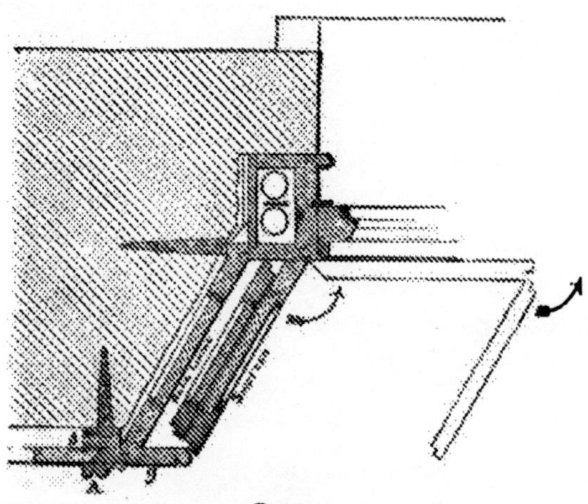

FIG. 212.
Scale, 1 inch = 1 foot.

In Fig. 212 and some of the following figures the dotted lines show the position of the shutters and flaps while in the act of being closed.

*Shutter and Two Flaps.*—When a window opening is wide, or the wall in which it is formed is not very thick, there is not so much room for shutters in proportion to their width, and they have to be folded into a greater number of leaves in order that they may take up less room in the thickness of the wall.

Fig. 213 is the half-plan of a window with the same opening as that in Fig. 212, but in a wall only 1 foot 6 inches instead of 2 feet thick.

The shutter in this case is necessarily folded into three leaves; the two back flaps, being very narrow, are not framed.

The lining, *l*, at the back of the ground, *g*, is only to preserve a neat appearance within the boxings when they are empty; it may be omitted and the back lining of the boxing prolonged to meet the back of the ground.

There are many methods of arranging folding shutters, which vary considerably according to the length of shutters required, and the space available for them to fold into.

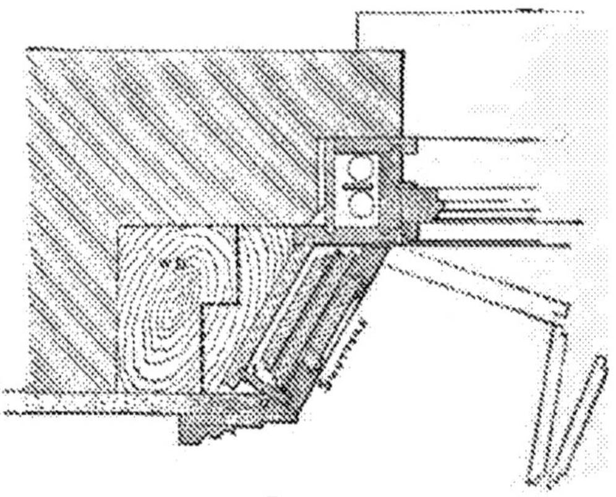

FIG. 213.
Scale, 1 inch = 1 foot.

One method of gaining room for shutters is to make the boxings project into the room, as shown in Fig. 214, or when the windows are separated by very narrow piers, the shutters may be arranged as in Fig. 215.

Where the masonry cannot be made to extend inwards far enough to form a support for the lining at the back of the shutters, such support is afforded by wooden brackets fixed to the back of the pier and extending inwards as far as may be required.

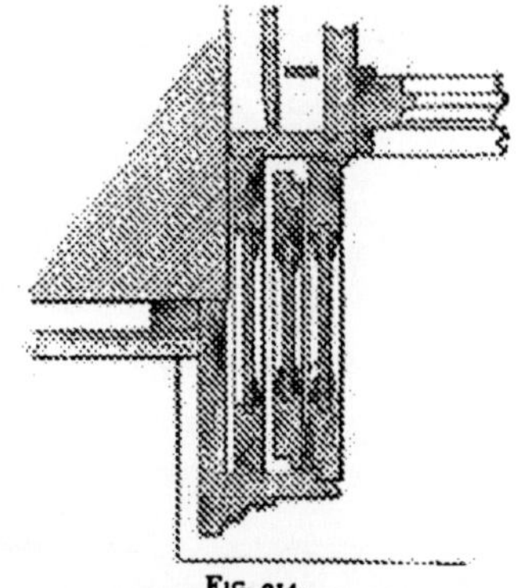

FIG. 214.
Scale, 1 inch = 1 foot.

Another arrangement for shutters to cover a window in a thin wall is shown in Fig. 216.

In this case the larger flap of the shutter folds back upon the inner side of the wall, and is exposed to view, being connected with the boxing of the window by a short flap which forms the jamb lining. The elbow of the wall is lined, in order to present a neat appearance when the shutters are closed.

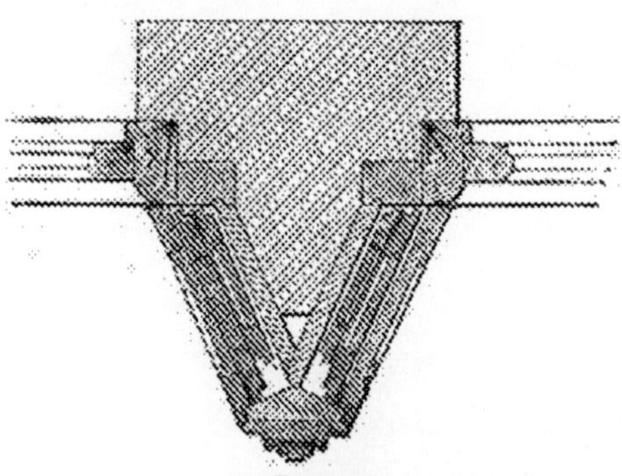

FIG. 215.
Scale, 1 inch = 1 foot.

This is rather an old-fashioned arrangement, but very useful in some situations.

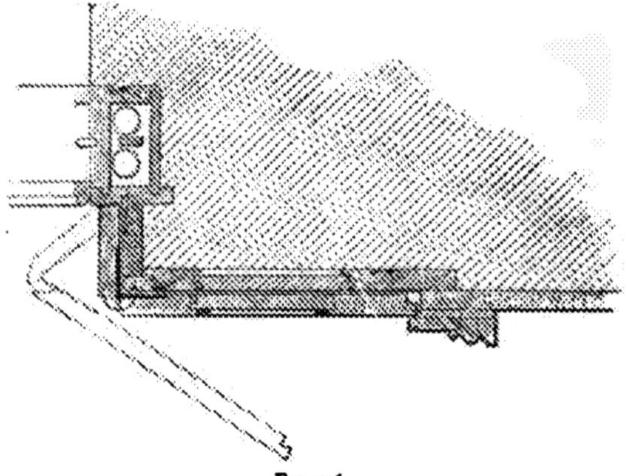

FIG. 216.
Scale, 1 inch = 1 foot.

*Shutters with Cover Flap.*—The different forms of folding shutters hitherto illustrated have one disadvantage in point of appearance, viz. that when the shutters are closed the recess formed to receive them is visible, and forms a break in the continuity of the panelling.

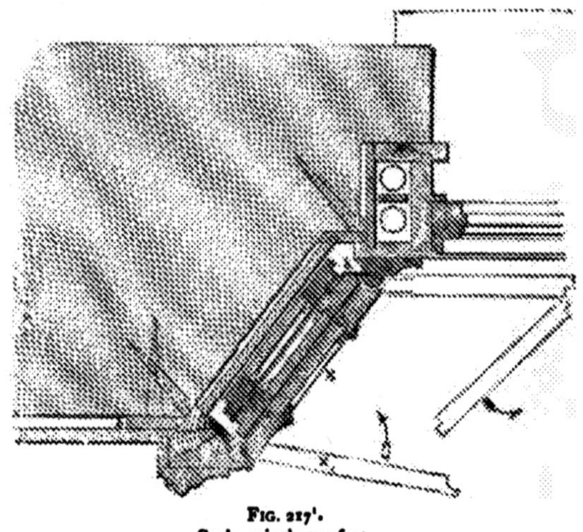

FIG. 217[1].
Scale, 1 inch = 1 foot.

[1] Modified from Plate 54, vol. iii., Laxton's *Examples of Building Construction.*

To avoid this, in very superior work the recess is covered by a separate flap, X (Fig. 217), which is hinged to the ground supporting it. When the shutters are to be closed, this flap is opened; and after they are shut against the sash the flap is returned, so that the appearance of the lining is preserved intact.

In order to throw the shutters back into the recess sufficiently to clear this flap, various arrangements are adopted.

That shown in the figure simply consists of a hinge, *h*, of peculiar form attached to a heavy moulding fixed to the inside lining of the cased frame. The action of this hinge will be clear upon examining the figure, in which the shutters are shown folded back into the recess, the position, $X_1$, of the flap, when partly closed, being indicated in dotted lines.

In some cases the shutter is thrown back clear of the covering flap by inserting a very short flap,[1] which lies across the ends of the shutters nearest the sash frame, and answers the same purpose as the peculiar hinge shown in Fig. 217.

SLIDING SHUTTERS may move either vertically or laterally; in the former case they are often called *lifting shutters.*

*Lifting Shutters* are hung in exactly the same way as sliding sashes; immediately behind the boxed frame of the sash is a similar frame for the shutters (Fig. 218).

The leaves of the shutters slide down into a rectangular well formed for them in the floor, so that their upper rails are nearly level with the window sill.

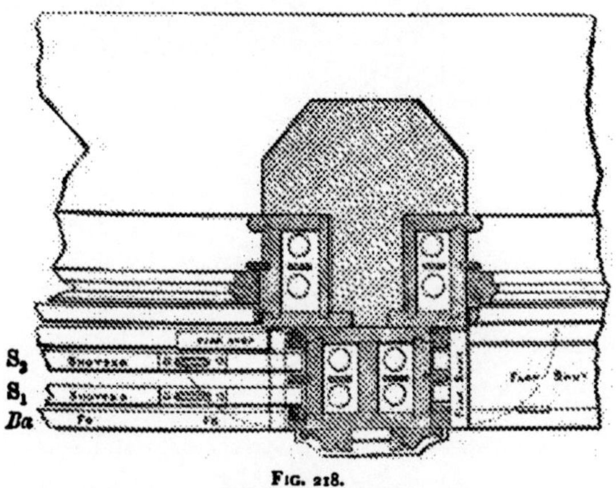


FIG. 218.
Scale, 1 inch = 1 foot.

[1] A good example of this arrangement is shown in Laxton's *Examples of Building Construction*, Plate 55, vol. iii.

On the front side they lie close to the inside of the wall, and on the other they are screened by a framed *back* (*Ba* in Fig. 219).

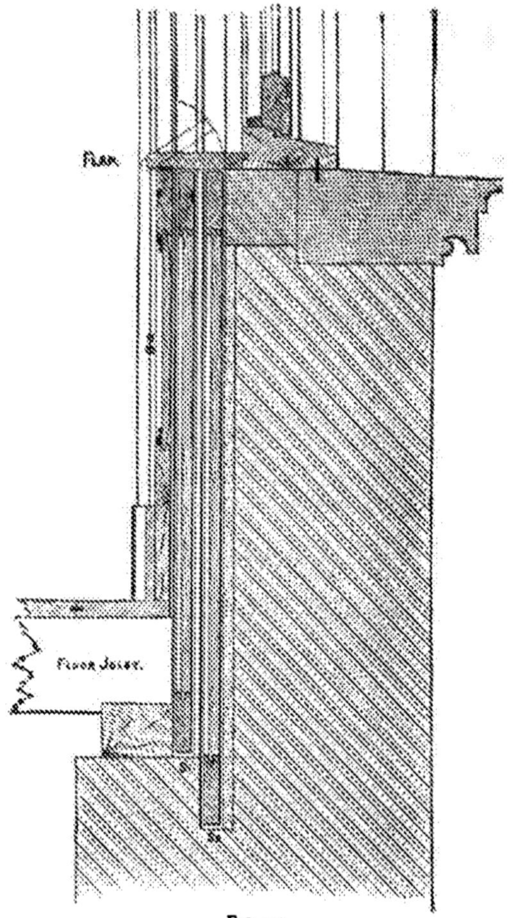


Fig. 219.
Scale, 1 inch = 1 foot.

The two leaves of the shutter slide in different and parallel paths,—the upper one, $S_1$, between the bead on the front lining of the shutter frame and the parting bead: the other,

$S_2$, between the parting bead and a bead fastened on to the inside lining of the sash frame.

The shutter $S_2$, nearest to the wall, is the lower of the two when they are closed. It is somewhat larger than the other, being of such a height that it will extend from the top of the flap or capping to the upper edge of the meeting rail. The other shutter fills up the space between the upper edge of the meeting rail and the top of the window.

The top of the well is closed when the shutters are down by a horizontal hinged flap, and vertical flaps conceal the parting bead, etc., when the shutters are not closed.

Sliding shutters are useful when there is not a sufficient thickness of wall behind the sash to receive folding shutters.

Fig. 218 is a plan of part of two adjacent windows separated by a narrow pier or mullion, and fitted with lifting shutters, and Fig. 219 is a vertical section of the same.

On the left of the plan the flap over the well for the shutters is supposed to be standing vertically open along FO FO, so that the upper rails of the shutters are visible with the flush handles for lifting them.

The vertical flap is also open and folded back.

On the right of the figure both flaps are closed.

In some cases the boxing for shutters is so arranged that its outside lining is formed by the inside lining of the cased frame for the sashes, which is a more economical construction than that shown in Fig. 218, but not so convenient.

*Sliding Shutters* are those in which the flaps slide laterally into recesses formed on each side of the window.

Such an arrangement can only be adopted when there is a considerable space on each side of the window. It possesses no particular advantages, and cannot here be described.

A good illustration of shutters sliding laterally will be found in Laxton's *Examples of Building Construction*, vol. iii. Plate 37.

**Outside Shutters** for dwelling-houses are generally hung somewhat like doors—in two leaves, one on each side—which are fixed to the outside lining (or to a fillet plugged to the wall in front of the outside lining) with *parliament hinges*, by which it is enabled to clear the reveal, and fold back upon the wall; see Fig. 220

Fig. 220.

For shop fronts shifting shutters are used, the appearance of which is familiar to all. Any description of them would be beyond the range of this course.

## SKYLIGHTS AND LANTERNS.

*Skylights* are windows, either fixed in roofs, or themselves forming the roof of a staircase or other building lighted from above.

They are very varied in form, according to the position in which they are fixed.

In many cases the skylight is raised upon vertical or slightly inclining frames filled in with sashes which form its sides (Figs. 224, 225); it is then frequently called a *Lantern*.

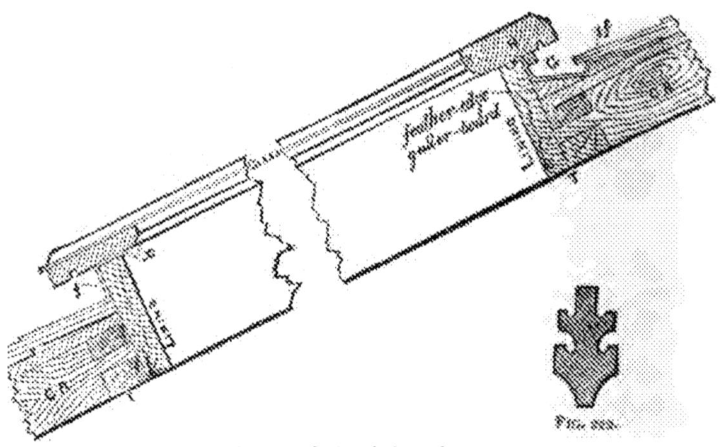

FIG. 221.—Scale, 1 inch = 1 foot.

The most common form of skylight is perhaps that in which the sash is parallel to the slope of the roof, and slightly raised above the surface of the slating, as in Fig. 221.

An opening is formed in the slope of the roof (by trimming the common rafters CR), for the same size as the proposed skylight; a lining[1] is attached to the inner sides of the trimmers TT, and of the trimming rafters, extending a few

[1] Usually called a "*curb*" or "*kerb*," and dovetailed at the angles.

inches above them. Upon this the sash rests; its styles and rails project over the frame, and may be rebated to fit it, or a projecting piece may be nailed on, as shown in Fig. 221, to cover the joint.

Lead flashings, *ff*, are also fixed as shown to prevent the wet from getting in; and any that may penetrate finds itself in a groove cut in the upper surface of the top and side linings, down which it runs, escaping at the lower end of the latter.

The sash bars run down the slope of the roof like rafters, and should be made strong enough to resist the weight of glass and snow, force of wind, etc. The rebates should be grooved, so as to carry off any moisture that may pass round the edges of the glass.

The lead apron at the lower extremity of the inside of the skylight should be formed into a sort of gutter, as shown in dotted lines at *x*, to receive and carry away the moisture which condenses on the lower surface of the glass. It is also desirable to form gutters in the sides of the sash bars for the same purpose, as in Fig. 222.

The panes should run continuously through from top to bottom of the skylight, without cross bars to intercept the wet running off the glass.

If it be necessary to have the panes in shorter lengths, they should overlap, as in Fig. 223, and be secured by metal clips, shown in thick black lines which hang the bottom edge of each pane to the top edge of the pane below it.

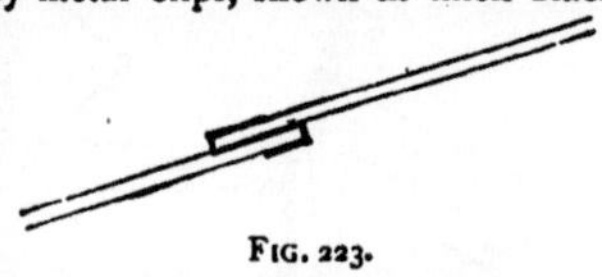

Fig. 223.

It is sometimes necessary, for want of space, to obtain more light, or for other reasons, to make the side linings vertical instead of at right angles to the rafters as shown, but the latter is the stronger construction.

It is becoming usual, especially where a skylight is of considerable length, to avoid the gutter by lowering the head H of the skylight 2 or 3 inches below the lower edge of the slates of the roof. The end at *x* remains at the same level, so that the slope of the skylight is flatter than that of the roof.

If such a skylight as that shown in Fig. 221 be required to open it must be hinged at H; and in some cases the joint is protected by a strip of lead fastened round the sash, which hangs down over the lead flashing on the sides of the frame.

The glass in skylights is sometimes secured by means of a capping fixed to the upper surface of the sash bars, which holds the glass more firmly and prevents the wet from penetrating.

Another kind of skylight consists of a pair of sashes fixed above the apex of a roof and parallel to its sides.

Two varieties, surmounting a queen-post roof, are shown in Figs. 224, 225.

The skylight, of which half is shown at A, consists of a pair of sashes similar in construction to that just described, raised a few inches above the surface of the side slopes of the roof by means of linings fixed to the purlins resting upon the queen posts.

The inner sides of the queen posts have backing pieces fixed to them, carrying a lining so as to convert the interval immediately under the skylight into a shaft or boxing.

In some cases, for the sake of appearance, the lower extremity of this shaft is filled in with a sash, *Sa*, called a ***counter skylight*** or ***ceiling light***, containing glass, so as to keep the plane of the ceiling almost unbroken.

The skylight or lantern at B is raised two or three feet above the roof by means of framed sides containing sashes, which may either be fixed, or made to open by being hinged at the top, or (as in Fig. 225) hung on centres.

The sill of the framed sides is fixed to a capping or curb, which rests upon a cross bearer supported by the heads of the queen posts.

This form of skylight gives more light and ventilation than that at A, but is of course considerably more expensive.

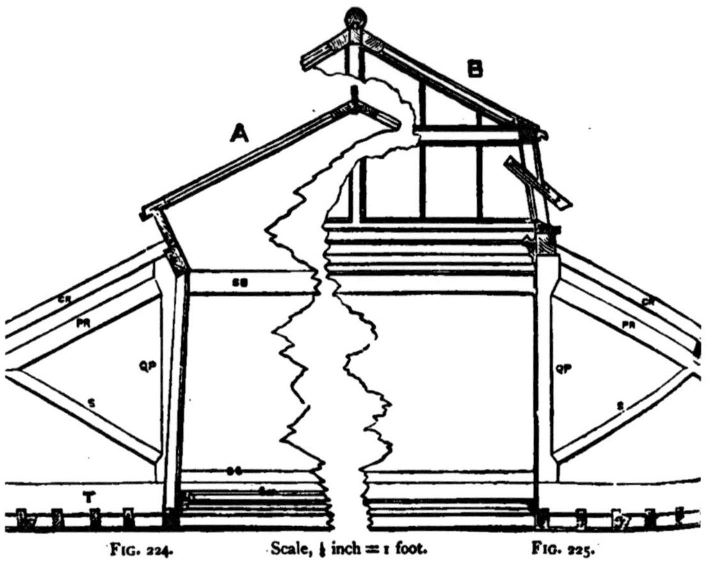


FIG. 224. Scale, ¼ inch = 1 foot. FIG. 225.

Figs. 226, 227 show a skylight or lantern over a room covered by a lead flat.

This example is taken from the lecture-theatre of an hospital near London, but is in many particulars similar to one over the Museum of Economic Geology, and illustrated in Laxton's *Examples of Building Construction.*

The lantern, being large and heavy, is supported on two sides by cast-iron girders,[1] AB, CD (Fig. 227), extending across

[1] In these days rolled beams would be better.

the room. The other sides are covered by binders fixed between these girders.

Fig. 226.
Scale, 1 inch = 1 foot.

Fig. 227 is a plan showing the arrangement of these girders, and of the binders and joists supporting the lead flat, the larger portion of which is broken away to show the bearers beneath.

Fig. 226 is a sectional elevation of half the lantern, showing the different parts in sufficient detail to render much explanation unnecessary. The moisture condensed upon the inside of the upper portion of the skylight runs down and is caught in a small zinc gutter formed in the upper portion of the moulding at W, and from thence is led through a hole (dotted in the figure) to discharge upon the lead flat outside.

The details of the side sashes hung on centres are similar to those already given for such sashes in E.B.C.D.

It will be noticed that the inside bead, *x*, Fig. 226, is so fixed upon the sill that the skylight when closed does not shut up against it, but an interval is left, which forms a gutter to receive the condensed moisture from the sash. A groove cut in the sill enables this water to escape.

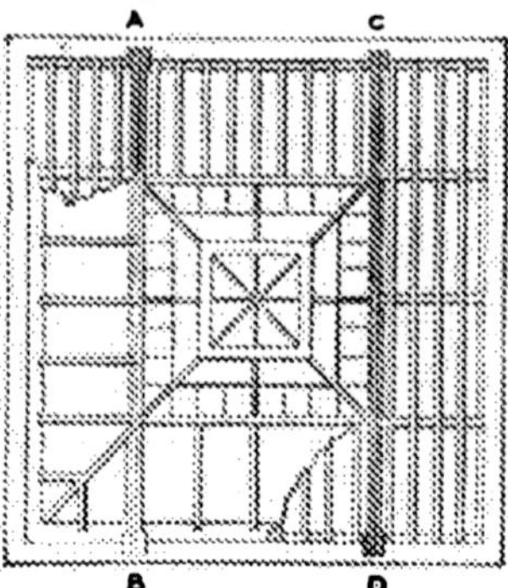


FIG. 227.
Scale, $\frac{1}{12}$ inch = 1 foot.

Such a lantern as that shown in Fig. 226 may itself form the roof of a staircase, in which case the oak sill, forming the base of the sash, would rest upon the coping of the walls of the staircase.

When the side sashes of a lantern are fixed, ample provision should be made for carrying off the moisture which condenses on the inside of the glass, and has a tendency to run down into the room below.

This may be prevented by providing a wide oak sill projecting inwards an inch or two, so as to give room for a deep groove formed on the inside, into which the condensed moisture runs, and from whence it is led outwards by holes bored through the sill.

Or the inside bead on the oak sill may be kept a little back from those on the sides, so as to form a gutter as explained above and shown in Fig. 226.

*Sliding Sash in Skylight.*—It is sometimes advisable to construct the slightly inclined sashes of a skylight so as to open by sliding.

In such a case it is important to keep the rain from penetrating between the frame and the sash.

This may be done by arranging as in Fig. 228.

The sash, S, slides down the frame, F, upon a little brass friction roller, *r*, fixed in the frame. *st* is a stop on the sash which strikes against the block, *bl*, attached to the frame, and arrests the fall of the sash when it has gone far enough.

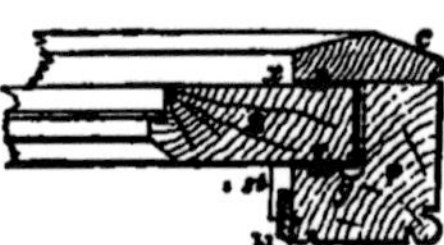

FIG. 228.
Scale, 1 inch = 1 foot.

*c* is a capping protecting the upper surface of the joint between the sash and frame. As an additional precaution an angle-iron water bar may be inserted as shown, so as to prevent any water running off the sash from penetrating sideways at the point *x*. If, in spite of this, any water should penetrate, it will find itself in the groove *g*, which leads it off through the lower end of the frame.

# CHAPTER VIII.

## *STAIRS.*

***Subjects required by Syllabus, and (in brackets) the pages at which they are treated upon.***

*Stone stairs* [p. 146]. *Wooden stairs* (*both doglegged and open newel*) [pp. 161, 163].

*Stairs* are arrangements of steps for conveniently ascending and descending from one level to another.

They are generally constructed either in stone, wood, concrete, or iron.

The consideration of iron stairs does not come within the range of this course.

The terms common to all stairs will first be mentioned, and also a few general principles universally applicable; after which

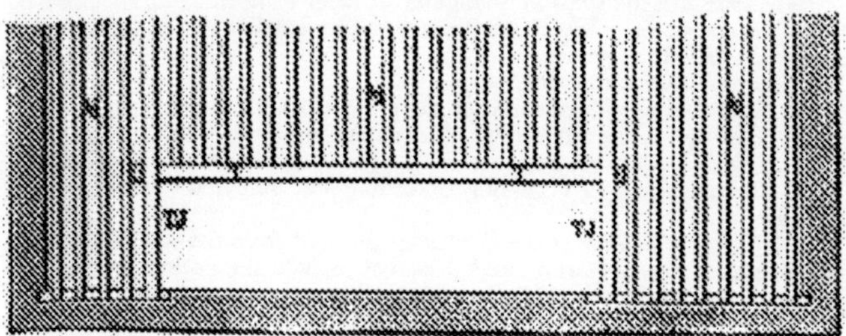

FIG. 229.

the construction of stone and wood stairs respectively will be considered more in detail.

The following are terms used in connection with all stairs, whatever may be the material of which they are constructed.

*The Staircase* is the chamber or space which contains the stairs.

This may be a room of the exact size required, the walls of which closely surround and support the steps, as in Fig. 263, or the stairs may be in a large apartment, such as a passage or hall, openings being left in the upper floors so as to allow headway for persons on the steps, and to furnish communication between the stairs and the different stories of the building.

In such a case the stairs are generally, though not necessarily, placed against a wall, as shown in Fig. 229, and the opening is trimmed round (see E.B.C.D.).

In Factories, or similar large buildings, the staircase should be in a tower projecting from the building, so that it may in case of fire be intact. The best materials for fireproof stairs are, first, wrought iron, then cast iron, then hard wood with plastered soffit. With regard to stone steps, see note, p. 146.

*Tread* is the horizontal upper surface of the step upon which the foot is placed.

*Rise* is the vertical height between two treads.

*Riser*[1] is the face or vertical portion of the step.

*Nosing* is the outer edge of the tread. In most cases it projects beyond the face of the riser and is rounded or ornamented by a moulding, being known, accordingly, as a "rounded" or "moulded" nosing[2] (see Figs. 220, 221).

*Fliers* are the ordinary steps of rectangular shape in plan.

*Winders*[3] are the steps of triangular or taper form in plan, required in turning a corner or going round a curve. The small ends of winders are sometimes called the *quoins*.

*A Curtail Step* is described at p. 168.

*A Flight* is a continued series of steps without a landing.

*A Landing*[4] is the flat resting-place at the top of any flight.

*A Half Space* is a landing extending right across the width of the stair.

*A Quarter Space* is a landing extending half across the width of the staircase.

*The Going of a Stair* is the horizontal distance from the face of one riser to the face of the next riser, and does not include the nosing or the projection of the tread beyond the face of the riser.

The term is, however, sometimes taken to mean the width of the stair, that is, the length of the steps.

*The Going of a Flight* is the horizontal distance from the first to the last riser in the flight.

*The Line of Nosings* is tangent to the nosings of the steps, and thus parallel to the inclination of the stair.

*Newels* are posts or columns used in some kind of stairs to receive the outer ends of steps (see Figs. 258, 259). The name "newel" is sometimes applied to the final baluster on a curtail step.

When the newels surround a central opening, as in Fig. 261, the staircase is said to have an "*open newel.*"

*The Handrail* is a rounded or moulded rail, parallel nearly throughout its length to the general inclination of the stair, and at such a height from the steps as to be conveniently grasped by a person on the stairs.

*Balusters* are slight posts or bars supporting the handrail.

---

[1] Sc. *Breast.*
[2] Sc. *Bottled* or *Bottle-nosed step.*
[3] Sc. *Wheeling steps.*
[4] Sc. *Plat.*

**Dimensions of Stairs.**—The dimensions of staircases and steps are regulated by the purposes for which they are intended.

*Length of Steps.*—Sometimes spiral staircases are constructed in very cramped positions, with steps only 1 foot 9 inches long; but, as a rule, steps should not be less than from 3 to 4 feet long, so as to allow two people to pass, and in superior buildings they are very much longer.

The stairs in the illustrations given with these Notes are necessarily shown narrow for want of space.

*Tread and Rise.*—The angle of ascent for a stair will depend upon the total height to be gained between the floors, and the space that can be afforded in plan.

The wider the step the less the rise should be, as steps which are both wide and high require a great exertion to climb.

Authorities differ slightly as to the proportion between the tread and riser; the following table is given by Mr. Mayer in Newland's *Carpenter's and Joiner's Assistant.*

| Treads, inches. | Risers, inches. | Treads, inches. | Risers, inches. |
|---|---|---|---|
| 5 | 9 | 12 | 5½ |
| 6 | 8½ | 13 | 5 |
| 7 | 8 | 14 | 4½ |
| 8 | 7½ | 15 | 4 |
| 9 | 7 | 16 | 3½ |
| 10 | 6½ | 17 | 3 |
| 11 | 6 | 18 | 2½ |

The following rule is often adopted for steps of the dimensions ordinarily required in practice, *i.e.* those with treads from 9 inches to 14 inches wide:—

Width of tread + height of riser = 66 inches.

Thus with a tread of 12 inches riser would be 5½ inches; with a riser of 6 inches the tread would be 11 inches.

The rule adopted in France, where they have given great attention to the subject, is as follows: "Inasmuch as on the average human beings move horizontally 2 feet in a stride, and as the labour of rising vertically is twice that of moving horizontally, the width of the tread added to twice the height of the rise should be equal to 2 feet."

The proportion that the tread and riser bear to one another cannot always in practice be fixed by rule, but is regulated by the space—as regards both plan and height—that can be afforded for the staircase.

The tread of a step should, however, never be less than 9 inches in width, even for the commonest stair; while, for first-class houses and public buildings, the stairs may have treads from 12 to 14 inches wide.

*Flights* should, when possible, consist of not more than 12 or 13 steps, after which there should be a landing, so that weak people may have a rest at short intervals.

Two consecutive flights ought not to be in the same direction.

## DIFFERENT FORMS OF STAIRS.

*N.B.*—In the Figures connected with stairs the handrail is drawn in the elevations and sections in order more clearly to show the direction of the steps, but omitted from the plans so as not to obscure them.

**A Straight Stair** is one in which all the steps are parallel to one another and rise in the same direction—thus a person ascending moves forward in a straight line.

Figs. 233, 234, 256, 257, show plans and sections of straight staircases, the former in stone, and the latter in wood; these are described at pages 148, 160.

Such a stair is, for some reasons, very convenient, but can only be used when there is a considerable length of space available for the staircase compared with the height to be gained.

When this is not the case, the flight of steps are made to run in different directions, so that they are doubled up into a shorter space.

Flights running alternately in opposite directions are found to be a great relief in ascending a considerable height, and therefore a very long straight stair is objectionable.

**A Dog-legged Stair**[1] is so called from its being bent or crooked suddenly round in fancied resemblance to a dog's leg.

In this form of stair the alternate flights rise in opposite directions, as indicated by the arrows in Figs. 235, 238, and 259.

[1] This term is generally used with reference to wooden stairs, but there is no distinct name for stone stairs of similar form. Stairs with rectangular well holes, such as those in Figs. 243, 261, are sometimes called *dog-legged*.

The ends of the steps composing each of these alternate flights are in the same plane with those of the other flight, so that there is no opening or well hole between them.

It is evident that—putting landings out of consideration—dog-legged stairs require only half the length of staircase that would be occupied by an equal number of steps of the same size arranged as a straight stair. On the other hand, the dog-legged stair requires twice the width of the straight stair.

Figs. 235–237 show a dog-legged stair in stone with a half-space landing. Figs. 258, 259, show a similar stair in wood. In Fig. 238 there is no intermediate landing, the whole space being taken up with winders.

It will be noticed that all the winders converge to a point in the stair itself, so that they are very narrow near this end, and most inconvenient to ascend. This is a great drawback to the dog-legged form of stair, which, indeed, should never be used when winders are required, if there is room for a well hole between the flights.

**A Geometrical Stair** is one in which there is an opening or well hole between the backward and forward flights.

Such a stair requires of course a little more width, but only about the same length of space as a dog-legged stair.

The effect of the well hole is that the winders converge to a point between the flights, and have a certain amount of width even on the verge of the well hole. At a short distance inwards, where the person ascending places his foot, the winder is so broad as to afford a very convenient tread.

Figs. 240–242 show a geometrical stair in stone without intermediate landings, the space being occupied entirely by winders. Fig. 263 shows a similar stair constructed in wood.

**Circular Stairs** are composed of steps contained in a circular or polygonal staircase, towards the centre of which they all converge.

All the steps are necessarily winders.[1]

A Circular Newel Stair is one in which the converging steps are supported by a newel at the centre of the staircase.

[1] Sc. *Wheeling steps.*

This newel may be either solid or hollow (see p. 153).

A CIRCULAR GEOMETRICAL STAIR is in form the same as the last described, but there is no newel. The steps converge as before, but rise round an open well hole instead of resting upon a newel (p. 154).

## STONE STAIRS.

*Stone Stairs* have an advantage over those of wood, inasmuch as they are much simpler in construction,[1] but the steps are heavy and require substantial walls for their support; moreover, they become smooth under the friction of continued wear, and then are slippery and dangerous.

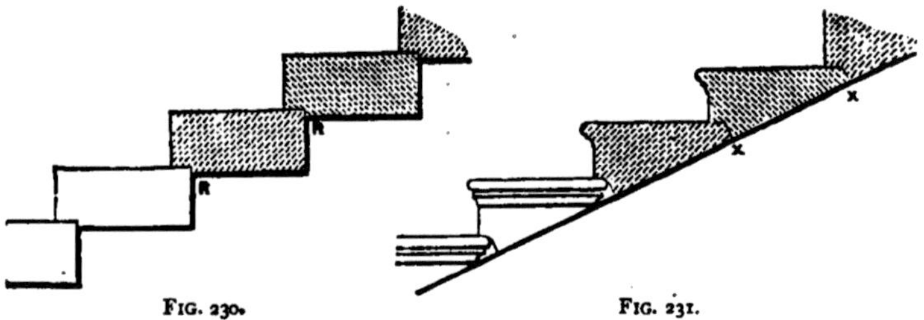


FIG. 230. FIG. 231.

The hatched portion of these figures is in section, the remainder in elevation.

**Stone Steps** are generally solid blocks, and should be worked on the tread and rise, the former being for external steps slightly weathered, or the stone set with a slight inclination outwards.[2] In superior buildings the soffit also is worked, and the nosing may be moulded,[3] as shown in Fig. 231.

Steps and landings that cannot be got out in one stone must be of pieces jointed, joggled, and plugged together; in some cases it is necessary to support the landings on girders. Stone steps are sometimes formed with thin flags forming treads and risers, similar to those of wooden steps. Such

[1] Hanging stone steps are soon destroyed by fire; the part exposed to the heat expands, that embedded in the wall does not, hence the steps snap off at the wall.

[2] Sc. This inclination is called the *kilt* of the stone.

[3] Sc. *Bottled* or *bottle-nosed*.

steps require no further description. The following remarks refer to solid steps.

SQUARE STEPS are rectangular in section, as shown in Fig. 230.

SPANDRIL[1] STEPS have the lower side cut away so as to form a raking soffit, as in Fig. 231. This is sometimes useful where headway is required under the stairs; it also makes the steps lighter, and is considered to have a better appearance.

FIXING STONE STEPS.—Stone steps may in some forms of staircase be supported at both ends by walls; in other cases one end only of each is built into the wall; these latter are called *hanging steps*.

The lowest step of a stair is sometimes sunk slightly into the ground to prevent it from sliding on its bed.

*Steps supported at both ends* are of most simple construction. The stone is rectangular in section, of a height exactly equal to the rise, and in width a little more than that of the tread (Fig. 233).

They are about 12 inches longer than the width of the stair, so that a length of 6 inches at each end is built into the adjacent walls.

When, however, these walls do not rise higher than the sides of the stair, the steps are of a length exactly equal to the width of the stair, and the ends are supported by walls built underneath them.

*Hanging Steps* are each fixed at one end only; the outer end projects and is without support other than that afforded by the steps below it.

The fixed ends of hanging steps should be let into the wall about 9 inches, and very solidly and firmly built in.

As each step is supposed to depend to a certain extent on the support of the step below it, the joint between the two is so made that the pressure may be transmitted from one step to the other, and the parts in contact may be kept from slipping.

In square steps this is often done by cutting a rebate[2] (R R, Fig. 230) along the lower edge of the front of each step, into which fits the upper edge of the back of the step above, or a deeper rebate may be formed along the lower edge of the breast of each step, and the back-joint cut off at right angles to the soffit, as shown at Y Y in Fig. 232.

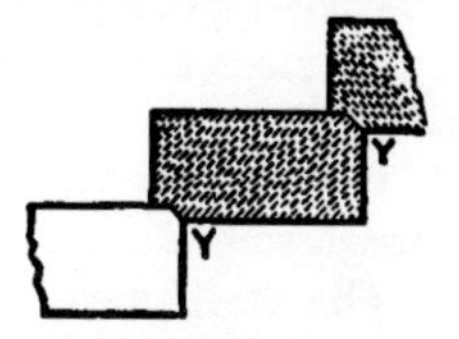

FIG. 232.

If the ends of the steps are securely built into the wall the steps cannot slide, and the rebate is of very little use; in fact, in the very best work it is sometimes omitted, unless the steps have a low rise, and would otherwise be too thin to bear the weight upon them, in which case their thickness can be increased by introducing the rebate.

A plain chamfered joint at right angles to the soffit, like that in Fig. 232 but without the rebate, is sometimes used.

Hanging steps may be built in as the wall is carried up; or, to avoid

[1] Sometimes called Feather-edged steps.
[2] Sc. *Piend-check*.

risk of damage to the steps, indents about 9 inches deep may be left in the walls, and the steps inserted afterwards; they should be pinned in with cement, and iron packing of hoop iron, pieces of old saws, etc.

Sometimes about 12 inches of the walling above and below the steps is built in cement.

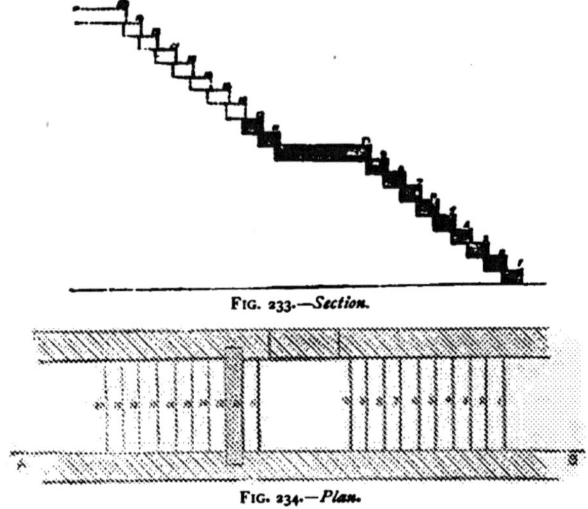

FIG. 233.—*Section.*

FIG. 234.—*Plan.*

**Different Arrangements of Stone Stairs.**[1]—STRAIGHT STAIRS.—Figs. 233, 234 show a straight stair composed of square steps supported at each end by being built into the side walls.

Fig. 234 is a horizontal sectional plan (looking downwards) through step No. 12.

The steps have 9 inches tread, and 7 inches rise, and between the flights (each consisting of 9 steps) is placed a landing.

DOG-LEGGED STAIRS in stone are generally composed of hanging steps, the inner ends of which are firmly built into the walls of the staircase, while the outer ends of one flight are in the same plane as those of the other flight.

Fig. 235 is a sectional plan (looking downwards) on the sixteenth step. Fig. 236 is a sectional elevation on the line

[1] Figs. 233–249 are on a scale of ¼ inch = 1 foot.

A B, through the lower flight; and Fig. 237 is a front elevation of the stairs, showing the front of the lower flight

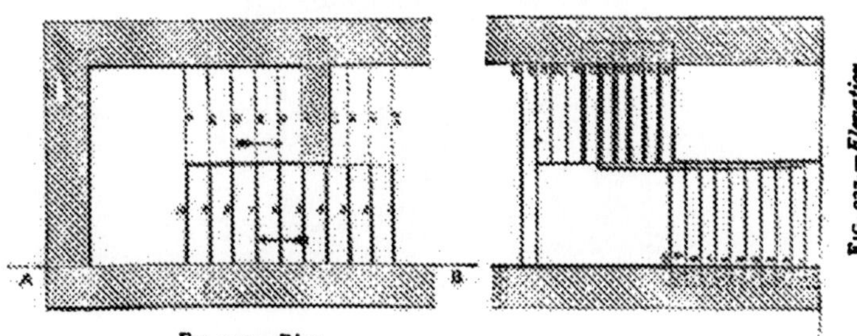


Fig. 235.—*Plan.*

Fig. 237.—*Elevation.*

and the back of the upper flight of steps.

The stairs in Fig. 235 are shown with a half-space landing; but if the same height has to be gained when there is a smaller space available for the staircase, winders may be added so as to have only a quarter-space landing, similar to that in Fig. 261, or the whole space may be occupied by winders as in Fig. 238.

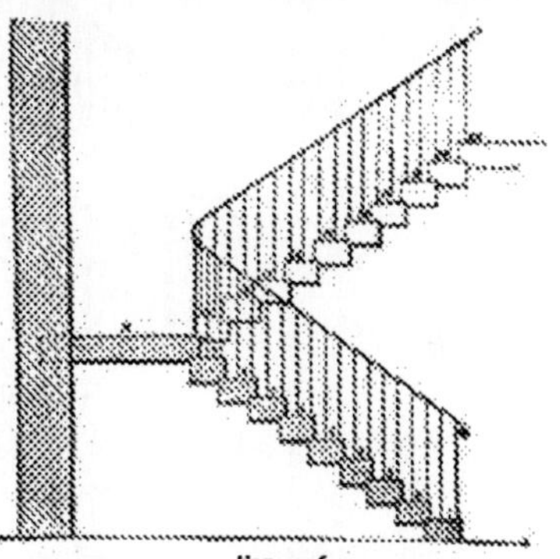

Fig. 236.
*Sectional Elevation on* A B.

Winders would be necessary also in case a greater height had to be gained, without increasing the area of the staircase.

Figs. 238, 239 show a dog-legged stair with winders communicating between three floors. These figures make clear the importance of having a sufficient headway between the flights running in the same direction (see *x y*), and also between the landings (see *o p*).

A Geometrical Stair in stone consists entirely of hanging steps, the outer ends of which are built into the walls of the staircase, while the inner ends abut upon the well hole of the stair, having no support but that derived from their successive connection, until they reach the floor.

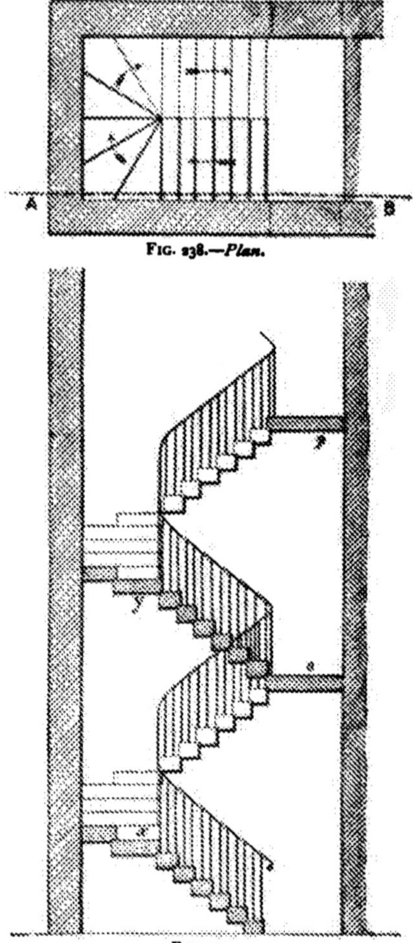


FIG. 238.—*Plan.*

FIG. 239.
*Sectional Elevation on* A B.

Figs. 240, 241, 242 give illustrations of a geometrical stair in stone, with a narrow well hole, having a semicircular end.

Fig. 240 is a sectional plan made through the sixteenth step looking downwards; Fig. 241 a vertical section through the lower flight, and elevation of the upper flight beyond; and Fig. 242 a front elevation of the staircase, showing the faces

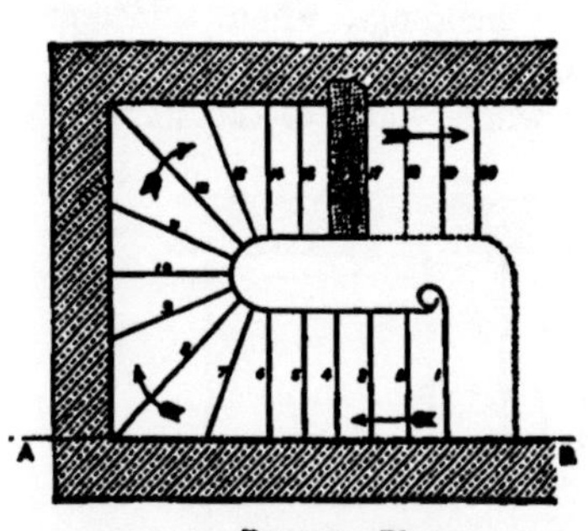


FIG. 240.—*Plan.*

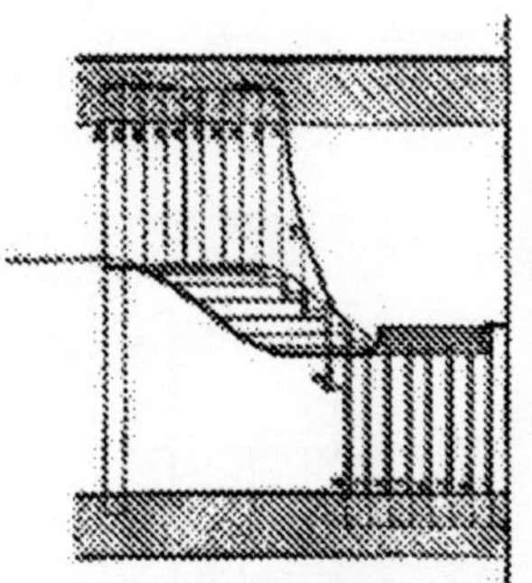

FIG. 242.—*Elevation.*

of the risers of steps of lower flight, and the backs of the steps of the upper flight.

The stair is constructed with spandril steps, and without a landing except at the floors, the space being entirely filled with winders, the improved form of which, as compared with the triangular winders of the dog-legged stair, will be evident upon comparing Fig. 240 with Fig. 238.

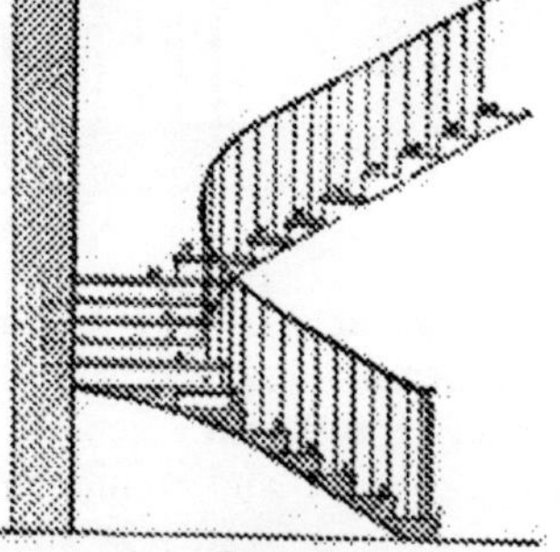

FIG. 241.
*Sectional Elevation on* A B.

Fig. 243 shows a geometrical stair adapted for a large and wide staircase.

This stair consists of three flights and two quarter-space landings, besides a large and wide landing (to which the stairs lead) on the level of the floor above.

The position and direction of the steps will be easily understood from the plan, without elevations, sections, or further explanation.

In some cases the inner corners of the quarter-space landings abutting on the well hole are cut off and made in plan of a quadrant shape, by which the curve of the handrail is improved at these points.

Such a stair takes up a great deal of room, and is only suitable for large and important buildings, where sufficient space can be afforded for the staircase.

In Fig. 243 a landing of the whole width of the staircase

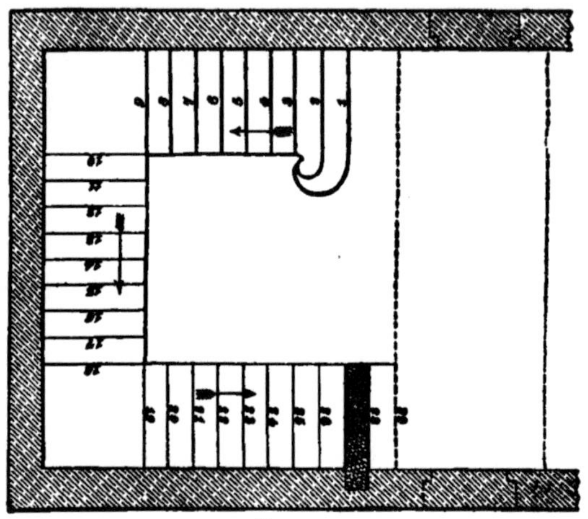

Fig. 243.

is shown at the level of the 29th step. Of course, if the arrangements required it, a quarter space landing at this point would be sufficient; from it would lead a flight parallel to steps 10 to 18, and running in the opposite direction.

Circular Stairs in stone may be composed either of steps supported at both ends, or of hanging steps converging toward a well hole; in either case, of course, all the steps are winders.

Circular Newel Stairs consist of square steps supported by the wall at one end, and at the other end by a "newel" or column of masonry, towards which they converge in the centre.

This newel may be either hollow or solid.

Fig. 244 shows an example of a circular stair with a hollow newel, consisting of a brick cylindrical shaft into which the inner ends of the steps are pinned, the other ends being built into the outer wall of the staircase.

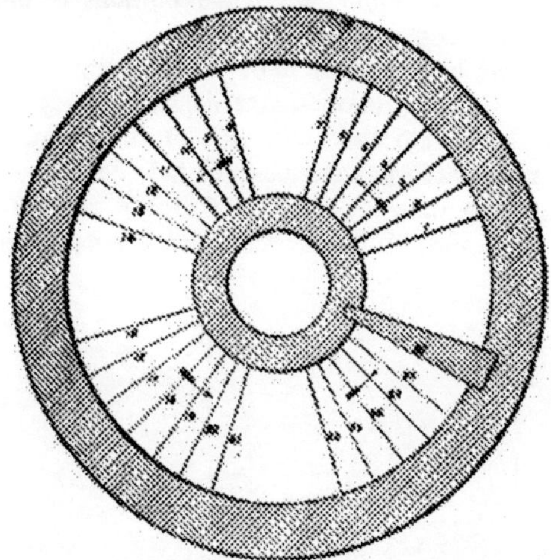

Fig. 244.

In some cases a thin wall is built round the centre newel, and also round the inside of the external wall, to support the ends of the steps, instead of building them in.

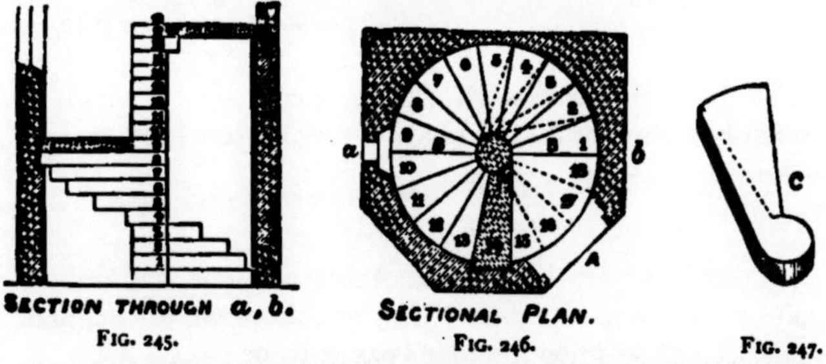


SECTION THROUGH a, b. Fig. 245.

SECTIONAL PLAN. Fig. 246.

Fig. 247.

A very common construction, especially for circular staircases of small diameter such as those in turrets, is shown in Figs. 245, 246.

Each step is worked in the form shown in Fig. 247, with a circular portion on the inner end, having a diameter equal to that of the intended newel.

As the steps are built up the outer ends are secured in the wall of the staircase, while the circular portions at the inner extremity, being laid one upon another, give the step the required support, and form the newel of the stair.

CIRCULAR GEOMETRICAL STAIRS consist entirely of hanging winders built into the outer wall of the staircase, and converging toward an open circular well hole down the centre.

Figs. 248, 249 show illustrations of such a stair, Fig. 248 being a sectional plan on No. 20 step, and Fig. 249 a sectional elevation.

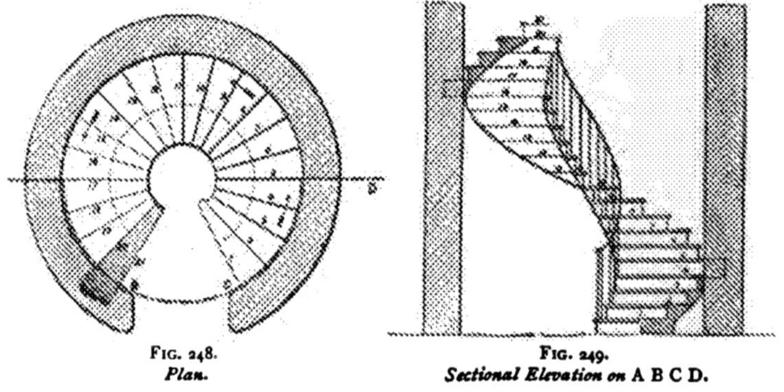

FIG. 248. *Plan.*

FIG. 249. *Sectional Elevation on* A B C D.

The steps are of spandril section, except No. 1, which is necessarily square, or it would have a very narrow base to rest upon.

## WOODEN STAIRS.

*Wooden Steps* are lighter than those of stone, and do not require such strong supports. They are also more elastic, and do not become so smooth under wear as to be dangerous.

On the other hand, they are subject to decay, they may be more rapidly destroyed in case of a fire, and may thus cut off all exit from the upper floors.

Letters of reference in the figures connected with wooden stairs :—

| | | | |
|---|---|---|---|
| Apron lining | *al* | Laths | *l* |
| Balusters | B | Outer strings | OS |
| Bearers | *b* | Pitching piece | P |
| Blocks | *bl* | Plaster | *pl* |
| Brackets | Br | Riser. | *r* |
| Bridging joists of floor | *bj* | Rough brackets | *rb* |
| Cross bearers | *cb* | Rough strings | RS |
| Fillets | *fi* | Soffit joists | *sj* |
| Furrings | *f* | Tread | *t* |
| Glued block | *gb* | Trimmer | T |
| Handrail | HR | Trimming joists of floor | TJ |
| Joists of landing | *j* | Wall strings | WS |

*N.B.*—The handrails are shown in the elevations in order to make the direction of the steps more plainly evident; but they are omitted in the plans for fear of rendering them obscure. The skirtings are also omitted from the plans. The plaster of the wall is also omitted from both plans and sections of the figures on a small scale.

**Parts of Wooden Stairs.**—STRINGS[1] are thick boards or pieces of timber placed at an inclination to support the steps of a wooden stair.

*Cut Strings.*—Wooden stairs of the commonest description are thus constructed.[2]

Two "*strings*," SS, are fixed at the slope determined upon for the stairs; in these rectangular notches are cut, each equal in depth to the rise, and in width nearly equal to the tread of a step: upon these boards are nailed, forming the treads, *t*, and risers, *r*.

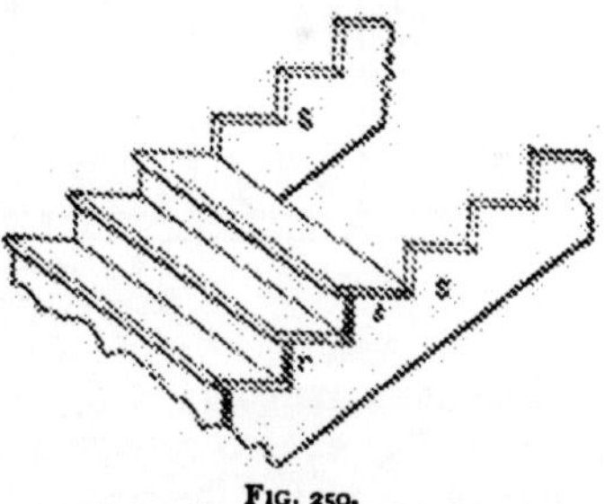

FIG. 250.

*Cut and Mitred Strings.*—In stairs of a better description the outer strings are cut as above described; but the ends of the risers, instead of coming right through and showing on the outer surface of the string, are mitred against the vertical part of the notch in

[1] Sc. *Stringers.*

[2] Stairs of this construction are never used in ordinary house-building.

the string, as shown at *a a* in Fig. 252, the other end of the step being, as before, housed into a groove formed in the wall string.

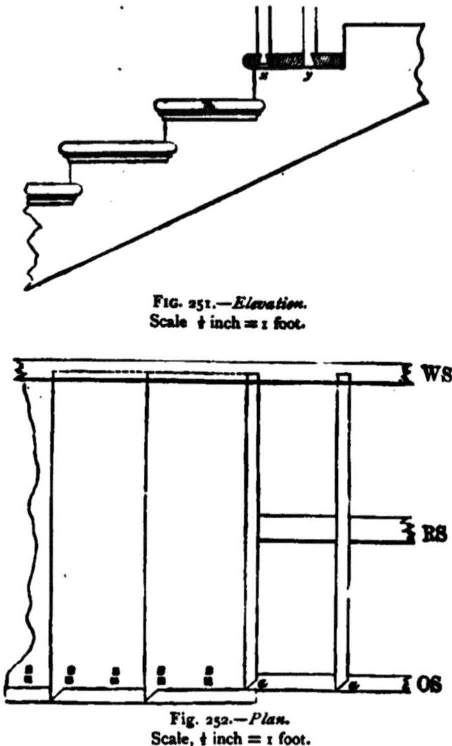


Fig. 251.—*Elevation.*
Scale ½ inch = 1 foot.

Fig. 252.—*Plan.*
Scale, ½ inch = 1 foot.

The outer extremity of the tread is also cut and mitred, as shown in Fig. 252, to receive a return moulding, forming the nosing of the end of the step.

B B show the mortises for the balusters, which should be dovetailed into the treads;[1] the dovetails may be formed as at *x* or as at *y*, Fig. 251.

[1] In speculative work the ends of balusters are simply skew-nailed to the treads or let into them without dovetailing, so that the balusters simply hang from the handrail.

*Housed Strings.*—In many staircases the strings, instead of being notched out to receive the steps, are left with their upper surfaces parallel to the lower, and grooves are cut into their inner sides to receive the ends of the treads and risers; these grooves are called "*housings*," and the steps are said to be "*housed*" into the strings.

Fig. 254 is an elevation of the inner side of a housed string, showing the sinkings or housings formed to receive the steps.

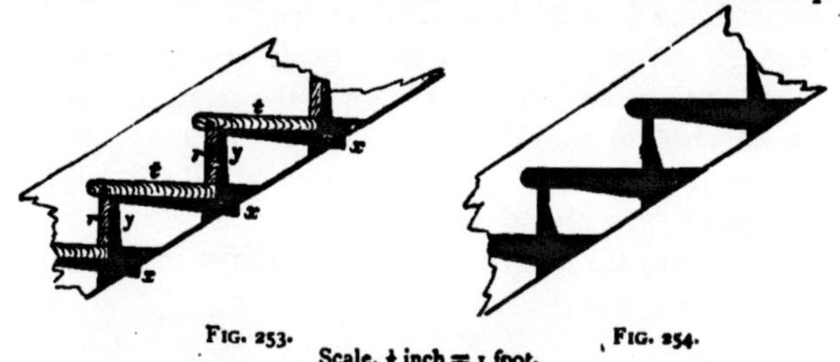


FIG. 253. Scale, ½ inch = 1 foot. FIG. 254.

Fig. 253 is a sectional elevation through the steps, showing the treads, *t*, and the risers, *r*, in position. These are secured by means of wedges, *x y*, which should be well covered with glue before insertion.

The treads are sometimes formed with two tenons at each end, which fit into mortises cut through the string.

*Open Strings* are those, such as the cut strings, or cut and mitred strings, described above, which are cut so as to show the outline of the steps.

*Close Strings* have their upper and lower surfaces parallel, the steps being housed into them as above described (see Fig. 253).

*A Wreathed String* is one formed in a continuous sweep round the well hole of a geometrical stair.

*The Wall String* is the string up against the wall, and plugged to it. WS, Fig. 260.

*The Outer String* is the string at the end of the steps farthest from the wall. OS, Fig. 260.

*Rough Strings.*—With stout treads and risers the two strings above mentioned are sufficient for stairs of 3 or 4 feet in width.

For wider stairs, however, the steps require additional support, and this is afforded by means of one or more "rough strings," or "*carriages*," fixed in the interval between the wall string and outer string, already described.

Two rough strings are shown in Fig. 257, for the sake of illustration, but one only would be necessary in so narrow a staircase; one rough string is shown in Fig. 259.

The scantling for rough strings may be about the same as those for bridging floor-joists of the same length.

The rough strings sometimes have small notches on their upper surfaces to receive the back edge of the tread, and their ends are attached to trimming joists TJ (see Figs. 256, etc.), or into pitching pieces P (Fig. 263), or trimmers T (Fig. 257), where trimming joists are not available.

WOODEN STEPS are formed of boards, as shown in Fig. 255.

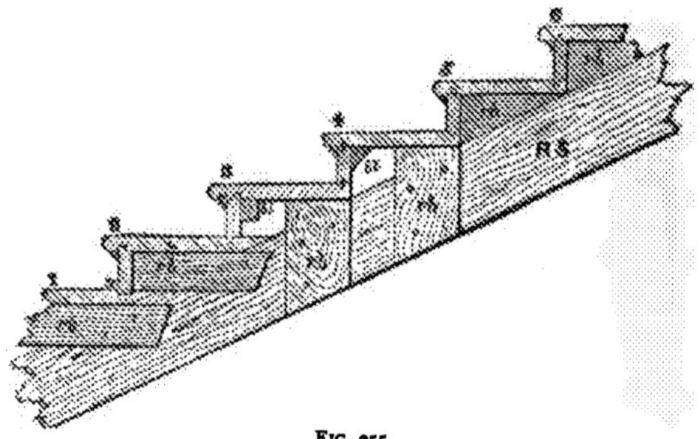


FIG. 255.
Scale, ¼ inch = 1 foot.

The risers are united to the treads by joints, which may be grooved and tongued, as in steps 5, 6; feathered, as in step 4; or rebated, as No. 3: in every case the joint is glued. The riser often has only its upper end tongued, the lower butting upon the tread below. This is not so good a construction as that shown at 3. A common practice is to house the lower edge of the riser into the tread below, as at *x*. The tread is sometimes tongued into the riser, but that is not a good construction.

The joint between the tread and riser is strengthened by small blocks, *bl*, glued into the inner angle, as shown in steps 3 and 4; these may be either rectangular or triangular in section.

The inner ends of the treads rest upon the rough strings, RS (if any), and they are frequently further supported by rough brackets, *rb*, attached to the rough strings or carriages.

These brackets may be pieces nailed alongside the string, as in steps 1, 2, 3, 4, or triangular pieces fixed to its upper surface, as in 5 and 6.

Occasionally vertical brackets are made of a width equal to that of the tread of the step, as at *xy* in Fig. 258.

In some cases a board is notched out like a cut string and nailed alongside the rough string, to answer instead of the rough brackets (see Fig. 262).

The treads project over the risers and are finished with a rounded or a moulded nosing, the projection of the nosing being generally equal to the thickness of the tread. When a moulded nosing is adopted with an open string, the moulding is returned at the end of the step, being mitred at the angle, as shown at Fig. 252.

The mouldings are generally planted on under the rounded nosing of the tread.

The treads should be of oak or other hard wood, and may be $1\frac{1}{8}$ inch thick for steps 4 feet long—the thickness being increased by $\frac{1}{8}$ inch for every 6 inches added to the length of the step.

In very common stairs the risers are sometimes dispensed with.

In some cases, especially in geometrical stairs of a high class, the upper edges of the risers are dovetailed to the treads, and the back of the treads screwed up to the lower edge of the risers.

**Different Forms of Wooden Stairs.**—STRAIGHT STAIRS.—In very narrow stairs of ordinary construction, with a wall on one side only, the following is the arrangement usually adopted.

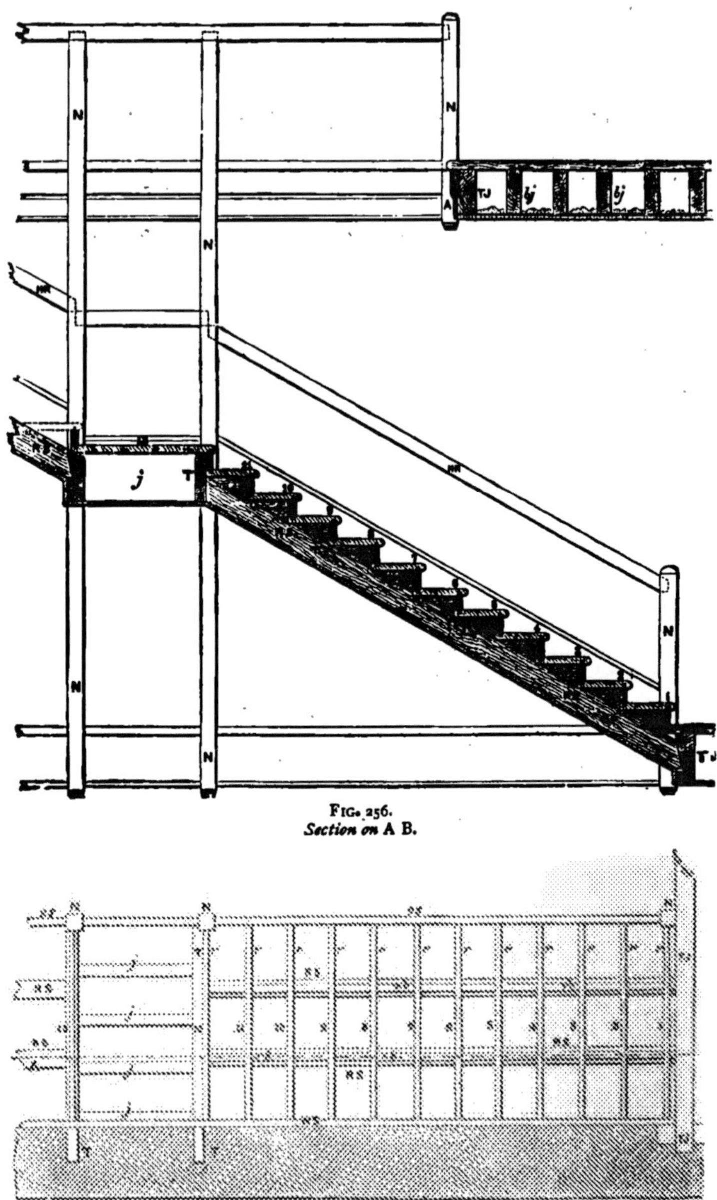


FIG. 256.
*Section on* A B.

FIG. 257.
*Plan (with treads and boarding removed).*
FIGS. 256, 257.—STRAIGHT STAIRS. Scale, ¼ inch = 1 foot.

Two grooved strings, OS and WS, Fig. 257, are placed at the required slope, at a distance apart equal to the length of the steps.

The wall string, WS, is fixed by being plugged to the wall. The ends of the treads and risers are keyed into the housings or grooves worked in the inner and outer strings.

The upper and lower ends of these strings are framed into newel posts, and so are the outer ends of the first and last risers of each flight. When the flight of steps extends uninterruptedly from the lower to the upper floor, these newels are attached to the trimming-joists, TJ, provided in the floors to receive them.

When the flight is broken by a landing, additional newel posts are provided on each side of the landing, and extending the full depth between the floors, as in Fig. 256.

To these are secured the trimmers, T, fixed and wedged into the wall, and projecting from it to carry the landing.

As already mentioned, the two strings are sufficient for stairs with stout treads and risers up to a width of 3 or 4 feet.[1]

For wider stairs, however, additional support to the steps is necessary, and this is afforded by one or more rough strings (RS, Fig. 257) or carriages placed in the interval between the strings already described.

The ends of these rough strings are framed or housed into the trimming-joists provided to receive them in the floors, between which the stairs extend.

When there is a landing the upper ends of the rough strings are fixed to the special trimmers which carry the landing.

The treads are further supported by rough brackets, *rb*, Fig. 256, secured to the rough strings.

The landing itself is formed like a floor, of boards laid upon joists framed in between the trimmers just mentioned.

When there is a wall on each side of the steps, of course the newels are not required.

When the floor is continued under the lowest flight of a stair, the space between the soffit of the stairs and the floor is called the *spandril.*

This space is often utilized as a cupboard by enclosing it with a panelled front (containing a door, and sometimes a window), known as the *spandril framing.*

DOG-LEGGED STAIRS.—Fig. 259 is the plan of a dog-legged stair with a half-space landing. The treads of the steps in the lower flight are omitted, so as to show the strings and risers. A portion of the steps of the upper flight is broken away in order to expose to view the construction of the flight below.

In this stair the wall string, WS, and outer string board, OS, are constructed as before, with intermediate rough strings if necessary.

[1] When the outer string is a *cut-string* it is never desirable to omit the carriage, however narrow the stair may be, as it would cause creaking, if not positive weakness. Even when both strings are close a carriage is an advantage.

M

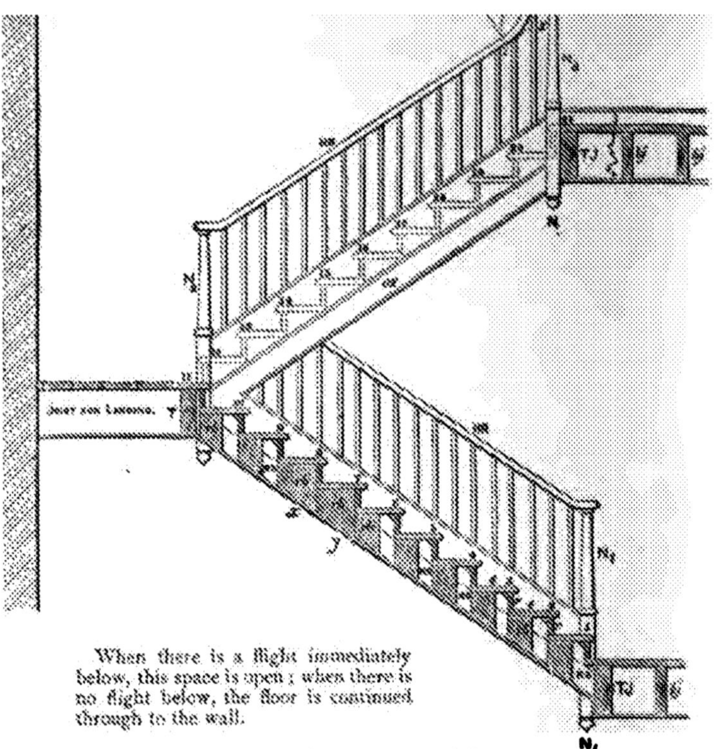


Fig. 258.—*Sectional Elevation on* A B.

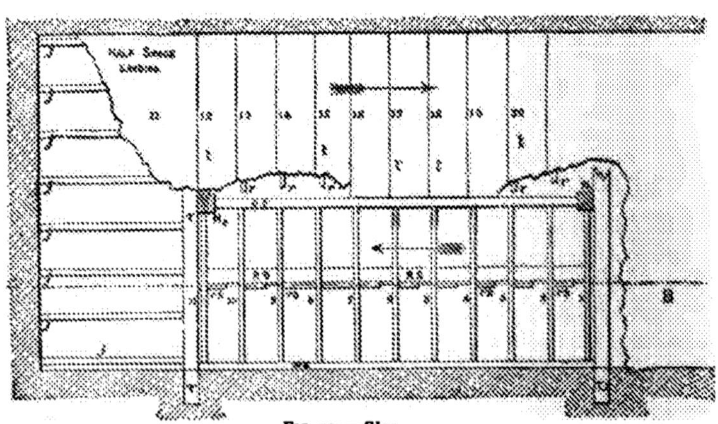


Fig. 259.—*Plan.*

Figs. 258, 259. Dog-Legged Stairs. Scale, ⅛ inch = 1 foot.

The outer strings are tenoned into the newels, and so are the first and last risers of the flight.

The outer string of the upper flight and that of the lower flight are in the same vertical plane, so that if the plan of the upper flight were complete the outer string of the upper flight would overlap and hide the outer string of the lower flight.

In the same way, if the number of steps in each flight were the same, the newel, $N^2$, of the upper flight would in plan exactly cover the newel, N, of the lower flight, being immediately over it.

The handrail in the plan is omitted as before.

Fig. 258 gives the elevation of the upper flight, and the section of the lower flight of the stairs shown in Fig. 259; but no portion of the elevation is broken away, and the treads of the lower flight are shown in section, though omitted from the plan.

The newels are fixed to trimming joists TJ, provided in the floors, and to trimmers T across the staircase at the landing.

The rough strings, RS, are framed in between these trimmers, and rough brackets, *rb rb*, are nailed alongside of them to support the steps.

The tread of the top step is frequently united to the boarding of the landing by a rebated joint. This is advisable if the space below the steps, known as the spandril, is to be made use of as a cupboard. In such a case the landing and the parts of all the steps should be put together with tongued joints, so that dust may be prevented from getting through them. Such joints are often used in superior work even when there is no cupboard below.[1]

NEWEL STAIRS is another name given to dog-legged stairs, because the newels form a conspicuous part of the structure.

OPEN NEWEL STAIRS have newels ranged round an opening or well hole in the centre between the flights of steps.

Fig. 261 shows the plan of such a stair, with a quarter-space landing.

The boarding of the landing and the treads of the lower flight are omitted on plan, in order to show the construction below.

Fig. 260 is a sectional elevation on A B. The treads of the lower flight are shown in elevation, though omitted from plan.

The construction of the straight portion of the stairs is similar to what has already been described. The winding steps are constructed as follows:—

Bearers, *bb*, carrying the risers, *rr*, are framed into the newels, their outer ends resting in the wall of the staircase. Between them are fixed cross bearers, *cb*. These would not be necessary in a narrow staircase, but are inserted in Fig. 261 for the sake of illustration.

In this example four winders are introduced to show the defects of such an arrangement as pointed out at p. 145.

In Figs. 261–263 the skirting is omitted in that portion of the plan where the treads are shown.

---

[1] It is more cleanly to lath and plaster soffits of stairs even in cupboards.

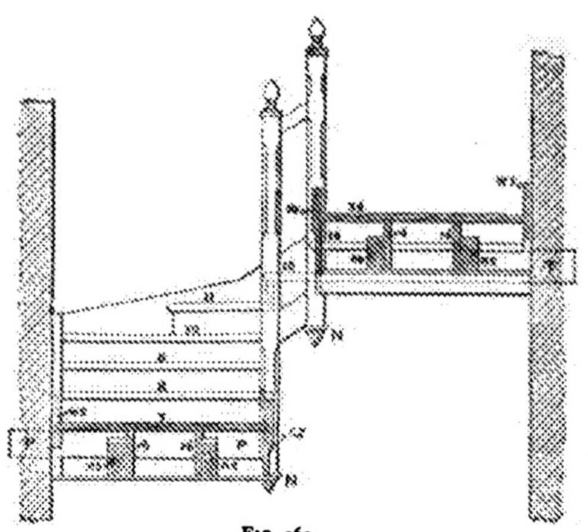

FIG. 260.
*Sectional Elevation on* A B.

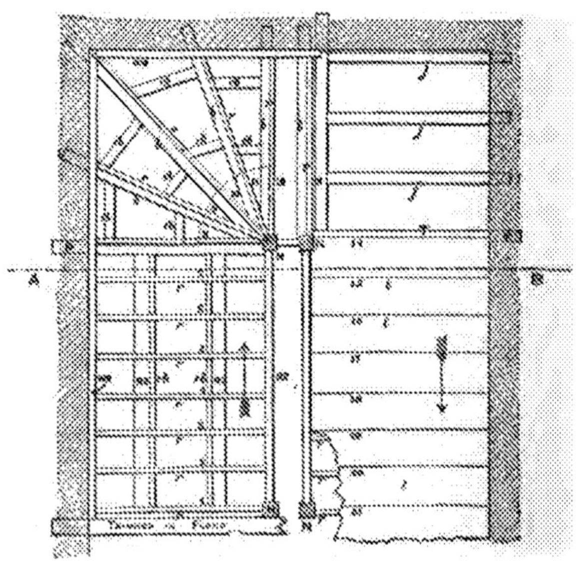

FIG. 261.—*Plan.*
FIGS. 260, 261.—OPEN NEWEL STAIRS. Scale, ¼ inch = 1 foot.

**Geometrical Stairs** have no newel posts. The flights are arranged round a well hole in the centre—sometimes called an "*open newel*"—and each step is secured by having one end housed into the wall string, the other end resting upon the outer string, but partly deriving support from the step below it.

The handrail is uninterrupted in its course from top to bottom.

The treads for geometrical stairs should be substantial.

The string may be greatly strengthened by a flat iron bar screwed to its under side.

Figs. 263, 262 give a plan and sectional elevation of a geometrical stair with winders.

The portion of the staircase shown in Fig. 263 consists of six fliers, then eight winders, then seven more fliers, making 22 steps, leading to a half-space landing on the floor above; from this the stairs again rise, commencing with the step marked 23, the remainder being broken off to show the first flight.

The treads of the lower flight and winders are also omitted, in order to show the supports below.

The steps are formed in the way described at p. 156, with (in this case) feather-tongued joints between the treads and risers.

The handrail has, as before, been omitted from the plan for the sake of clearness.

The treads and risers are housed into the wall string, the outer ends resting upon a cut and mitred string, and intermediate support is afforded by a rough string, to the side of which is nailed a rough notched bracket, cut to fit the under side of the steps, and to serve instead of brackets.

The strings themselves are framed in between the trimming joists provided in the floors, and *pitching pieces*, P, projecting from the wall at the level of the first and last winders; one of these latter is shown at P, but the other is covered by the fifteenth step.

The trimming joist just below No. 1 step extends of course right across the staircase—but it is in the plan (Fig. 263) supposed to be broken off just under the outer string in order to avoid confusing the plan of the curtail step.

The winders are supported throughout their length by bearers, *bb*, the inner ends of which are built and wedged into the wall of the staircase, the outer ends being tenoned into the circular or wreathed portion of the outer string.

The risers are nailed to these bearers, and the widest ends of the steps are supported by cross bearers dovetailed in between the risers and the longitudinal bearers above mentioned.

The lowest step of this staircase is formed with a curtailed end which, when the tread is on, in form somewhat resembles that shown in the stone staircase, Fig. 243.

In this illustration, however, the tread of the curtail step has been omitted in order to show the construction of the riser below, which is built up in a

Fig. 262.—*Sectional Elevation on* A B C D.

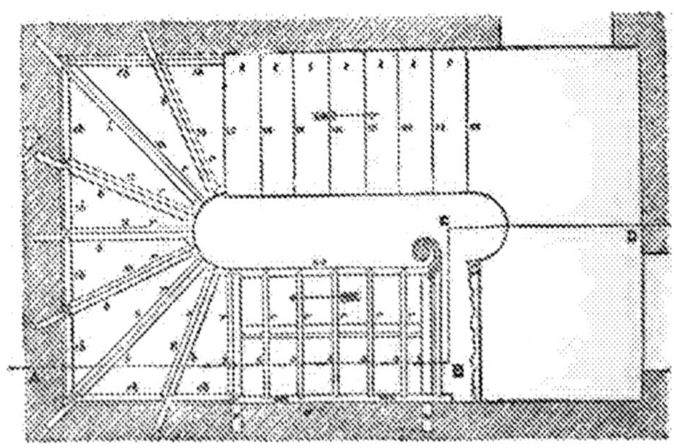

Fig. 263.—*Plan.*

Figs. 262, 263.—Geometrical Stairs. Scale, $\frac{3}{16}$ inch = 1 foot.

curved form, terminating in a circular block, which forms the base to support the last baluster or newel.

The inner side of the staircase is finished and embellished by a skirting notched on the under side to fit the steps, and secured to narrow grounds plugged to the wall.

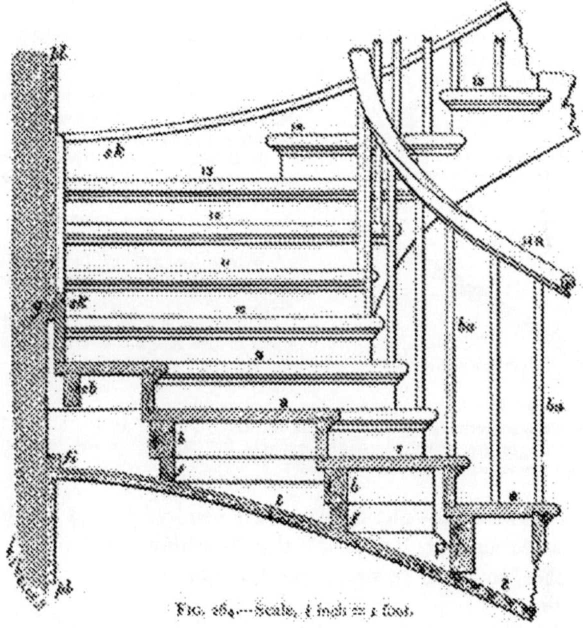

Fig. 264.—Scale, [illegible] inch = 1 foot.

In some cases two cross bearers are provided for each winder, one being framed in between the longitudinal bearers in the centre as well as that at the wide end, as in Fig. 261.

If very thick treads are used, the bearers and rough strings may be omitted altogether, the steps being wedged into the wall and projecting without further support till they reach the outer string.

Fig. 264 is a portion of a stair similar to that in Fig. 262, but with different descriptions of joints between the treads and risers, enlarged in order to show the plaster and other details, which could not be made clear upon a very small scale.

Solid steps, like those of stone, are sometimes formed in wood for geometrical staircases, and make strong but expensive work.

A Bracketed Stair is one which has ornamental brackets, B (Fig. 265), fixed on the end of each step above the outer string and mitred to the outer end of the riser.

They are put on merely for the sake of appearance, and play no part in supporting the steps.

*A Curtail Step* is one of which the end is projected or curved (as shown in Fig. 240) to receive the newel balusters that support the scroll terminating the handrail.

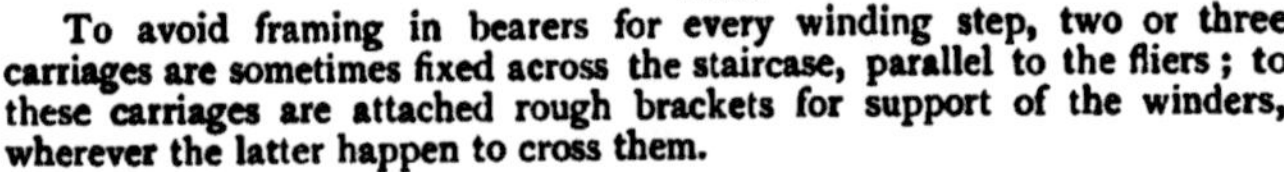

Fig. 265.
Scale, 1 inch = 1 foot.

It is not unusual, especially in stone stairs, to make the last two steps of curtail form, as shown in Fig. 243; in some cases three or more steps are curtailed.

When the end of the step is circular it is called a *round-ended* step.

*Carriages* is a general name applied to the rough timbers, such as strings, etc., used for supporting a stair.

To avoid framing in bearers for every winding step, two or three carriages are sometimes fixed across the staircase, parallel to the fliers; to these carriages are attached rough brackets for support of the winders, wherever the latter happen to cross them.

Handrailing.—The height of the handrail should not be uniform throughout, but varied slightly within the limits of a few inches, so as to secure a graceful line at the changes of inclination.

The handrail should be higher on the landing, where the person using it is erect, than on the steps, where he will be inclining either forward or backward, according as he is ascending or descending the stairs.

[The height from the treads (at the nosings) to the upper surface of the handrail should be 2 feet 7½ inches; to this there should be added at the landings the height of half a riser.—*Newland.*]

For winding stairs regard should be had, in adjusting the height of the rail, to the position of the person using it—who may be thrown farther from it, not only by the narrowness of the treads, but by the oblique position of the risers.

The handrail should be raised over winders, especially those of a steep pitch.

Nicholson recommends that the upper surface of the handrail should have a diameter of 2½ inches; but the sizes vary greatly—3 or 3½ inches by 2 or 2½ deep being common dimensions, while, for very important staircases, the handrail may be 6 × 4 inches, or even larger.

The different sections of handrails are distinguished by peculiar names, according to their shape, such as "Mopstick handrail," a nearly circular form; "Toad's back," which has a flattish, curved upper surface, etc., etc.

The handrail may be secured to the balusters by means of a flat bar of wrought-iron about ⅛-inch thick, and in width equal to that of the top of the baluster.

Fig. 266.

Fig. 267.
Scale, 2 inches = 1 foot.

This bar, C in Figs. 266, 267, is called a "*core*," and it is screwed down upon the heads of the balusters, and up to the under side of the handrail, as shown in the figure, which represents a piece of the horizontal portion of the handrail to a landing.

The balusters supporting the inclined handrail over the steps have their tops splayed to fit the lower surface of the rail. In common work the balusters are nailed to the handrail direct, without the intervention of a core.

*A Wreathed Handrail* is one which ascends in a continuous curve round a circular well hole, as in Fig. 249.

*A Ramp* is the sudden rise, concave in form, made by a handrail where it is stopped, as against the newel in Fig. 258.

*A Knee* is the convex part of the sudden rise in a handrail, as in Fig. 258.

*A Swan Neck* is a ramp and knee combined, being concave in one part and convex in another; see Fig. 258.

The method of setting out the handrailing for different forms of stairs is quite a science in itself, and is fully treated upon by Mr. Mayer in Newland's *Carpenter's and Joiner's Assistant*, whence many of the above hints have been taken, and to which the student must be referred if he should wish to pursue the subject farther.

Balusters are intended to support the handrail and to prevent any one from falling over the ends of the steps.

They should not be more than about 5 inches apart.

They are sometimes vertical wooden bars, square, turned, or carved, according to the class of work.

An iron baluster of the same pattern as the wooden ones should be introduced at intervals (generally about 1 in every 10) to strengthen the whole.

Iron balusters are frequently used throughout.

Wooden balusters should be dovetailed into the treads of the steps, and secured to the handrail as above described.

The balusters are sometimes fixed to the outer string, being bent or kneed so as to clear the ends of the steps, in order to give as much width as possible to the stairs.[1]

Generally there are two balusters fixed on the end of each step—one flush, or as nearly as possible flush, with the face of the riser, the other midway between the risers.

On each of the narrow ends of winders one baluster only is required.

---

## CHAPTER IX.

### *RIVETING.*[2]

RIVETS are small fastenings made of the best wrought iron or mild steel either by hand or by machinery, and before they are fixed consist each (see Fig. 268) of a small spindle or shank surmounted by a head, which may be pan-shaped as in Fig. 270, or formed like a cup or button as in Fig. 269.

About half of the shank of the rivet farthest from the head is slightly tapered.

When the rivet has been made red-hot, and put througn

[1] This is the French system, and involves the use of iron balusters, or iron balusters and iron brackets, or of iron brackets alone.

[2] Neither riveting, rolled beams, nor plate girders are mentioned in the Syllabus for this Course, but they are included in this volume because it is desirable to understand them in connection with floors and iron roofs.

the hole it is to occupy, the tail end of the shank is formed, either by hand or by machinery, into a button or point of the shape required, which differs in the various kinds of rivets, as described below.

Rivets are chiefly used to connect plates of iron. They are preferable to small bolts, because, being hammered close to the face of the plate, they hold more tightly, and the shanks of rivets are not so likely to become oxidized as those of bolts; moreover, as rivets are nearly always fixed when hot, they contract in cooling, and draw the plates together with great force.

Fig. 268.

They are much used in connection with building for uniting the parts of plate-iron and braced girders, also for wrought-iron tanks and boilers.

*Caulking* is a process adopted when it is found that the head or point of the rivet is not quite close to the plates, or that some opening exists between the plates themselves.

This process consists in knocking down the edges of the plates with a blunt steel caulking tool, so as to bring the edges together and to close the opening. In the case of rivets, the edges of the head or point are beaten down until they indent and slightly penetrate the surface of the plates, and thus completely close the opening.

**Different Forms of Rivets.**—There are various names given to rivets, according to the shape to which the point is formed.

*Snap rivets* are those of which the points formed while the iron is hot are finished with a tool containing a nearly hemispherical hollow, which shapes it as shown in Fig. 269.

Fig. 269.

That figure represents a snap rivet in a punched hole. This form of rivet is very frequently used in the best girder work.

*Button or cup-ended rivets.*—These are names sometimes applied to snap rivets.

*Hammered rivets* have points finished, by hammering only, to a conical form as in Fig. 270, which shows such a rivet in a drilled hole.

They are more liable to leak than those with button points, but are used for rivets of large size, which, if finished with snap points, would require very large hammers in order that the points might be beaten down quickly enough.

Fig. 270.

Rivets with conical points are sometimes called *staff rivets.*

The rivet in Fig. 270 has a *pan head*, a modification of it in which the sides of the head are vertical is called a *cheese head*, and shown in Fig. 271.

*Countersunk rivets* are those in which the point is hammered down while hot flush with the surface of the plate, as in Fig. 272.

This is necessary wherever a smooth surface is required,

Fig 271.

Fig. 272.

free from the projection that would be caused by ordinary rivet heads.

The countersinking is drilled, and may extend right through the plate.

It is frequently the practice, however, to have a shoulder at the upper edge of the lower plate, as shown at *a a*, so that the countersink does not extend right through the plates.

The sides of the countersunk portion may be directed upon the centre of the rivet hole at the edge of the plate, as in Fig. 272, or in many cases they are not inclined so much as shown.

Steel Rivets require very careful treatment, or their heads will be apt to fly off upon receiving a sudden jar. They require to be rather larger, in proportion to the thickness of the plate, than iron rivets, and should be raised to a dull red heat, and their points knocked down as quickly as possible.

**Proportions of Rivets.**—The aggregate section of the rivets in any joint must be determined by the stress that will come upon them, but the diameter of the individual rivets in punched holes will depend upon the thickness of the plates through which they pass; for in punching holes it is advisable, in order to avoid breaking the punch, that its diameter should be greater than the thickness of the plate.

*Sir William's Fairbairn's rules for the proper diameters for rivets* passing through punched holes in plates are as follows:—

For plates less than ½ inch thick the diameter of the rivet should be about double the thickness of the plate.

For ½ inch and thicker plates the diameter of the rivet should be about 1½ time the thickness of the plate.

When holes are *drilled* they may be smaller in proportion to the thickness of the plate.

When plates of different thicknesses are joined, the rivet is proportioned with reference to the thickest of the plates.

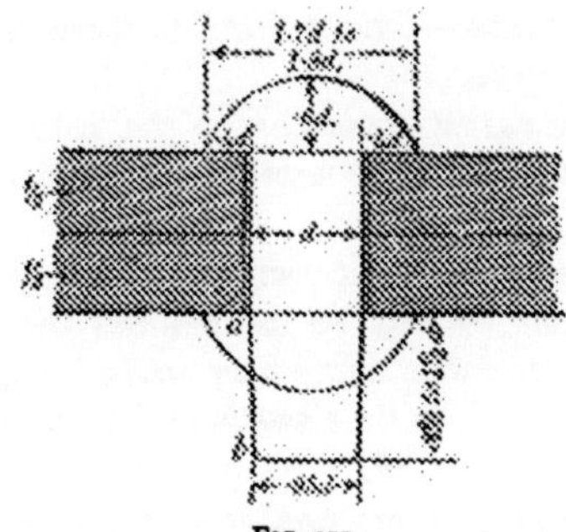

FIG 273.

*Professor Unwin's rule* for the diameter of rivets joining plates is as follows:—

$$d = 1{\cdot}2\sqrt{t}.$$

Where $d$ is the diameter of the rivet and $t$ the thickness of the plate.

The hole is generally practically from 4 to 20 per cent. of the diameter larger than the cold rivet, which will more than allow for the expansion of the latter when heated before insertion.

DIMENSIONS OF RIVET HEADS, ETC.—*The height of the head of a snap rivet* should be about ⅝ of the diameter of the shank, and the diameter of the head should be from 1½ time to twice that of the shank.

*The length of the rivet before clenching*, measuring from the head = sum of thicknesses of plates to be united + 1¼ to 1½ time the diameter of the rivet (see Fig. 273). For machine-riveting, *a b* should be made ⅛" to ¼" longer.

*The proportions for heads of different forms are used as follows* (see Figs. 269, 272) :—

| | Height. | Width of base of head. | Length of *ab*, Fig. 211. |
|---|---|---|---|
| Conical heads | ·75 *d.* | 2 *d.* | 1·2 *d* to 1·5 *d.* |
| Pan heads | ·7 *d.* | 1·6 *d.*<br>1·45 *d.* top of head | not formed by riveter |
| Cheese head | ·45 *d.* | 1·5 *d.* | ,, |
| Countersunk | ·4 *d* to ·5 *d* | 1·5 *d* to 1·6 *d.* | ·75 *d* to 1 *d.* |

Where a number of plates have to be joined, $\frac{1}{32}$ inch for each plate is added to *a b.*

The above are general dimensions, but some engineers provide a special drawing of the rivet head they require.

**Pitch of Rivets.**—The "*pitch*" of rivets is their distance from centre to centre.

The distance varies according to the nature of the stress upon the joint and with the number of rivets necessary to be inserted in a given space.

The pitch used for girder work varies from 3 to 5 inches, but it should not exceed 10 to 12 times the thickness of a single plate, as otherwise damp may get in between the plates and cause rust, which in time swells and bursts them asunder.[1]

*The distance between the edges of rivet holes*, to prevent the danger of breaking two into one, should not be less than equal to the diameter of the rivets. This, it will be seen, leads to the rule that the minimum pitch of rivets should not be less than twice their diameter.

*The distance between the edge of a rivet hole and the edge of the plate in which it is formed*, to prevent it tearing through, should not be less that the diameter of the rivet. Thus the *centre* of the rivet will be $1\frac{1}{2}$ diameter from the edge of the plate. Sometimes for thick plates $\frac{1}{16}''$ or $\frac{1}{8}''$ is added to the distance.

[1] Stoney.

## RIVETED JOINTS.

**Lap Joints** are formed by riveting together plates that overlap one another, as in Figs. 274–277.

The overlap should not be less than 3¼ to 3½ times the diameter of the rivets in single riveting (Fig. 274), or 5½ to 6 diameters in double riveting (Fig. 276).

There are formulæ[1] for finding the length of the overlaps,

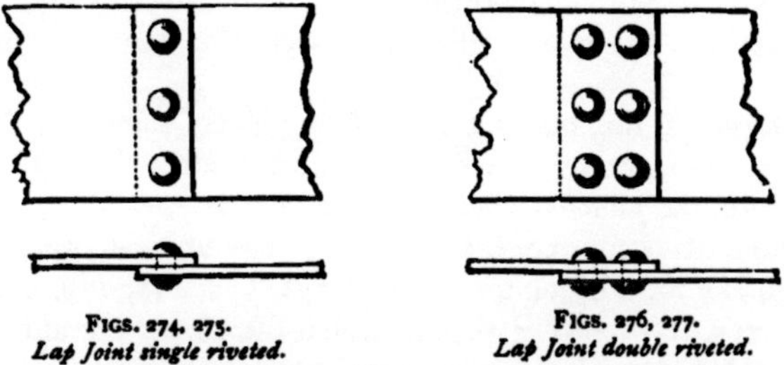

Figs. 274, 275. *Lap Joint single riveted.*

Figs. 276, 277. *Lap Joint double riveted.*

so that the joints may be of equal strength throughout; but the above rules will be a sufficient guide in ordinary cases.

**Fish Joints** are those in which the ends of the plates meet one another, the joint being "fished" either with a single

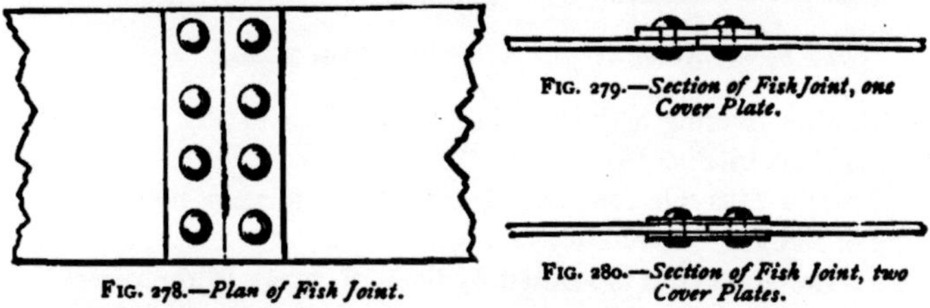

Fig. 278.—*Plan of Fish Joint.*

Fig. 279.—*Section of Fish Joint, one Cover Plate.*

Fig. 280.—*Section of Fish Joint, two Cover Plates.*

"cover plate," as in Fig. 279, or with one on each side, as in Fig. 280.

When a single cover plate is used it should be of somewhat greater thickness than that of either of the main plates to be united, in order to allow for the extra stress caused by the cover plate being out of the direct line of stress.[1]

[1] See Part IV. N.B.C.

When two cover plates are used each of them should be of not less thickness than half the thickness of either of the plates to be united.

BUTT JOINTS is the name given to fished joints that are in compression, so that the ends of the plates butt evenly against one another.

This seldom occurs in practice, for the very process of riveting draws the plates slightly apart, and the edges are generally caulked to conceal the gap.

Sometimes the gap is filled with cast zinc run into the interval.

If, however, the plates are carefully planed square at the edges, and brought very carefully into close contact throughout their width, the joint is called a "*jump joint.*"

SINGLE RIVETING consists of a single row of rivets uniting plates in any form of joint, as in Figs. 274, 275, 278, 279, 280.

DOUBLE RIVETING is that in which the plates are united by a double row of rivets, as in Figs. 276, 277, 281.

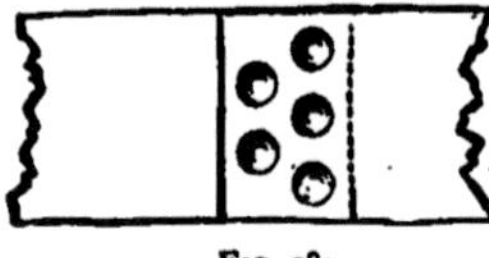

FIG. 281.
*Zigzag Double Riveting.*

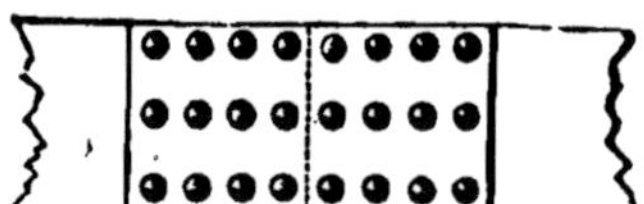

FIG. 282.
*Chain Riveting.*

Double riveting may be either "*chain,*" as in Fig. 276, or "*zigzag,*" as in Fig. 281.

TRIPLE AND QUADRUPLE RIVETING are formed by 3 or 4 rows of riveting respectively.

CHAIN RIVETING is formed by lines of rivets in the direction of the stress, parallel to one another on each side of the joint, as in Fig. 282.

ZIGZAG RIVETING consists of lines of rivets so placed that the rivets in each line divide the spaces between the rivets in the adjacent lines, as in Figs. 281, 283.

**Joints in Tension.**—*Lap Joints.*—Fig. 284 shows the arrangement of rivets generally adopted for lap joints which are to undergo a tensile stress.

The object of so placing the rivets is to keep the strength of the joint as nearly equal to that of the original plate as possible.

In this case the strength of the joint may be arranged so as to be equal to that of the cross section of the plate, less one rivet hole.[1]

It is true that the weakest section of the plates themselves is at A B, where they are pierced by three rivet holes; but before either plate could break at this line, the three rivets, *opq* or *rst*, within the line must be shorn in two.

Thus, before the upper plate can tear at A B, *o p q* must be shorn; and before the lower plate can give way at A B, the rivets *r s t* must be shorn.[2]

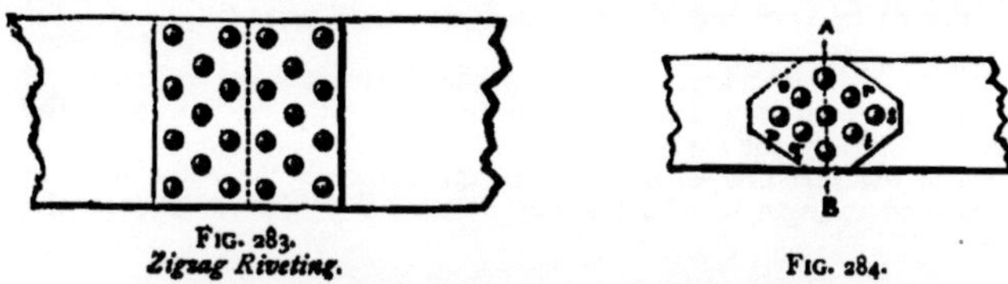


FIG. 283.
*Zigzag Riveting.*

FIG. 284.

**Butt Joints.**—The same principle may be applied to

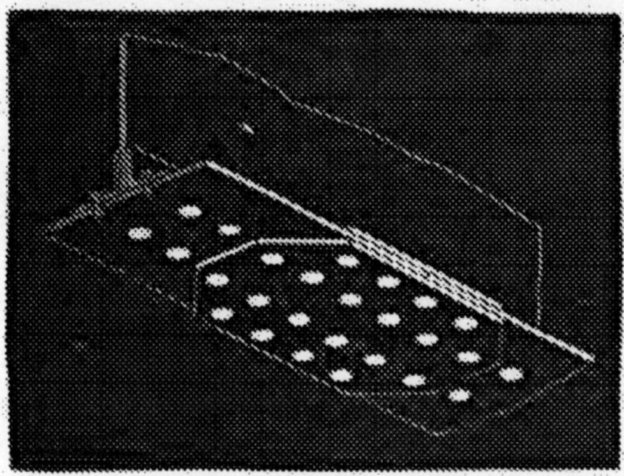

FIG. 285.

a joint with cover plates, as shown in Fig. 285. The arrangement is similar to that in Fig. 284, but with two rivets at the weakest part.

[1] To ensure this, the loss of tensile strength in a plate caused by a rivet hole must not be greater than the shearing strength of a rivet.

[2] *Shearing.*—A rivet is shorn when by the sliding movement of one or both of the plates through which it passes it is cut through horizontally.

N

The riveted joints of tension flanges of girders are very commonly arranged in plan, as shown in Fig. 285.

**Joints in Compression.**—It was at one time thought that for a butt joint under compression very few rivets were necessary; that the whole strain was communicated by the end of one plate to the other upon which it pressed; and that the rivets would be required only to keep the plates in their places.

Experience has shown, however, that in practice we cannot depend upon the plates being so closely butted against one another as to transmit the thrust direct (see p. 176).

"Very slight inaccuracy of workmanship may cause the separation of the butting plates, and then the whole thrust is transmitted through the rivets and through the cover plates."

"For the best bridges it is now assumed that all the joints shall be of sufficient strength to take the whole strain, if necessary, through the rivets."

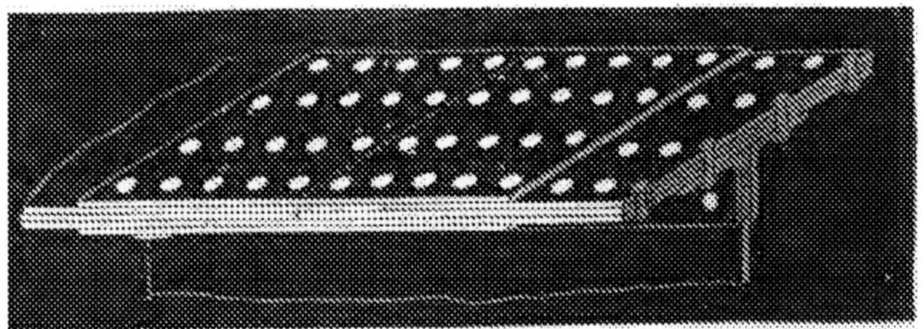

Fig. 286.—*Grouped Joint.*

"The only way in which compression joints may safely differ from tension joints is, that the rivets may be more closely spaced across the plate, the quantity punched out in any section not affecting the strength of a compression joint as it does that of a tension joint."[1]

*Grouped Joints.*—The joints that occur in the plates of riveted girders are generally formed with cover plates.

When there are several layers of plates, as in the booms of a large girder, the joints may with advantage be collected into groups, so that several may be covered by one pair of plates, as shown in Fig. 286.

[1] Unwin, *Iron Bridges and Roofs.*

Fig. 286 shows the joints in the three plates of the boom of a heavy girder collected under cover plates. The joints may be chain or zigzag riveted in plan; or in some cases the cover plates are cut off obliquely, so as to have triangular ends, and the rivets are arranged somewhat as in Figs. 284, 285.

---

## CHAPTER X.

### *WROUGHT-IRON GIRDERS.*

*Cast-iron Girders form part of the Elementary Course, and were dealt with in E.B.C.D., p. 196. Rolled Wrought-iron Beams and built-up Plate and Box Girders are not mentioned in either Course, but will be briefly described here, as some little knowledge regarding them will be useful.*

**Proportion of Flanges.**—It was pointed out in E.B.C.D. that, because the resistance of cast iron to compression is about six times as great as it is to tension, the flange of a cast-iron girder which is in tension requires about six times the area or section that is required in the flange subjected to compression. In practice the tension flange is often much larger, so that the ratio is often only three or four to one. Hence a cast iron girder is made with the tension flange having an area three to six times as great as that of the compression flange (see Figs. 30 and 31, p. 10). With wrought-iron girders, however, the case is different. The working resistance of wrought-iron to compression is $\frac{4}{5}$ of its resistance to tension (see Table, p. 36). The sectional area of the tension flange may therefore be made $\frac{4}{5}$ of that of the compression flange. In many cases, for the sake of simplicity, it is made practically equal to it.

**Rolled Wrought-iron Beams.**—The manufacture of wrought-iron beams or joists has been so much improved of late years that they can now be rolled to any size that is likely to be required in ordinary buildings.

In section (see Fig. 287), they consist of two flanges, *f f*, and a web, *w*, the flanges being both of the same size.

f
w
f

Fig. 287. *Rolled Beam.*

Rolled beams may ordinarily be obtained of various sections, from 3 to 20 inches in depth, and have been manufactured up to a depth of even 3 feet; but for a greater depth than 12 inches a built-up girder, such as one of those described below, is usually preferable.

The reason for this is that the number and thickness of the plates used in a built-up girder may be varied at different parts of it, in proportion to the stresses which come upon those parts; whereas, in a rolled girder, the thickness of the web and of the flanges is necessarily unvarying throughout its length, and if, therefore, these are thick enough to withstand the greater stresses, they are too thick in those portions where the smaller stresses occur.

*Compound Rolled Iron Girders.*—Sometimes two or three rolled iron beams are riveted together with or without plates attached to them (see Figs. 288, 289).

Fig. 288.

Fig. 289.

*Compound Rolled Iron Girders.*

**Plate Girders.**—If for any particular position rolled beams cannot be obtained of the necessary form or dimensions, girders may be built up by riveting plates and angle irons together in different ways.

Riveted, or, as they are more usually called, plate girders may be constructed of sizes far exceeding those of the largest rolled beams.

The best depth for these girders is about $\frac{1}{12}$ the span.

The simplest form of plate girder consists of angle irons (*f f*) riveted to a vertical plate (*w*), as shown in Fig. 290, the former being the flanges [1] and the latter the web of the resulting girder. The rivets are generally at a *pitch* (or distance between centres) of from 3 to 5 inches—most frequently 4 inches.

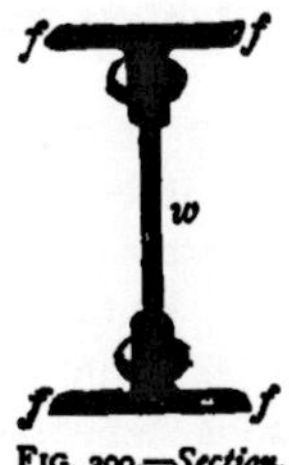


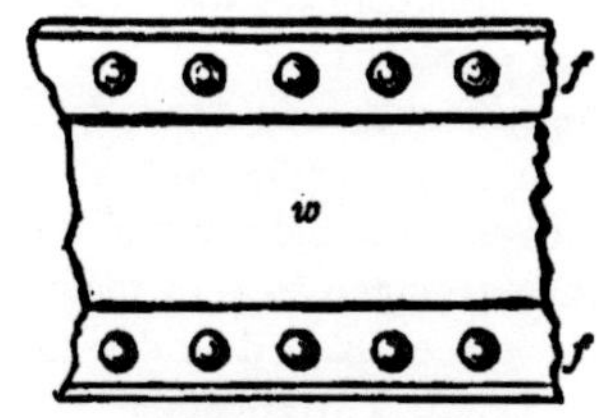


FIG. 290.—*Section.* FIG. 291.—*Elevation.*
*Plate Girder.*

Some particulars regarding riveting are given at p. 170. In some cases the rivets of the lower or tension flange of the

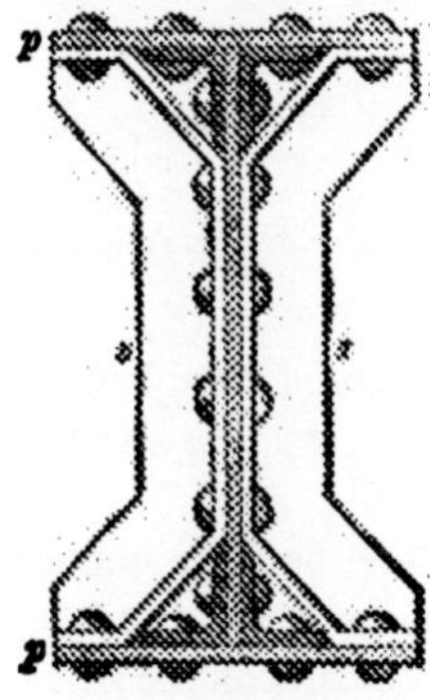


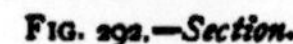

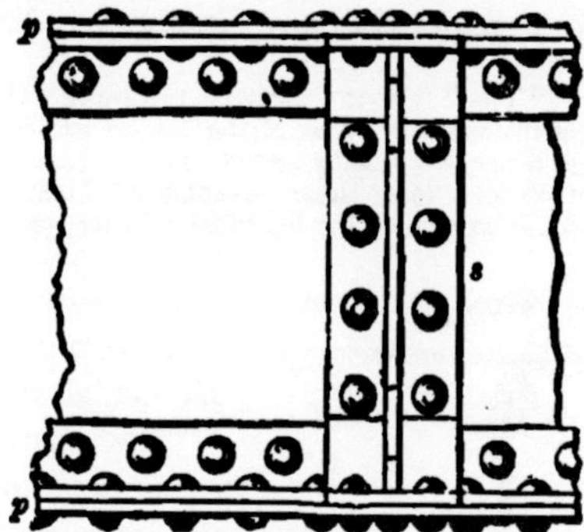


FIG. 292.—*Section.* FIG. 293.—*Elevation.*
*Plate Girder.*

girder are pitched at wider intervals than those in the upper or compression flange.

In larger girders separate plates *p p* may be used for the flanges, and are fixed to the web by angle irons riveted as shown in Figs. 292, 293.

When the web is deep, or of slight thickness, it has a tendency to buckle sideways, and requires support.

[1] Called also "*booms*" in large girders.

This may be afforded by stiffeners (*s*) of T iron riveted vertically to both sides of the web along the girder, at distances varying according to the load, depth of girder, and thickness of web.

Extra stiffeners are also placed under points where heavy loads are expected.

The stiffeners may either be bent outwards at an angle as shown, or they may be cranked or joggled, that is bent close round, over the angle irons of the girder (which latter is a more expensive arrangement), or they may be kept out by means of distance pieces placed under them so as to clear the angle irons. This last arrangement is simple, but adds unnecessary weight to the girder.

In girders to carry great loads several plates are required in each flange, and when the flange-plates are wide, gussets or vertical plates are added; but such heavy girders are not likely to be required in any ordinary building.

> "There are in existence plate-girder bridges of almost all possible dimensions, and some of the largest are objects of universal admiration; yet it may be broadly stated that the plate girder, if made beyond a span of 50 feet, loses those advantages which, up to that span, its simplicity affords as against the lightness of other systems."[1]

**Box Girders** are made up of plates united by angle irons and rivets into a hollow rectangular box section, as shown in Fig. 294.

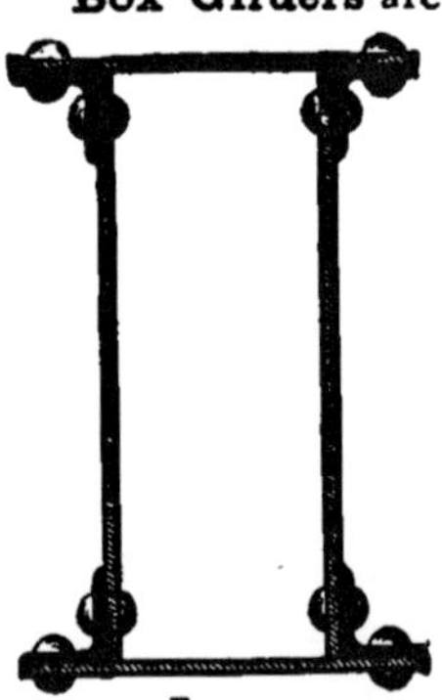

FIG. 294.
*Section of Box Girder.*

Box girders should be large enough to admit a man or boy, so that they can be painted periodically on the inside to prevent corrosion.

When the girder is necessarily too small to allow of this, the plates are made of extra thickness to allow for corrosion; and sometimes the interior of the girder is filled with concrete to protect the iron from the action of the air and to prevent oxidation.

[1] *Works in Iron*, by Ewing Matheson.

*Comparison of Plate and Box Girders.*[1]—The comparative advantages of plate and box girders are summed up by Sir W. Fairbairn as follows: "On comparing the strengths of these separate beams, weight for weight, it will be found that the box beam is as 1 : ·93, or nearly as 100 : 90.

"This difference in the resisting power of the two beams does not arise from any difference or excess in the quantity of material in either structure, but from the better sectional form of the box beam. The box beam, it will be observed, contains a larger exterior sectional area, and is consequently stiffer and better calculated to resist lateral strain, in which direction the plate form generally yields before its other resisting powers of tension and compression can be brought fully into action.

"Taking this beam, however, in a position similar to that in which it is used for supporting the arches of fireproof buildings, or the roadway of a bridge, when its vertical position is maintained, its strength is very nearly equal to that of the box beam.

"But while the plate beam, in the position thus described, is nearly equal, if not in some respects superior, to the box beam, it is of more simple construction, less expensive, and more durable, from the circumstance that the vertical plate is thicker than the side-plates of the box beam, and is consequently better calculated to resist those atmospheric changes, which in this climate have so great an influence upon the durability of the metals.

"Besides it admits of easy access to all its parts for purposes of cleaning, painting, etc."

---

## CHAPTER XI.

### *FIREPROOF FLOORS.*

*Subjects required by the Syllabus, and (in brackets) the pages at which they are treated upon.*

*Fireproof floors (such as brick arches supported on rolled or cast-iron girders)* [p. 186]; *Fox and Barrett's* [p. 191] *and Dennett's patent concrete floors* [p. 188].

**General Remarks.**—Fireproof floors are of great service in preventing flames from spreading throughout a building.

A great many different systems of fireproof construction have been proposed during the last few years; and before describing the most important of these it will be desirable to

[1] Sir W. Fairbairn, *On the Application of Cast and Wrought Iron to Building Purposes.*

state what characteristics should be looked for in a good fireproof floor.

## Characteristics of Good Fireproof Floors.

In estimating the efficiency of any system of fireproof flooring the undermentioned points should be attended to.

### A, PROTECTION OF IRONWORK.

The structure of a fireproof floor is generally dependent upon the ironwork; if that is destroyed or gives way the floor must follow. Iron girders and columns may be protected by terra-cotta blocks, see Figs. 297, 310, 311, etc., or by concrete, see Figs. 305, etc.

### B, RESISTANCE TO FIRE OF THE MATERIAL COMPOSING THE FLOOR.

*Brickwork and hard-burnt clay* are the best fire-resisting materials.

*Wrought iron*, if not protected by a non-conductor of heat, will warp and twist under the action of fire and destroy the structure.

*Cast iron* cracks and gives way suddenly, especially when it is heated and then drenched, as it is likely to be during a fire. In the Chicago fire the ends of cast-iron columns were actually melted off.

*Timber* in large scantlings will resist the action of fire for a long time if the flames cannot get round its sides or ends. After it becomes charred to a certain depth the charcoal formed on its surface, being a non-conductor, protects it.[1]

*Wooden floors* will resist a considerable action of fire if well embedded in mortar, which, however, leads to their premature decay.

*Wood* may be rendered partially fireproof by being coated with cyanite, asbestos paints, or other substances similar.

*Concrete* is generally a good fire-resisting substance, but this depends to some extent upon the materials of which it is composed.

*Gypsum* (sulphate of lime) is weaker than Portland cement, but resists fire better, as it does not lose its cohesive power even when raised to a white heat and then drenched with water.

---

[1] Lawford, *Transactions*, Society of Engineers, 1888.

*Broken brick or stone*, for the aggregate, stand fire better than breeze, which will burn away under very high temperatures.

*Slag Cement* is likely to be largely used for concrete floors in this country. It is cheaper and lighter than Portland cement, while its fire-resisting properties exceed those of Portland cement or gypsum.[1]

*Plaster* also resists fire well, especially when it is nearly entirely made with gypsum, as in the Hitchins Company's and Robinson's plasters.

*Stone* is a very bad material for fireproof structures; when subjected to great heat it suddenly cracks and gives way without warning. For this reason arches of fireproof construction should never rest upon projecting stone corbels.

In the Chicago fire, sandstone was found to stand better than limestone. Granite was quite disintegrated, or, under less heat, scaled.[1]

*Silicate cotton, slag wool*, and similar materials are fireproof, and very useful for pugging floors or partitions.

C, COST.—Under this head must be considered not only the cost of the floor itself, but the expense it leads to.

Thus a deep floor will involve extra height of walling, and an arched floor, having a thrust upon the walls, will necessitate their being of extra thickness.

D, STRENGTH.—The floor must, of course, be strong enough to bear the weights it may be required to carry.

This can easily be arranged for, as it is a mere question of the thickness of arches and dimensions of the girders, and other parts of the floor.

E, PERMANENCY.—Floors of materials subject to decay from dry rot and other causes must, of course, be carefully avoided.

Recapitulating, we see that a good fireproof floor should be of good fire-resisting material—all ironwork being protected by non-conductors—that it should not lead to expense in other parts of the building, should be strong enough to carry the weights required to be placed upon it, and not liable to decay.

The student should test each floor described by seeing which it possesses of the characteristics described above. In selecting a floor for any particular purpose some of these characteristics will be more important for that purpose than others, and it is impossible to say abstractly that any system is the best under all circumstances.

[1] Gass, *Transactions*, R.I.B.A., 1886.

## DIFFERENT FORMS OF FIREPROOF FLOORING.

A great many different forms of fireproof flooring have been proposed and made use of during the last few years.

They may be generally classed under four heads.

A. Arches of brick or concrete supported upon walls or girders.

B. Hollow bricks or tubes supported between girders and filled in with concrete.

C. Concrete filled in between and around girders.

D. Solid timber of considerable thickness.

E. Iron plates resting on girders.

*The only systems required by the Syllabus to be dealt with are those under A, and Fox and Barrett's under C.* One or two more systems are briefly described in this volume, but fuller particulars and other systems are given in Part II., N.B.C.

### Arched Systems.

GIRDERS AND BRICK ARCHES.—Among the earliest forms of fireproof floors were those consisting of brick arches of small or moderate span, supported by cast or wrought iron girders.

Such constructions are still in use for mills, warehouses, sugar factories, and other buildings, where great weights have to be stored.

Fig. 295 is a transverse section of part of a floor composed

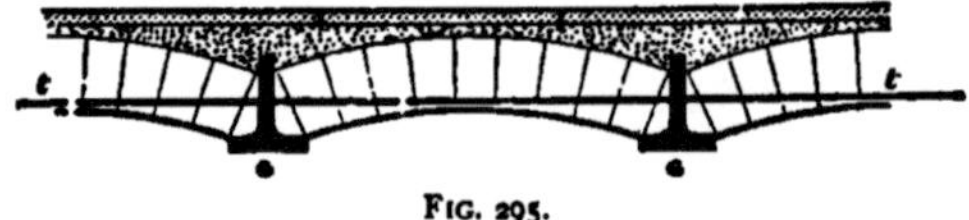


FIG. 295.

of brick arches resting upon cast-iron T girders, G G. Wrought-iron rolled joists would, of course, be far better.

The girders may be placed from 4 to 12 feet apart; the arches turned from one to the other; the spandrils filled in and levelled up with concrete, and covered with a floor of any material.

A tension rod, *t t*, unites the girders, and prevents their yielding under the thrust of the arches. The nearer the tension rod is to the springing of the arch the better, but it is frequently kept high up within the arch in order that it may not be visible.

The tension rod is often used only for the outer arches of a series; these, being thus prevented from yielding, form an abutment for the others.

In arches of a larger span the thickness of the brickwork may be increased toward the haunches, as shown in Fig. 296.

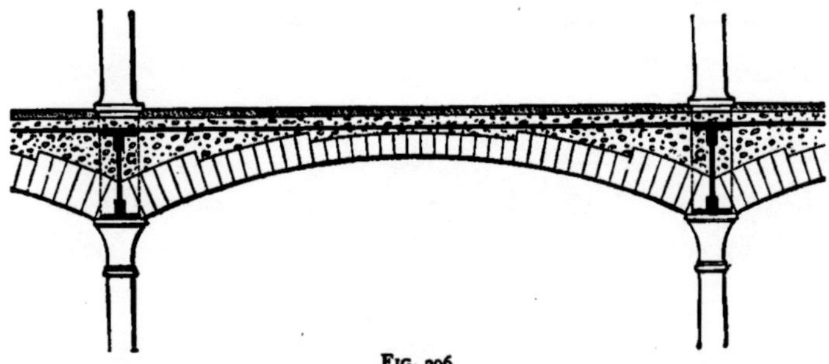

Fig. 296.

This increase of thickness is useless unless the extra rings are bonded in with the others, or built with bricks the full depth of the arch, which amounts to the same thing.

Sir W. Fairbairn recommends that the rise of such arches should be $\frac{1}{10}$ the span for floors of mills, and $\frac{1}{8}$ the span for warehouse floors to carry heavy weights.

Fig. 296 shows an arch of about 10 feet span, carried by wrought-iron plate girders, with angle iron flanges. These girders run at right angles to the arches, their ends rest upon the heads of columns, and the girders are laterally tied together by flat iron bars, *t t*, secured to their upper flanges.

WHICHCORD'S FIREPROOF BLOCKS.[1]—It will be seen that in the systems above described the lower surfaces of the iron girders are exposed to the direct action of fire.

To prevent this, the late Mr. Whichcord embedded them in fireclay blocks, which protect them from fire, and, at the same time, form skew-backs for the arches.

Fig. 297 shows in section a rolled girder with protecting fire blocks, BB. These are made in lengths of 9 inches, and with a minimum thickness at any point of 1½ inch of fireclay, which has been found to resist the greatest heat to which such a structure is likely to be subjected.

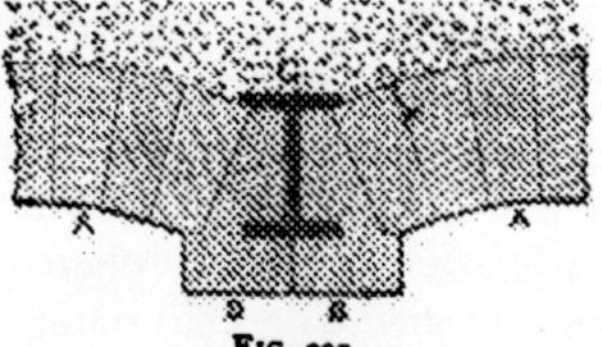

Fig. 297.

Where ceiling joists are used, they may be supported on the lower ledges of the fire blocks.

DOULTON-PETO SYSTEM, Fig. 298.—In this the blocks or voussoirs of the arch are of hollow fireclay

[1] Used at the National Safe Deposit Co.'s Warehouse.

blocks, which are stated to be ⅓ lighter than bricks or concrete. The under sides of these are dovetail grooved so as to form a key for the plastering.

This flooring is capable of sustaining great weights; the girders are well protected; the arches being light may be of considerable span, though large spans increase the depth and cost of the floor, and, moreover, they do exert a certain amount of thrust upon the walls.

This flooring has been used at Whiteley's, The London Pavilion, National Provincial Bank, and in several warehouses.

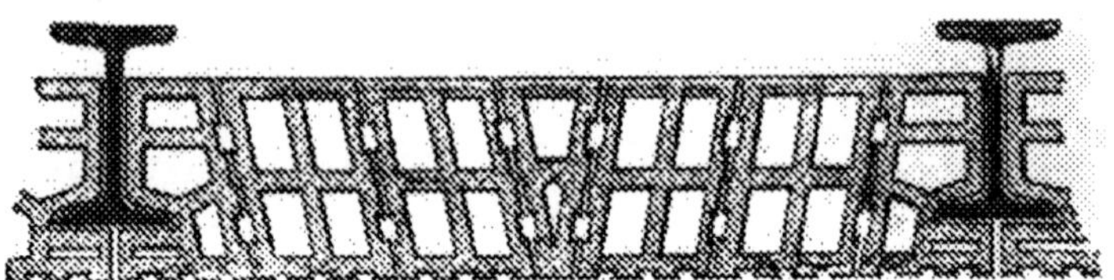

FIG. 298.—*Section of 8-inch Flooring.*
DOULTON-PETO'S SYSTEM.

DENNETT'S FIREPROOF FLOOR consists of concrete arches supported where they abut upon the walls by projecting courses, and at intermediate points by rolled or riveted iron girders, as shown in Fig. 299.

The arches should have a minimum rise of 1 inch to every

FIG. 299.
DENNETT'S SYSTEM.

foot of width up to spans of 10 or 12 feet, and are sustained by centering until they are thoroughly set.

The concrete used has sulphate of lime (gypsum) for its matrix. It has been proved that this substance does not lose its cohesive power even when it is raised to a white heat and then drenched with cold water.

The floor above the arch may be formed by simply bringing the concrete itself to a smooth surface. Joists may be nailed to fillets laid upon the concrete, in a similar manner to that shown in Fig. 300, or the surface may be paved as in Fig. 299.

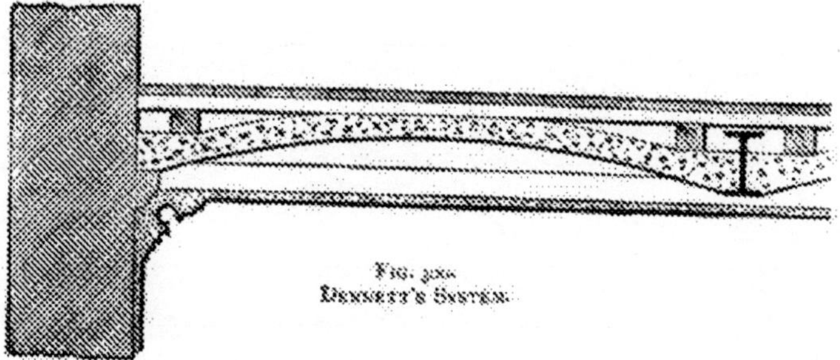

Fig. 300.
Dennett's System.

The soffit of the arch may be finished at once with the setting coat of plastering;[1] or, if a flat ceiling is necessary, joists must be fixed to the lower flanges of the girders to carry the lath and plaster. The laths are not shown in Fig. 300.

Figs. 299, 300 are taken from Messrs. Dennett's pamphlet.

*Disadvantages of Arched Floors.*—Arched floors, especially when composed of voussoir blocks, are complicated and heavy. The arches depend greatly upon one another, and if one gives way it may lead to the failure of the whole floor. In any case they exert a thrust upon the walls.

These disadvantages have led to the adoption of other forms of fireproof flooring.

## Systems with Hollow Bricks or Tubes.

In order to avoid the lateral thrust of arches upon the walls, various systems have been proposed in which hollow bricks or tubes are suspended by means of T or L irons between I joists, and the spaces between and above them filled in with concrete.

HOMAN AND RODGERS' SYSTEM (Figs. 301, 302) consists of purpose-made hard-burnt bricks with moulded projections, protecting the iron joists upon which they rest, and filled in with concrete.

As the concrete is tough the boarding of the floor may be nailed to it direct, but inch sleeper fillets are recommended so as to leave a space for ventilation, gas and water pipes, etc.

---

[1] Concrete arches are often laid upon a soffit of corrugated iron, which supports the concrete while it is being laid and protects it afterwards.

The soffits of the hollow bricks are dovetail grooved as a key for the plaster ceiling, and the depth of the finished floor is only 6 to 9 inches.

Fig. 302 is a longitudinal section, and Fig. 301 a cross section, of the floor.

FIG. 301.—*Cross section.*
HOMAN AND RODGER'S SYSTEM.

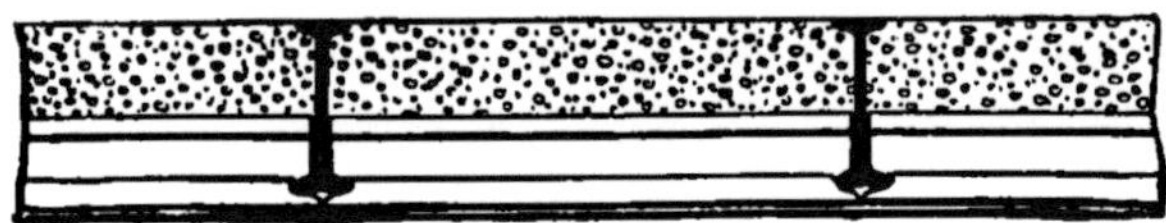

FIG. 302.—*Longitudinal Section.*
HOMAN AND RODGER'S SYSTEM.

*Fawcett's system* (Figs. 303 to 304) *consists of Fireclay* or red clay tubes, or, as they are called by the inventor, "lintels," of the section shown at *L*,

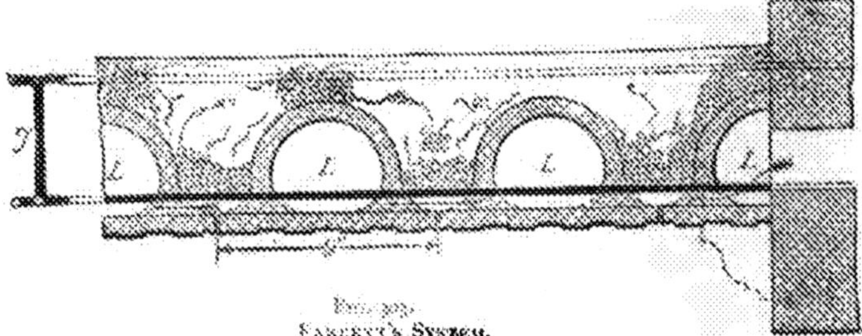

FIG. 303.
FAWCETT'S SYSTEM.

Transverse section, showing the air passage under the joists and the admission of cold air into the side of the lintel.

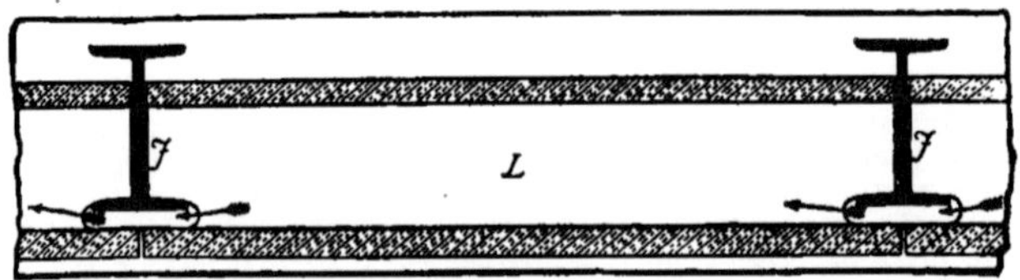


FIG. 304.
FAWCETT'S SYSTEM.

Longitudinal section, showing the tubular lintel encasing the joist, and the admission of cold air into the end of the tubular lintel.

Fig. 303, which rest upon the lower flanges of wrought-iron rolled I joists 2 feet apart. The lintels are placed obliquely between the joists—their own diagonals being at right angles to the joists. The spaces between and above them are then filled in with concrete—their lower sides are grooved as a key for plastering. The weight of the floor is taken by the joists and concrete, the lintels acting merely as a permanent centering and casing to the ironwork, which is well protected.

This system has been used for a warehouse in Southwark.

## Girders filled in with Concrete.

In these systems there is no thrust upon the walls, and they are efficient if the ironwork is well covered by non-conducting material.

Fox and Barrett's Floors consist of wrought-iron girders placed about 20 inches apart, at right angles to which, and resting on their bottom flanges, are laid rough fillets or strips

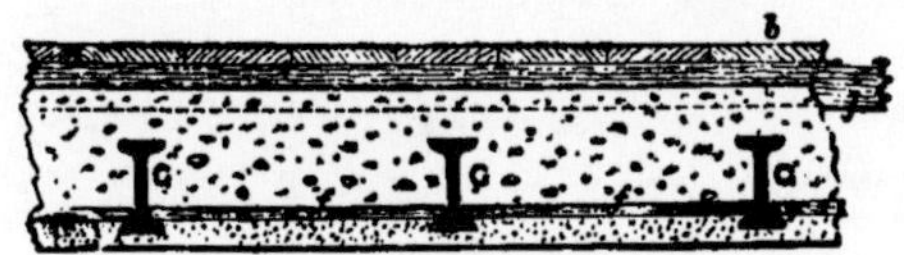


Fig. 305.—*Cross section.*
Fox and Barrett's System.

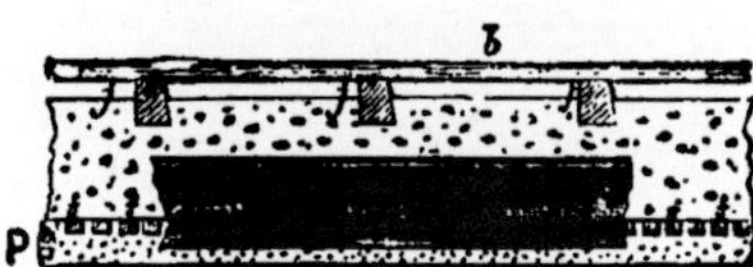


Fig. 306.—*Longitudinal section.*
Fox and Barrett's System.

of wood 1 inch or 1½ inch square, and about ½ inch apart. Concrete is then filled in between the joists—being supported by the fillets—which form a key to the plastering of the ceiling below.

In order to avoid all inflammable material, small earthenware drain pipes have been used instead of wooden fillets.

Fig. 305 shows a transverse section, and Fig. 306 a longitudinal section, of such a floor.

G G are the wrought-iron girders, *f f* the fillets, P the plaster of the ceiling below.

The surface of the floor in the example shown is covered with boards laid upon the joists, *j j*, which are embedded half their depth in the concrete, and cut to a dovetail section to keep them firm.

Sometimes the concrete is filled in only up to the upper surface of the girders, and floor joists or paving laid upon it.

The concrete used for fireproof flooring of this kind should be of a quick-setting lime or cement, for until it has set its full weight comes upon the girders, but when it is solid it forms a series of flat arches between the girders and strengthens the floor.

If the concrete is thick, it should be applied in two layers to hasten its drying.

Care must be taken that the floor has a good abutment on each side, or is well tied together.

When the lower flanges of the girders are so wide that they would interrupt the key of the plaster and prevent its adherence, light ceiling joists are sometimes secured to the under side of the fillets at right angles to them. These are lathed and plastered in the usual way.

LINDSAY'S SYSTEMS.—*a, With* I *Girders.* The first of these (Fig.

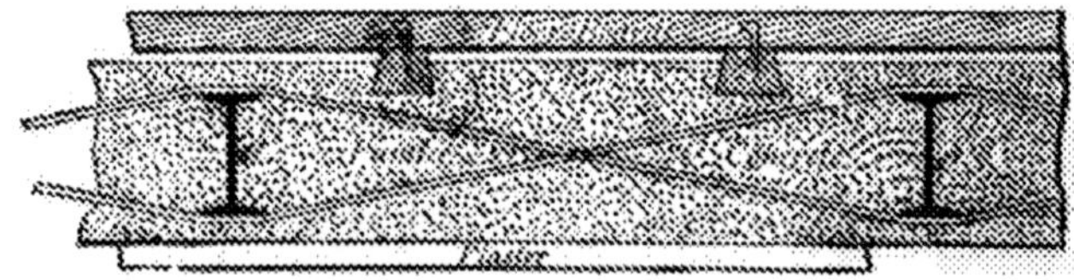

FIG. 307.—*Cross section for boarded floor with embedded sleepers.*
LINDSAY'S SYSTEM WITH I GIRDERS.

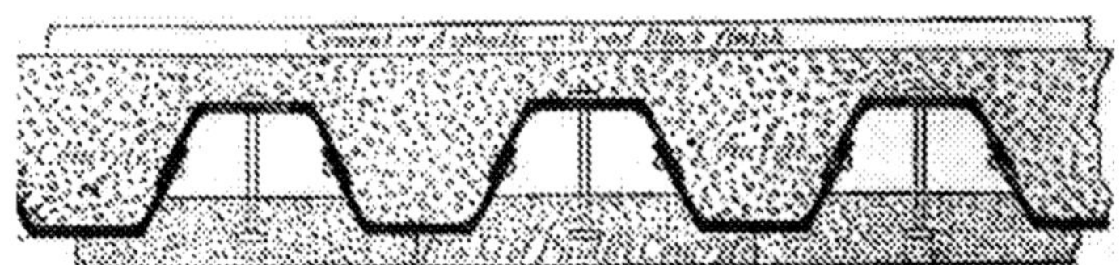

FIG. 308.—*Section of floor with concrete blocks under.*
LINDSAY'S SYSTEM WITH TROUGH GIRDERS.

307) consists of wrought-iron or steel I joists, spaced from 18 inches to 3 feet apart, and trussed by pairs of rods about 18 inches apart, as shown in Fig. 307, which clip on to the lower flanges of the girders. Very light concrete, made of coke breeze, mineral sand, and Portland cement—known as "pumice concrete"—is filled in and around the girders and rods.

This system has been used for the Branch Bank of England, Royal Infirmary (Liverpool).

LINDSAY'S SYSTEMS.—*b, With Trough Girders* (Fig. 308). In this system wrought-iron or steel girders of trough section riveted together are filled in with "pumice" concrete. When there is no substantial ceiling the lower surface of the ironwork is open to the action of fire, but this may be avoided by fixing pumice concrete blocks or slabs below instead of an ordinary plaster ceiling.

This system has been used at the National Liberal Club, Prudential Assurance Company (Brook Street), Messrs. Maples, Dublin Museum, and by several Railway Companies.[1]

## Solid Timber Floors.

EVANS' AND SWAIN'S SYSTEM (Fig. 309) consists of timber joists spiked close together without any spaces between. The depth of the joists varies from 4½ inches for 8 feet spans to 11 inches for 30 feet spans. The spikes are about 18 inches apart, holes being bored for them to prevent splitting.

All cracks or shrinkages in the upper surface of the floor are filled up with a grouting of liquid plaster, while the plaster ceiling may be attached, as shown, to the under surface of the joists, alternate joists being less deep, so as to form a key, or it may be attached to laths upon fillets.

The advantages of this floor are, that it is simple, and composed entirely of timber in large scantlings and plaster, both of which offer a very considerable resistance to fire.

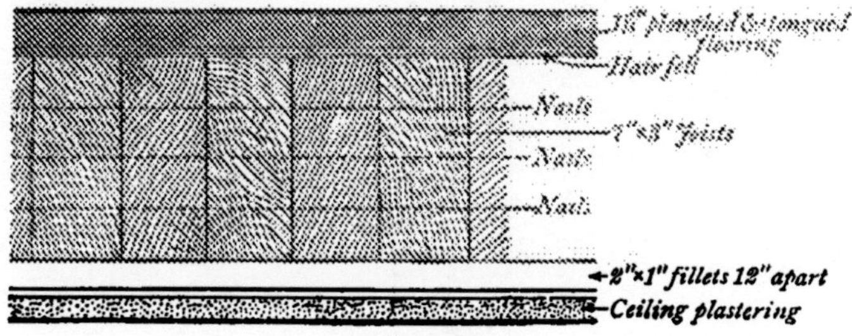


FIG. 309.

## American Systems.[2]

ARCHED FLOORS are much used in America—either brick arches supported by iron girders with "porous terra cotta,"[3] protecting blocks forming skewbacks, or arches of hollow blocks like those in the Doulton-Peto system (Fig. 298), or concrete arches like those of Dennett, but supported upon corrugated iron soffits.

PUGGED FLOORS.—A section of one of these is shown in Fig. 310. It consists of wooden joists on which 2" × 1" strips support a course of bricks whose upper surface is covered with a layer of concrete, and upon which is a tiled or boarded floor. The ceiling is of terra-cotta tiles fixed to the joists by iron clips—jointed, and plastered below.

---

[1] Cunnington, *Building News*, March 15, 1889.

[2] *Transactions*, R.I.B.A., 1886, p. 129, Mr. Gass's paper.

[3] Porous terra cotta is composed of clay mixed with combustible material, such as sawdust, cut straw, charcoal, etc. When baked the combustible material is consumed, leaving the terra cotta full of holes. It is fireproof, light, will hold nails, and gives a good surface for plastering (see Part III. N.B.C.).

*Slow-burning construction*[1] is a term applied to the kind of floor generally used for mills and warehouses. These consist of solid beams or beams bolted together and 8 or 10 feet between centres, upon these are laid floor planks 3 inches to 3½ inches thick, over which is spread a layer of mortar ⅝ inch thick, and over this again is laid a grooved and tongued

FIG. 310.

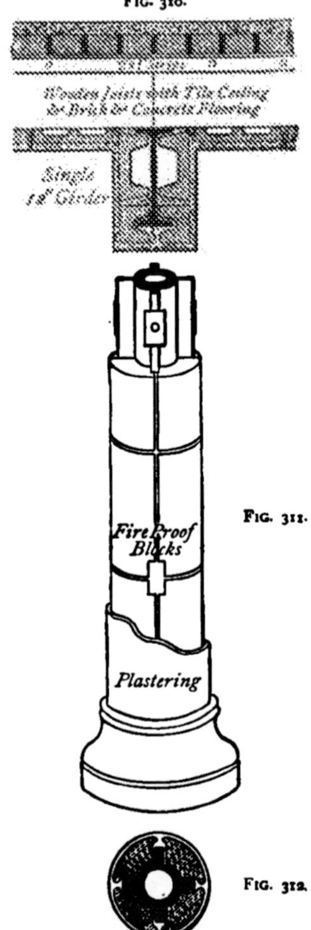


FIG. 311.

FIG. 312.

[1] Woodley's *Fire Protection of Mills*, New York.

floor of hard wood 1¼ inch thick. Sometimes two thicknesses of rosin-sized sheathing paper are substituted for the layer of mortar.

GENERAL.—Ironwork is always protected by terra-cotta blocks (Figs. 310–312 [1]), plaster, etc. Ceilings are of terra-cotta tiles, or plastered on wire-cloth netting with ⅜ inch squares. Exposed woodwork is protected by terra cotta or sheets of tin. Partitions are of hollow tiles.

---

## CHAPTER XII.

### *IRON ROOFS.*

*Subjects required by Syllabus, and (in brackets) the pages at which they are treated upon.*

*Roofs of Iron . . . for spans up to 60 feet.*

THIS Course includes roofs of from 40 to 60 feet span.

Such roofs can easily be formed with straight rafters, and it will therefore be unnecessary to notice roofs with arched rafters or mixed roofs in this volume.

**Forms for Roof Trusses.**—Plate III. shows various forms of trusses for iron roofs of spans up to 60 feet.

When the principal rafters are long they require support at intermediate points, which with roofs of ordinary construction should not be more than 8 or 9 feet apart. This support may be given in two distinctly different ways.

*Trussed Rafter Roofs*, Figs. 315–320.—In these the principal rafters are supported by one, two, or more struts at right angles or nearly at right angles to them, which together with tension rods form the principal rafters into a pair of trusses, joined at the ridge of the roof and prevented from spreading by the tie rod.

Sometimes, though rarely, the struts supporting the principal rafters are vertical, as in Fig. 316.

*King- and Queen-rod Roofs and modifications thereof*, Figs. 321–328.—In these the trusses are of the same skeleton form as in timber roofs, the principal rafters being supported by inclined struts, which with the tension rods and tie rod form the whole into a truss.

Occasionally, however, though but rarely, the struts are made vertical and the tension rods inclined, as in Figs. 324, 326. The vertical struts are more convenient when the roof has hipped ends.

**Trussed Rafter Roofs.**—In E.B.C.D., p. 208, illustrations and descriptions were given of a roof in which each

[1] From *Transactions*, R.I.B.A., 1886, Plate XVIII.

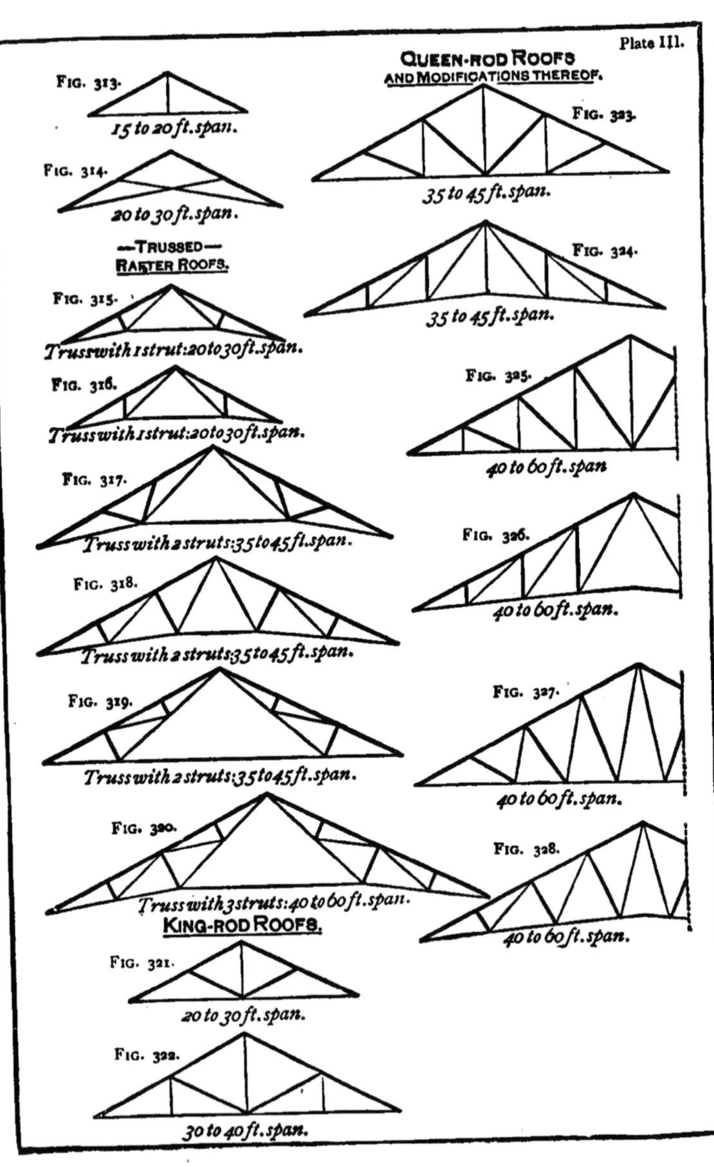
QUEEN-ROD ROOFS
AND MODIFICATIONS THEREOF.
FIG. 313.
15 to 20 ft. span.
FIG. 314.
20 to 30 ft. span.
—TRUSSED—
RAFTER ROOFS.
FIG. 315.
Truss with 1 strut: 20 to 30 ft. span.
FIG. 316.
Truss with 1 strut: 20 to 30 ft. span.
FIG. 317.
Truss with 2 struts: 35 to 45 ft. span.
FIG. 318.
Truss with 2 struts: 35 to 45 ft. span.
FIG. 319.
Truss with 2 struts: 35 to 45 ft. span.
FIG. 320.
Truss with 3 struts: 40 to 60 ft. span.
KING-ROD ROOFS.
FIG. 321.
20 to 30 ft. span.
FIG. 322.
30 to 40 ft. span.
FIG. 323.
35 to 45 ft. span.
FIG. 324.
35 to 45 ft. span.
FIG. 325.
40 to 60 ft. span
FIG. 326.
40 to 60 ft. span.
FIG. 327.
40 to 60 ft. span.
FIG. 328.
40 to 60 ft. span.

principal rafter was trussed by means of a strut supporting it in the centre (see Fig. 315, Plate III.), the strut itself being sustained by tension rods connecting it with the ends of the rafter.

Such an arrangement is best adapted for roofs up to 30 or 40 feet span; but when, as in larger roofs, the rafters become very long, they require support at more than one central point.

TRUSS WITH TWO STRUTS.—Figs. 317–319, Plate III., show various forms in which a truss with two struts to support the principal rafter may be constructed. Details of such a truss as that in Fig. 319 are given in Plate IV.

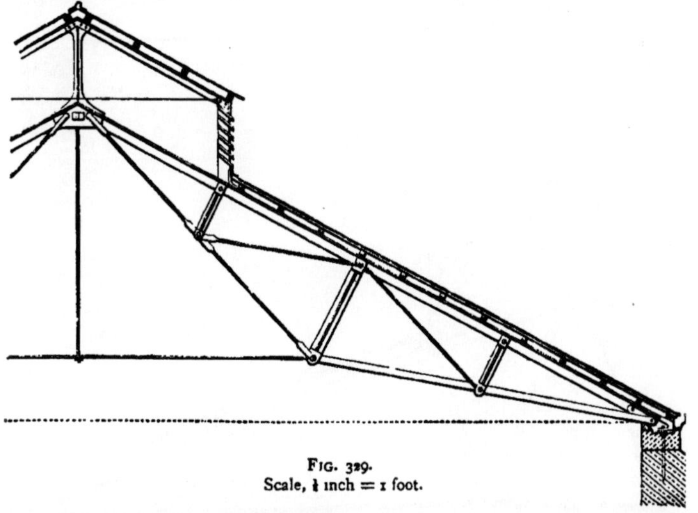

FIG. 329.
Scale, ½ inch = 1 foot.

TRUSS WITH THREE STRUTS.—In roofs of more than 40 feet span the rafters become so long as to require support at three intermediate points; the same principle of trussing may be continued as shown in Fig. 320.

Fig. 329 above is also an example of a trussed rafter roof with 3 struts. In this example the rafters are of T iron, the struts of double T iron riveted back to back. The tie rod and upper tension rod are of round iron, and the lower tension rod is of double flat bar iron.

The covering is of slates laid on boarding supported by angle iron purlins filled in with wood.

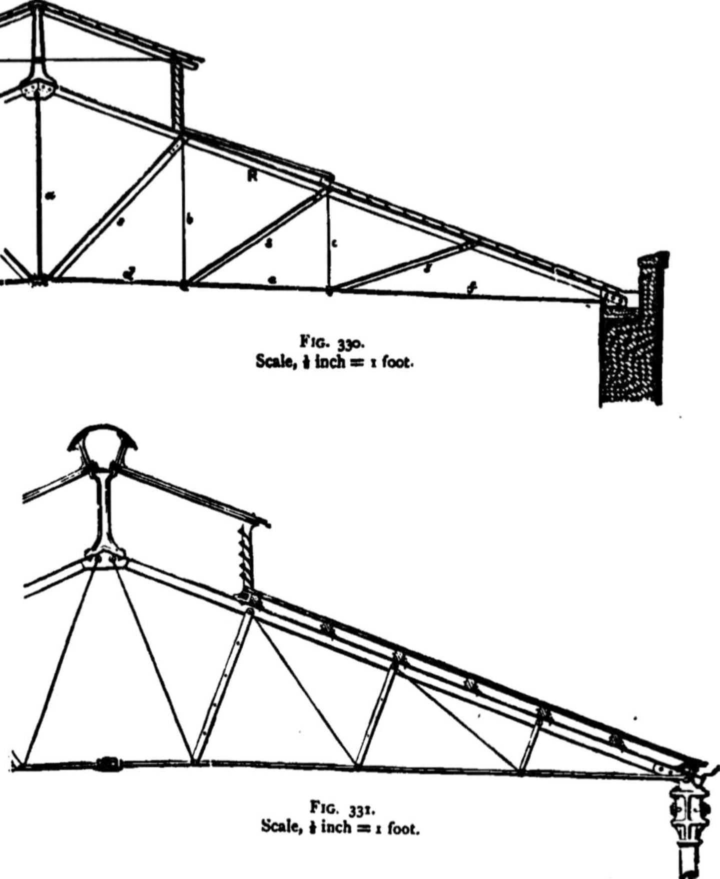

FIG. 330.
Scale, ½ inch = 1 foot.

FIG. 331.
Scale, ½ inch = 1 foot.

The roof is surmounted by a skylight, supported by a cast-iron standard, and provided with wooden or iron louvres.

With regard to trussed rafter roofs Mr. Matheson says,[1] the "forms just described are marked by an absence of vertical members, and for this

[1] *Works in Iron.*

reason the system is not a convenient one for hipped roofs, and for those roofs also where a longitudinal bracing between the principals is required in a vertical plane."

Detailed illustrations of this form of truss are given at p. 10, E.B.C.D.

**Queen-Rod Roofs.**—Figs. 323-328 show various forms of so-called queen-rod roofs adapted for spans from 35 to 60 feet.

An example of such a roof is also given in Fig. 329.

In this example the rafters and struts are of T iron, the tension and suspending rods of round iron. The covering is of Duchess slates laid on angle iron laths. The ridge lantern is of similar construction to that last described, covered with slates on angle iron laths, and supported by cast-iron standards.

MODIFICATION OF QUEEN-ROD ROOF.—Fig. 331 shows a modification of the queen-rod roof often used in practice.[1]

In this form of roof the struts are at right angles to the rafter, and are therefore of minimum length.

In the example given the struts are of double bar iron of the construction described at p. 201, the rafters of T iron, the tension and tie rods of round iron, the purlins of wood connected to the rafters by angle iron.

The tie rod is attached to chairs formed upon the heads of the columns supporting the roof, and is provided with a union joint in the centre by which it may be tightened.

## PARTS OF IRON ROOF TRUSSES.

The methods of constructing the different parts for iron roofs of small span have already been described in E.B.C.D. This section will be confined to the consideration of the forms to be given to members of somewhat larger roof trusses.

**Principal Rafters.**—The principal rafters of an iron roof of small span are generally of T-shaped section.

Bars of similar sections, but of larger dimensions, are also used for larger roofs; but in these many other forms are also adopted, a few of which may now be mentioned.

Rafters of I section have been sometimes used for spans

[1] This example was taken from the roof of a drill shed.

of over 60 feet, but are not convenient for the attachment of the struts

When T iron is used for larger roofs the upper flange may be strengthened by adding plates to it, as in Fig. 332.

"Bulb iron with a thin web and a bulb somewhat larger than the top table, gives a greater resistance with the same weight of metal than T iron, but its cost is considerably greater, and it is not quite so easy to connect with the other part of the truss."[1]

Fig. 332.

The increased strength required in long rafters has sometimes been given without increasing the depth of the iron used by placing two bars side by side, parallel to one another, and kept an inch or two apart by means of cast-iron distance pieces.

Double channel iron may be similarly used, thus—

Fig. 333.

or double angle iron, thus—

Fig. 334.

the latter are the more convenient for connecting with the heads of struts, etc.

Hip Rafters may be strengthened by the introduction of additional plates, as in Fig. 335, without much increasing the bulk of the rafter.

Fig. 335.

**Purlins** for roofs of from 40 to 60 feet span may be of timber (Fig. 331); of angle iron (Fig. 330); T iron, or channel iron. The angle and channel iron may be filled in with wood (Fig. 337) in order that the roof covering may be more easily attached.

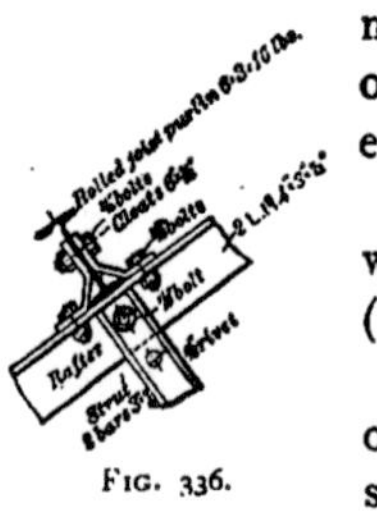

Fig. 336.

In larger roofs, where the principals are widely spaced, the purlins may be of I iron (Fig. 336), or trussed.

**Struts.**—Wrought-iron struts of angle or T iron, are frequently used for roofs of spans between 40 and 60 feet.

[1] Wray's *Theory of Construction*.

A better form, however, is the strut of cruciform section, consisting of two T irons riveted back to back, as in Fig. 329.

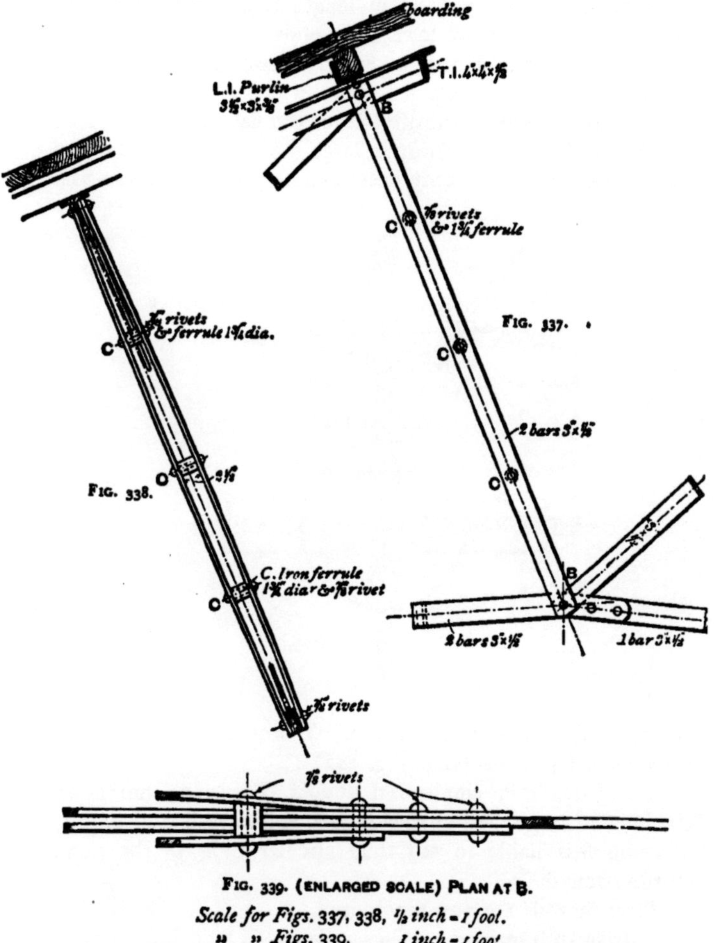


FIG. 339. (ENLARGED SCALE) PLAN AT B.

*Scale for Figs.* 337, 338, *½ inch = 1 foot.*
" " *Figs.* 339, *1 inch = 1 foot.*

Strong and light struts formed out of wrought-iron gas tubing fitted with cast-iron sockets at the ends are sometimes used.

Another very good form was noticed in E.B.C.D. It consists of two flat bars, Figs. 337–339, kept apart by cast-iron distance pieces, *c c c*, varying in length so as to form a strut tapering from the centre toward the ends.

Such a strut is shown in Fig. 331, also in Plate IV., and a similar one on an enlarged scale in Figs. 337–339. L or T irons are sometimes substituted for the flat bars.

**Tie and Tension Rods** in large roofs are of circular rod iron, or flat bars, as already described for smaller roofs—and

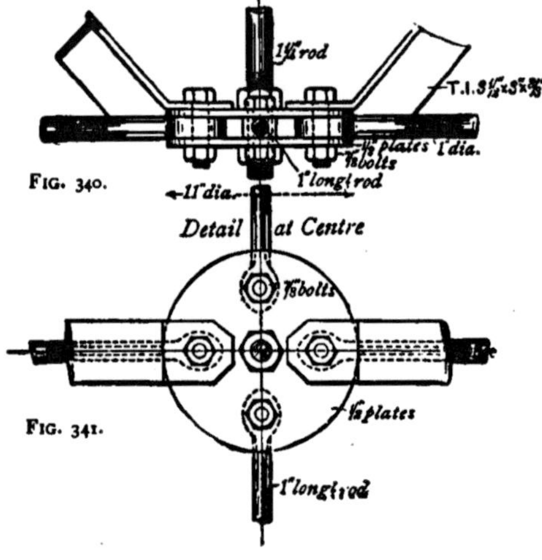


FIG. 340.

FIG. 341.

are secured in a similar manner. T iron tie rods are very convenient for connections (Fig. 342).

Flat bars, both single and double (Fig. 337), are more common in large than in small roofs, and have the advantage of being less liable to sag than circular roofs of the same tensile strength.

Steel tie rods are now much used.

**Joints in Tie Rod.**—When a tie rod is long it is severed at the centre, sometimes at two or more points. The joints may in a round tie rod be formed as shown in Figs. 340, 341 (which are details of an actual queen-rod roof of 40′ 3″ span), or the connecting plate may be oval, as in Plate IV. When the tie rod is a T iron or flat bar a very simple joint may be made, as in Fig. 342.

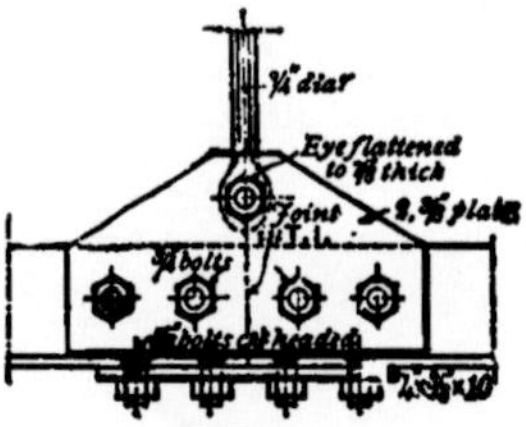

**Coupling Boxes.**—The tie rod should be so arranged with coupling boxes, shackles (p. 213, E.B.C.), or cottered joints that it can be altered in length in order to set up the roof when required.

FIG. 342.

In large roofs it is an advantage to arrange the tension rods in the same way, either with union screws—cottered joints—or with reverse screws at either end, so that by revolving the rod the screws turn opposite ways, and lengthen or shorten the rods.

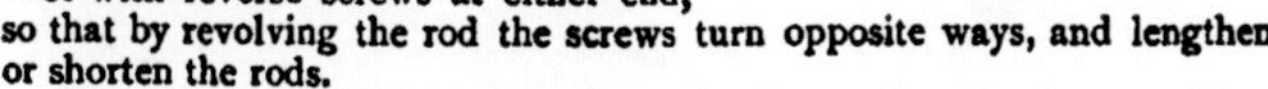

These shackles, etc., are not shown in the small scale figures. They are often omitted in practice, the result being that the tension rods either become slack or undergo a greater stress than they are intended to bear.

**Cottered Joints.**—Figs. 343, 344 show a simple example of a cottered joint applied to the end of a tie rod. This, being flattened out, passes between two plates which are bolted to the shoe, and lie on each side of the rafter.

FIG. 343.

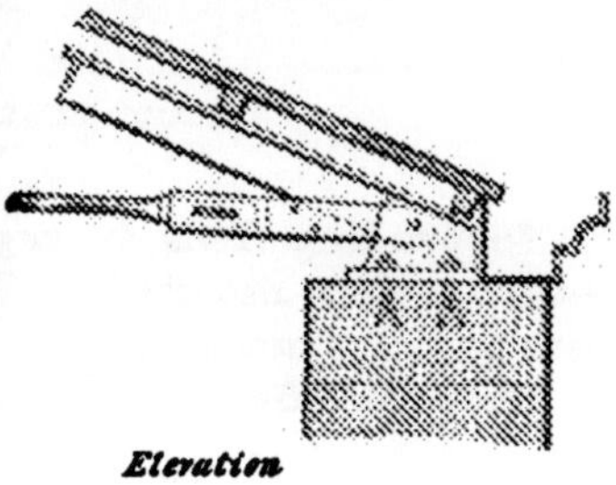

A rectangular slot is made through the plates and the end of the tie rod. In this slot are placed two iron wedges or "cotters" (*c c*), and the sides of the hole are protected and rendered smooth by means of wrought-iron *gibs* (*j j*), so that the wedges may slide easily when driven. As the wedges are driven inwards, they force the slot in the tie rod towards the shoe, so that it tends to coincide with the slot in the plates—thus the tie rod is shortened, and the roof tightened up.

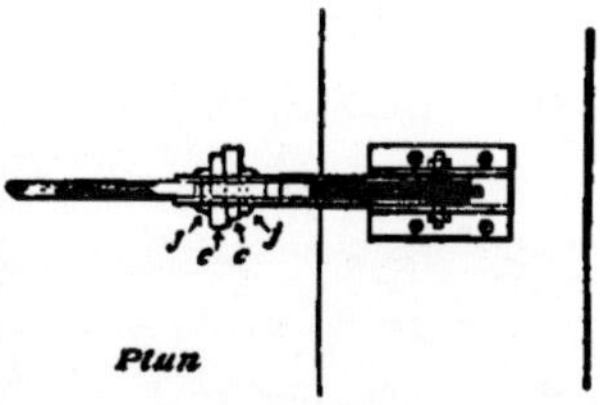

One cotter is frequently used instead of a pair, and has the same effect, for, as it is driven in, and the wider part enters the slot, it draws the two members in connection toward each other. In some cases the slot for the gib and cotters is formed in the shoe itself. A taper of from ¼″ to ⅛″ per foot of their length is generally given to the cotters.

FIG. 344.

**Connections at Heads and Feet of Struts.**—Several forms of these are shown in E.B.C.D., also in Figs. 337, 338,

339, 341, and in Plates IV., V. They require no explanation. Figs. 345, 346 show simple forms constructed with plates.

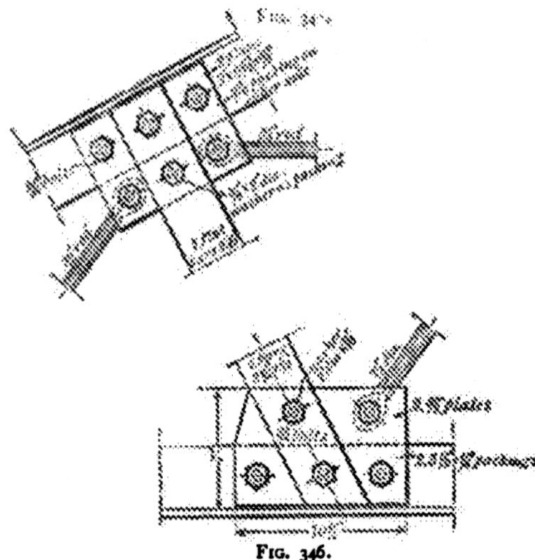

Fig. 346.

**Suspending Rods** for large roofs are similar in every respect to those described in E.B.C.D., and nothing more need be said regarding them.

**Shoes and Heads.**—The lower extremities of small prin-

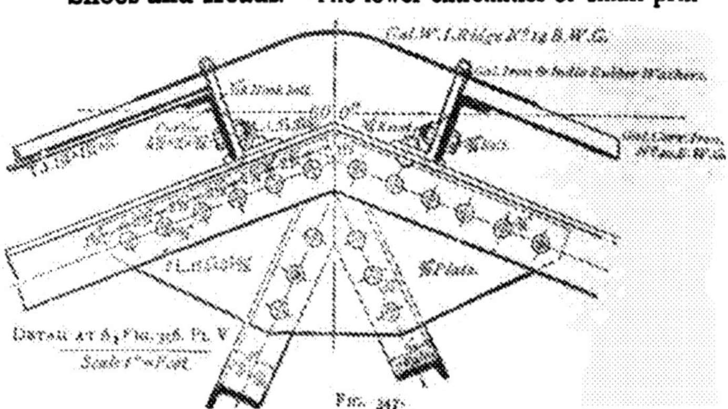

Fig. 347.

cipal rafters are sometimes secured in cast-iron shoes. Cast-iron heads and shoes are seldom used for large roofs.

Illustrations of cast-iron shoes are given in Figs. 343, 344. 353, and in 352, Plate IV.

Simpler joints are formed by the use of flat wrought-iron plates, to which the parts to be connected are bolted or riveted. When the principal rafter is of two angle irons one plate may be inserted between them, as in Figs. 347, 348, which are details of the joints A and E of the roof, Plate V.

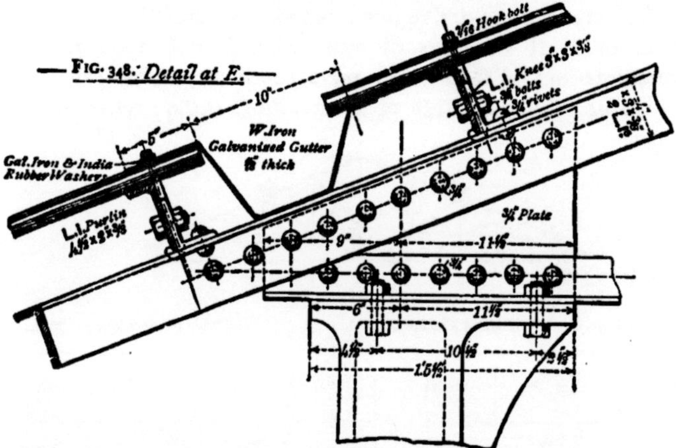

FIG. 348.: Detail at E.

When the principal rafter is of T iron then two plates may be used, one on each side of the web, as in Fig. 330.

Fig. 349 is a simple joint with plates connecting the foot of the principal rafter with a tie of T iron.

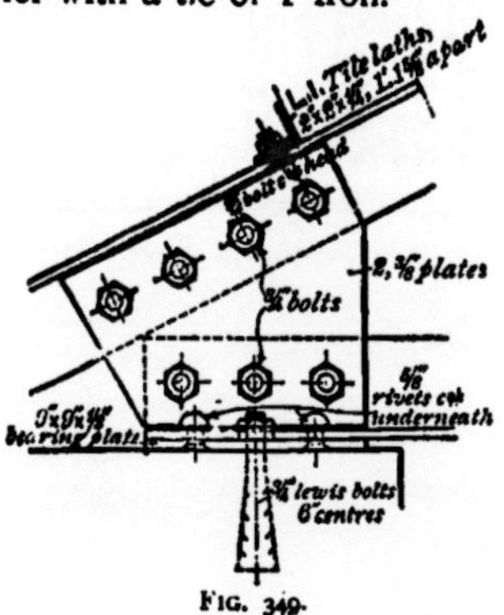

FIG. 349.

## Contract Drawings of Iron Roofs.[1]

**Plates IV., V.** are reduced copies of part of the contract drawings for roofs recently constructed.

There is no object in describing them in detail, but it should be mentioned that Plate V. is inserted by the kind permission of Sir Alexander Rendel, K.C.I.E., and Plate IV. by that of Messrs. Handyside and Co.

The student will derive more benefit by carefully studying these practical drawings of well-designed roofs than from representations of roofs drawn merely to illustrate the text.

**Table of Scantlings of Iron Roofs** (from actual practice):—

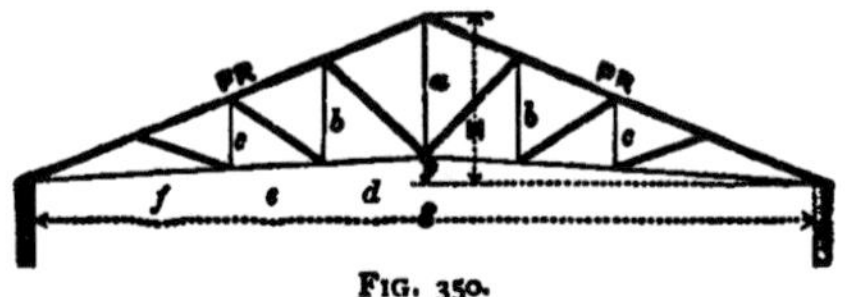


Fig. 350.

Rise, $H = \frac{s}{8}$. Rise of Tie Rod, $t = \frac{s}{4}$. Principals 6 feet 8 inches apart.

| Span, *s*. | Rafter, PR. | Struts, S. | King Bolt. | Queen Bolt. | | Tie Rod. | | |
|---|---|---|---|---|---|---|---|---|
| In Feet. | T iron. | T iron. | *a*. | *b*. | *c*. | *d*. | *e*. | *f*. |
| | Inches. | Inches. | | | | | | |
| 20 | 2½ × 2 × ⅜ | 2 × 2 × ⅜ | ¾ | ⅝ | ... | ⅝ | ¾ | ... |
| 25 | 2¾ × 2½ × ⅜ | 2 × 2 × ⅜ | ⅞ | ¾ | ⅝ | ⅞ | 1 | ... |
| 30 | 2⅞ × 2½ × ½ | 2½ × 2½ × ⅜ | 1 | ¾ | ⅝ | 1 | 1⅛ | ... |
| 35 | 3 × 2¾ × ½ | 2½ × 2½ × ⅜ | 1 | ¾ | ¾ | 1 | 1⅛ | 1¼ |
| 40 | 3½ × 3 × ½ | 2½ × 2½ × ⅜ | 1⅛ | ⅞ | ¾ | 1⅛ | 1¼ | 1⅜ |
| 45 | 4 × 3½ × ½ | 3 × 3 × ½ | 1¼ | 1 | ⅞ | 1⅛ | 1¼ | 1½ |
| 50 | 4 × 3½ × ⅝ | 3 × 3 × ⅜ | 1⅜ | 1 | ⅞ | 1¼ | 1⅜ | 1½ |
| 55 | 5 × 4½ × ⅝ | 4 × 4 × ½ | 1½ | 1⅛ | 1 | 1⅜ | 1½ | 1⅝ |
| 60 | 5 × 4½ × ¾ | 4 × 4 × ⅝ | 1⅝ | 1⅛ | 1 | 1½ | 1⅝ | 1¾ |

[1] From Molesworth's *Pocket Book*.

Plate IV

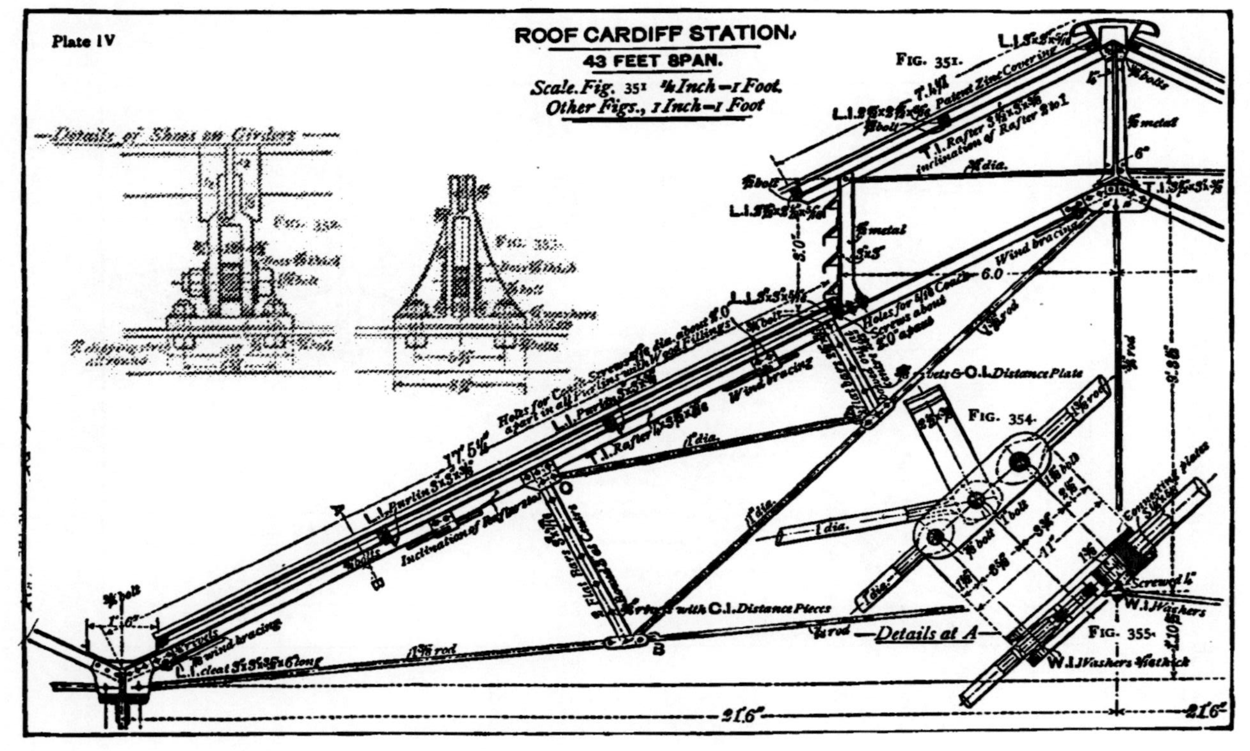
ROOF CARDIFF STATION,
43 FEET SPAN.
Scale. Fig. 351 ¼ Inch = 1 Foot.
Other Figs., 1 Inch = 1 Foot
Details of Shoes on Girders
Fig. 351.
Patent Zinc Covering
Wind bracing
Holes for Coach Screws about 2.0 apart
Holes for Coach Screws with Wood Fillings
L.I. Purlin
T.I. Rafter
Inclination of Rafter
Flat Bars
C.I. Distance Pieces
C.I. Distance Plate
Fig. 354.
Fig. 355.
Connecting plates
Screwed
W.I. Washers
Details at A
21.6"
6.0
8.0"
17.5¼"
B
O

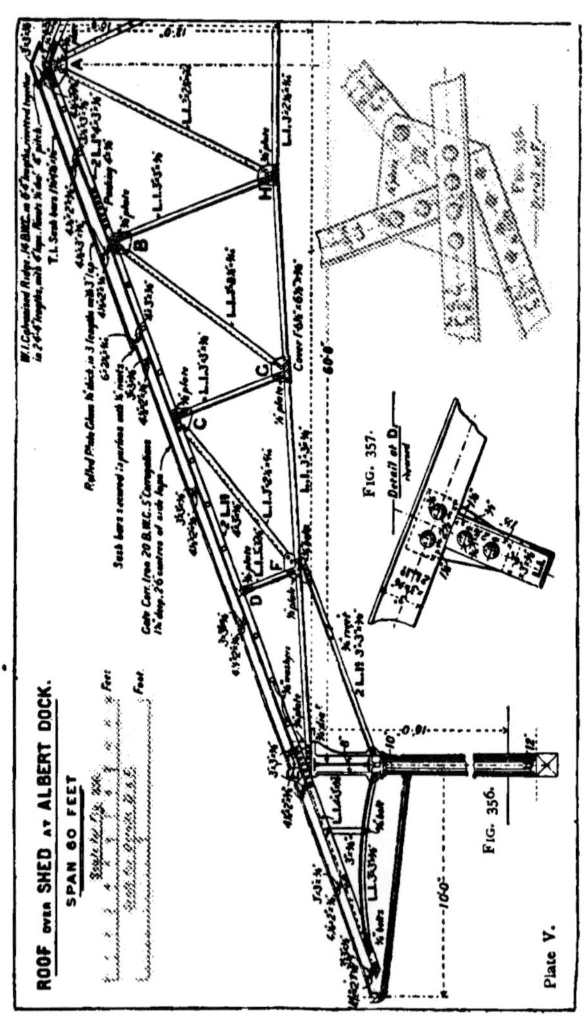
ROOF OVER SHED AT ALBERT DOCK.
SPAN 60 FEET
Feet
Feet
A
B
C
C
D
E
H
60·0"
10·0"
16·0"
FIG. 357.
Detail at D
FIG. 356.
FIG. 358.
Plate V.

# CHAPTER XIII.

## *PLASTERERS' WORK.*

***Subjects required by Syllabus, and (in brackets) the pages at which they are treated upon.***

"*Lath* [p. 210], *plaster* [p. 212], *and battening to walls*" [p. 211].

*Plastering* consists in applying different compositions resembling mortar to walls and ceilings, in thin layers, so as to form smooth surfaces, for the sake of appearance and cleanliness.

The plaster may either be laid on the face of the wall itself, or it may be spread over a screen of laths fixed in any required position.

The latter operation only is technically known as "*plastering*," the application to the wall itself being called "*rendering*."

Plastering and rendering are applied in one, two, or three coats, according to the importance of the building and the degree of finish required.

### Materials used by the Plasterer.

LIMES AND CEMENTS.—*Lime.*—The pure or fat limes (see p. 23) are generally used for plastering, because in using hydraulic limes minute unslaked particles are apt to get into the work, and to *blow*, throwing out bits of plaster, and injuring the surface.

*Plaster of Paris* is calcined gypsum. When mixed with water to form a paste it sets very quickly, expanding as it sets, and attains its full strength in an hour or two.

*Portland Cement* (see p. 24) is made from chalk and clay mixed together in water, then burnt and ground. It is the strongest cement in use, but sets more slowly than the other varieties.

*Roman Cement*, *Medina Cement*, *Harwich*, *Calderwood*, *Whitby*, *Mulgrave's*, and *Atkinson's Cement*, are all natural cements of the same description. They are made by burning nodules found in different geological formations. These cements set very rapidly, but attain no great ultimate strength.

*Keene's*, *Parian*, *Martin's*, *Robinson's Cements*, are all manufactured by recalcining plaster of Paris with different substances. These cements are useful only for indoor work; they set very quickly, and can be painted within a few hours.

*Whiting* is made by grinding white chalk to a fine powder.

SAND AND WATER.—Very clean sand and fresh water should be used for plasterers' work.

MIXTURES.—*Coarse Stuff* is a rough mortar, containing 1 or 1½ part of sand to 1 of lime by measure, thoroughly mixed with long ox hair (free from grease and dirt), in the proportion of 1 lb. hair to 3 cubic feet of mortar.

*Fine Stuff* is pure lime slaked with a small quantity of water, and afterwards saturated until it is of the consistence of cream; it is then allowed to settle and the water to evaporate, until thick enough for use. For some purposes a small quantity of white hair is added.

*Plasterers' Putty* is lime dissolved in water, and then run through a hair sieve. It is very similar to fine stuff, but prepared somewhat differently, and always used without hair.

*Gauged Stuff* consists of from ¾ to ⅘ plasterers' putty, and the remainder plaster of Paris. The last-named ingredient causes the mixture to set very quickly, and it must be gauged in small quantities. The proportion of plaster used depends upon the time to be allowed for setting, the state of the weather, etc., more time required in proportion as the weather is damp.

For cornices the putty and plaster are often mixed in equal proportions.

*Stucco* is a term vaguely applied to many mixtures containing common and hydraulic limes, also to some cements.

*Common Stucco* contains three or four parts sand to one of hydraulic lime.

*Trowelled Stucco* consists of ⅔ fine stuff (without hair), and ⅓ very fine clean sand.

*Bastard Stucco* is of same composition as trowelled stucco, with the addition of a little hair.

*Rough Cast* consists of sand, grit, or gravel, mixed with hot lime in a semi-fluid state.

*Size* is thin glue made by boiling down horns, skins, etc.

*Double Size* is boiled for a greater time so as to be stronger.

LATHS are thin strips of wood, generally fir, sometimes oak, split from the log, 3 or four feet long, about an inch wide, and varying in thickness according to their class.

| | | |
|---|---|---|
| *Single laths* | are about . . . | 3/16 inch thick. |
| *Lath-and-half laths* | ,, . . . | ¼ ,, |
| *Double laths* | ,, . . . | ⅜ ,, |

**Lathing.**—Laths to receive plaster may be fixed either in a horizontal position as for ceilings, vertically as a covering for walls and partitions, or in such a manner as to form inclined or curved surfaces.

*Lathing Ceilings.*—For this purpose the laths are nailed to the underside of the ceiling joists (see p. 89, E.B.C.D.), or in many cases to the bridging joists, which should, if necessary, be brought into a horizontal plane by adding slips of wood called "firrings."

The laths are fixed parallel to one another, and ⅜ inch

apart, so that the intervals afford a key for the plaster. Every lath is secured by nails, one being driven through the lath wherever it crosses a joist or batten. The moist plaster passes between the laths, forming protuberances at the back—these harden and form what is known as the "*key*," which prevents the plaster from falling away from the laths and keeps it in position. Care should be taken that the ends of the laths do not overlap one another, and that they are attached to as small a surface of timber as possible, so that the key may not be interrupted.

If the joists are of wood, a narrow fillet may be nailed along the under side of each to receive the laths, so as to interfere with the key of the plaster as little as possible.

The laths should be laid in "bays," so as to break joint in portions 3 feet wide (see Fig. 359).

The thickest laths should be used for ceilings, and for very important work they should be nailed with zinc nails, so that there may be no danger of their oxidizing, and the rust showing on the surface.

*Battened Walls*[1] are so called because wooden battens about 2 to 2½ inches wide, and from ⅝ to 1 inch thick, are fixed vertically at central intervals of about 12 inches, to receive the laths.

The battens are nailed to wood plugs in the wall, except where flues occur, in which case they should be secured by iron holdfasts.

The laths are nailed as above described. They should be fully ¾ inch clear of the inside of the wall, and about ⅜ inch apart—thus affording a key which is sufficient to support the plaster in its vertical position.

Lath-and-half laths should be used for walls and partitions subject to rough usage, and single laths for ordinary walls.

Walls likely to be damp should be battened, as the clear air-space between the masonry and the lathing ensures the plastered surface being constantly dry; but battened walls harbour vermin, the woodwork is subject to decay, and is injurious in case of fire.

[1] Sc. *Strapped walls.*

Figs. 359, 360 show a sectional plan and an elevation of a portion of a battened wall, with some of the plaster removed, in order to show the laths *l l* and battens *b b* below.

The laths are shown as breaking joints in bays. This is not absolutely necessary for walls, but is often done in vertical work as well as for ceilings.

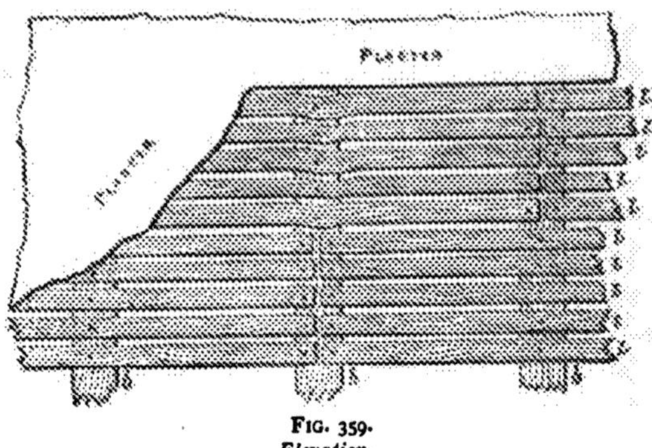

FIG. 359.
*Elevation.*

FIG. 360.
*Sectional Plan.*

*Counter-lathing* is necessary when plaster has to be applied close to a flat surface, such as that of a large beam. In such a case laths are nailed on to the surface of the beam about a foot apart, and across these is nailed the lathing to receive the plastering.

This second layer of laths is termed *counter-lathing.* Being clear of the surfaces of the beam, a key is afforded, and the plaster adheres to the first layer of laths, which it would not do if they were nailed on to the beam itself.

*Brandering* is a Scotch term applied to a kind of counter-lathing.

**Plastering.**—ONE-COAT WORK; known as "*Lath and Plaster one Coat;*" or, "*Lath and Lay.*"—This consists of a layer of "coarse stuff" of a uniform thickness, spread over the laths with a smooth and even surface. The plaster should be stiff enough to hold together, but just sufficiently soft to pass between the laths, being worked well in between them with the point of the trowel, and bulging out behind the laths into excrescences, which form a key, and keep the plaster in position.

This is the cheapest kind of plastering, and is used only in inferior buildings, or behind skirtings, plinths of partition shutters, window backs, etc.

In some parts of the country one-coat work is never used to cover lathing, but only for rendering on walls.

TWO-COAT WORK; described as "*Lath, Plaster, and Set;*" or, "*Lath, Lay, and Set.*"

*1st Coat.*—The first coat is laid upon the laths as above described, but the surface, instead of being smoothed, is roughed over by scratching it with a birch-broom, so as to form a key for the second coat.

*Setting.*—The second coat, or "setting," is a thin layer of fine stuff, or putty, or gauged stuff, and should not be trowelled on till the first layer is stiff. If the latter has become very dry, it must be moistened before the second coat is applied, or the latter in shrinking will have its moisture sucked out, crack, and fall away. As the fine stuff is laid on, the surface is smoothed by drawing backwards and forwards over it the wet brush used for damping the first coat.

THREE-COAT WORK.—Described as "*Lath, Plaster, Float, and Set;*" or, "*Lath, Lay, Float, and Set.*"

*Pricking-up* is the name given in this case to the first coat, which is laid as before described; but in order to form a good key for the next coat the surface is scored over with the point of a lath in deep scratches, crossing each other diagonally in sets of parallel lines about 3 or 4 inches apart.

Scratching tools, with several points, are sometimes used.

*Floating.*[1]—The second, or "floated" coat, is applied when the pricking-up is sufficiently dry to resist pressure.

It consists of fine stuff, with the addition of a little hair, and derives its name from its being laid on with "floats" in the following manner:—

[1] Sc. *Straightening.*

In order to ensure the surface of the plaster being in a true plane, narrow bands or "screeds" of plaster, about 6 or 7 inches wide, are formed at the angles, and at intervals of from 4 to 10 feet on the wall or ceiling. The surfaces of these are then brought into the required plane by passing long straight-edges over them.

Horizontal screeds for ceilings should moreover be levelled, and vertical screeds "plumbed" up from the skirting grounds (see p. 113), before proceeding farther.

The spaces between the screeds are then "filled out" flush with the fine stuff, and smoothed off with straight-edges, or with a large flat board, having two handles at the back, and known as a "Derby float."

The surface is then gone over with a smaller hand float, and any defects made good by adding a little soft stuff.

*Setting.*—Before applying the third coat or setting, the floated surface should be scratched over with a broom, and then allowed to become perfectly dry.

The setting is varied in composition to suit the nature of the finish intended for the surface.

If the surface is to be papered, it should be "set with fine stuff;" if it is to be whitened, it should be "set with putty and washed sand;" and if it is to be painted, it should be finished with "trowelled stucco" or plaster.

"*Set with Fine Stuff.*"—For surfaces to be papered the setting coat should be of fine stuff containing a little hair, and the finished work would be described as "Lathed, Plastered, Floated, and Set with Fine stuff."

"*Set with Putty and Plaster.*"—If the wall or ceiling is to be whitened or coloured, the third coat should be of plasterers' putty mixed with a little fine sand, and sometimes with a little white hair.

If required to set quickly, especially in damp weather, from $\frac{1}{6}$ to $\frac{1}{3}$ plaster of Paris is added to the stuff, which must be gauged (or mixed) in small quantities (see Gauged Stuff, p. 210).

This work, when finished, would be known as "Lathed, Plastered, Floated, and Set with Putty and Plaster;" or it would also come under the general designation of *Gauged Work.*

Great care should be taken to ascertain that the floated coat is dry before this setting is applied, otherwise the coats will shrink unequally, and the last coat will be full of cracks.

**Rendering** is the term used for the process of applying plaster or cements to the naked surface of walls.

With regard to plaster, it is applied in exactly the same way as upon laths, excepting a slight difference in the first coat.

The surface of the wall to be rendered should be rough, so as to form a key to which the plaster will firmly adhere. This may be secured by leaving the mortar joints unstruck and protruding when the wall is built; or the joints may be raked and the face hacked and picked over to give it the necessary roughness.

*Rough Rendering* is the first coat laid to receive more finished work.

It is of coarse stuff, but contains a little less hair than that used on laths, and is applied in a moister state, which causes it to adhere better to the wall.

The holes and crevices in the wall should be entirely filled up in applying this coat, but the surface of the plaster need not be scratched or scored over.

*Floating and Setting* are performed in exactly the same way as upon laths.

GAUGED WORK is formed by the addition of a proportion of plaster of Paris to any coat of plaster, in order to cause it to set more rapidly. Unless the process is very carefully conducted cracks will occur in the plaster. The quantity of plaster added depends upon the rapidity of setting required, the dampness of the weather, etc.

**Rendering in Cement.**—The wall to be rendered should itself be dry, but the surface should be well wetted, to prevent it from absorbing at once all the water in the cement; it should also be sufficiently rough to form a good key for the cement.

Screeds may be formed on the surface, and the cement should, if possible, be filled out the full thickness in one coat, and of uniform substance throughout.

Any excess of cement in projections, moulding, etc., should be avoided, by dubbing out with bits of brick.

When cement is put on in two or three coats, the coats already applied should on no account be allowed to dry before the succeeding layers are added.

The coats last applied are very liable to peel off under the effects of frosts or exposure.

Many of the quick-setting cements, such as those mentioned below as adapted for internal work, are rendered in one thickness of cement and sand, and the face afterwards finished and brought to a surface with neat cement.

Sand may be added with advantage to most cements, to prevent excess in shrinkage and cracking; sometimes a very large proportion is used.

*External Work.*—The material best adapted for rendering the external surfaces of walls is Portland cement. Other materials, such as Roman cement, are, however, frequently used, but have not the same adherence, appearance, or weathering properties.

The objection to Portland cement, from an economical point of view, is its first cost, the greater labour required in using it as compared with that necessary for other cements, and also the time frequently wasted upon it, for, in consequence of its setting slowly, there is a tendency for the men to go on working it too long.

In order that it may set as quickly as possible, the less heavy varieties should be selected for rendering.

External rendering is often marked with lines, so as to represent blocks of ashlar stone.

Both Portland and Roman cement are mixed with a proportion of sand for external work.

The Portland cement may be used in the proportion of 1 cement to 3 sand, and the Roman cement with 1 part of sand to 1 of cement for upright work.

For cornices, mouldings, etc., about half the quantity of sand should be used, but some is required to prevent cracking.

*Internal Work.*—Parian, Keene's, Martin's cement, and others of a similar character, are eminently adapted for internal work.

The treatment of the several descriptions varies slightly, but they are generally laid in a thin coating of about ⅛ inch depth on a backing of Portland cement and sand. In some cases the backing is formed of the quick-setting cement itself, mixed with 1 to 1½ of sand.

Most of them can be brought to a beautiful hard polished surface, and are ready to receive paint in a few hours.

These cements are largely used, not only for rendering walls, but for forming skirtings, mouldings, pilasters, angle beads, and other internal finishings of a building.

Portland cement is also used for internal work often with a very large proportion of sand, as much even as 9 parts of sand to 1 of cement being recommended.

**Rough-Cast** is used as a cheap protection for external walls.

The surface of the wall is first "pricked up" with a layer of "coarse stuff," upon which a coat of similar composition is evenly spread; while this is wet, and as fast as it is done in small portions, rough-cast (p. 210), in a semi-fluid state, is thrown upon it with large trowels from buckets, forming a rough adhering crust, which is at once coloured with lime-wash and ochre.

**Pugging** is a coat of coarse stuff of about 2 or 3 inches thiok laid on boards fixed between the joints of floor. It is intended to prevent sounds and smells from passing from one room to the other, but is rather apt to lead to decay in the woodwork.

**Arrises,** or sharp corners of plastered walls, require to be of extra strength, or protected in some way from being chipped and injured.

*Angle Staves* are substantial beads or cylinders of wood plugged to the salient angles of the walls, and splayed so as to receive the plaster on each side. They thus protect the angle of the wall from injury.

*Cement Angles* are often formed instead of angle staves. The angle of the wall, including a strip of 4 or 6 inches wide on each side, is rendered in cement, and is consequently harder and more able to withstand a blow than if finished in plaster. The corner of the wall or of the cement covering may with advantage be rounded.

*Cement Staff Beads* or *Quoin-beads* are similar in form to those in wood, described at p. 71, E.B.C.D., and are adopted in order to avoid an arris, and to answer the same purpose as angle staves.

# APPENDIX

## EXAMINATION PAPERS SET IN THE YEARS 1888, 1889, 1890, 1891, BY THE SCIENCE AND ART DEPARTMENT, SOUTH KENSINGTON,

IN

# BUILDING CONSTRUCTION.

### Second Stage or Advanced Course.

GENERAL INSTRUCTIONS.

*If the rules are not attended to, the paper will be cancelled.*

You may take the Elementary or the Advanced or the Honours paper, but you must confine yourself to one of them.

Your name is not given to the Examiner, and you are forbidden to write to him about your answers.

All figures must be drawn on the single sheet of paper supplied, for no second sheet will be allowed.

All drawings must show a correct knowledge of construction. Neat and accurate drawing to scale is required. Where only sketches are asked for the proportions must be approximately correct, though extreme accuracy, as in drawings to scale, is not necessary. The drawings may be left in pencil, provided they are distinct and neat. No extra marks will be allowed for inking in.

You are to confine your answers *strictly* to the questions proposed.

Put the number of the question before your answer.

Answers in writing must be as short and clearly stated as possible, and close to any figures to which they may refer.

The value attached to each question is shown in brackets after the question. But a full and correct answer to any easy question will in all cases secure a larger number of marks than an incomplete or inexact answer to a more difficult one.

A single accent (′) signifies *feet;* a double accent (″) *inches.*

Questions marked (*) have accompanying diagrams.

*The Examination in this subject lasts for four hours.*

## 1888.

### Second Stage or Advanced Examination.

INSTRUCTIONS.

*Read the General Instructions at the head of the Elementary paper.*
*You are only permitted to attempt* SIX *questions.*

21. Explain the meaning of "hydraulic lime," and how you would practically test a specimen of limestone in order to ascertain whether it would produce an hydraulic lime. (12.)

22. Describe the difference in both the behaviour and appearance of similar bars of cast and wrought iron—

(*a*) When broken under a tensile stress suddenly applied.

(*b*) When broken under a slowly applied tensile stress. (12.)

23.* Plans of two successive courses at the end of a brick wall built in English bond.

Draw, to a scale of ¾" to a foot, showing the use of diagonal bond in both courses, to strengthen the wall. (12.)

24.* Elevation of a beam loaded with 15 tons at a point out of the centre.

What proportion of the weight is borne at each of the two supports, A, B?

What portion of the beam is in tension, and which is in compression? (14.)

25.* Line diagram of a girder constructed for a uniform load, as shown.

Draw to twice the size, showing the members in tension by single, those in compression by double, and those under compression and bending stress by triple lines; the stresses due to their own weight to be neglected.

Draw a similar diagram, supposing the same load to be along the bottom instead of the top of the girder, omitting any bars you consider superfluous, and making any other alterations you think necessary. (14.)

26.* Section of part of a single floor with common joists 9" + 2½".

Draw, to a scale of $\frac{1}{8}$, a sectional elevation through A—A, showing the five floor battens, and four ordinary methods of forming a tight joint between them. (14.)

27. Draw, to a scale of 1½" to a foot, a cross section of a double-faced moulded skirting, 15" high, tongued to floor, and secured to wood grounds plugged to a brick wall. (16.)

28.* Line diagram of part of an iron roof truss for a 38-feet span, the rise being ¼ the span, and the camber of tie rod $\frac{1}{30}$ the span.

Draw a line diagram of the complete truss, to a scale of $\frac{1}{96}$.

Give an elevation of the joint at A, ½ full size, with any details required to fully explain its construction, *a a* being angle irons 2½" × 2½" × ⅜"; and *b b* (not continuous), as well as *c*, to be of 1¼" round iron. (16.)

29.* Plan of part of the top of a wall at the angle of a building, showing the wallplates to carry a hipped roof.

Draw, to a scale of ¾" to a foot, adding an angle tie and dragon beam. Give a vertical section through the dragon beam, showing its connection with the angle tie and the foot of the hip rafter. (16.)

30. Two iron plates 10" × ½" are to be connected by a riveted lap joint.

Draw, ¼ full size, a plan of a double riveted joint, the rivets being ¾", with a pitch of 2½".

Show by another plan a similar joint, but with the rivets arranged so as to weaken the plates as little as possible. (17.)

31.* Elevation of a brick archway.

Draw, to a scale of $\frac{1}{48}$, showing the centering you would use in its construction. Full details to be given, with the scantlings, including supports. (17.)

32. Give a horizontal section, to a scale of 1½" to a foot, through a cased

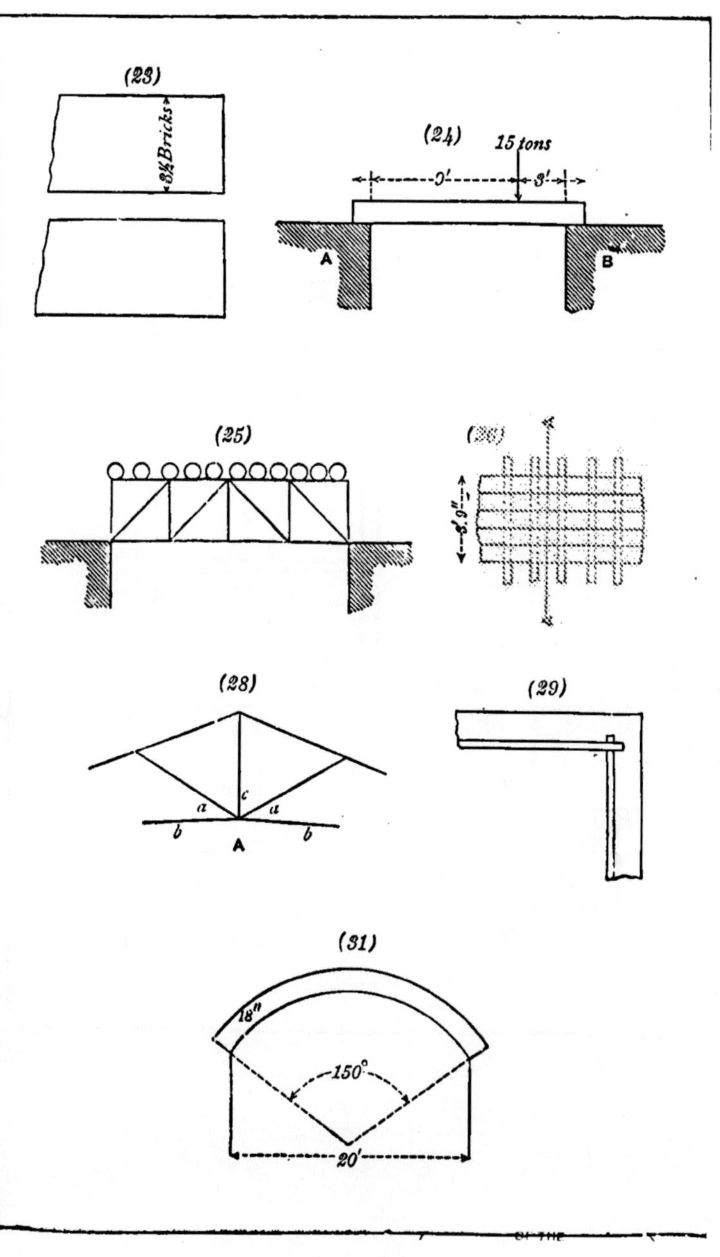
(23)
3½ Bricks
(24)
15 tons
9′
3′
A
B
(25)
(28)
c
a
a
b
b
A
(29)
(31)
18″
150°
20′

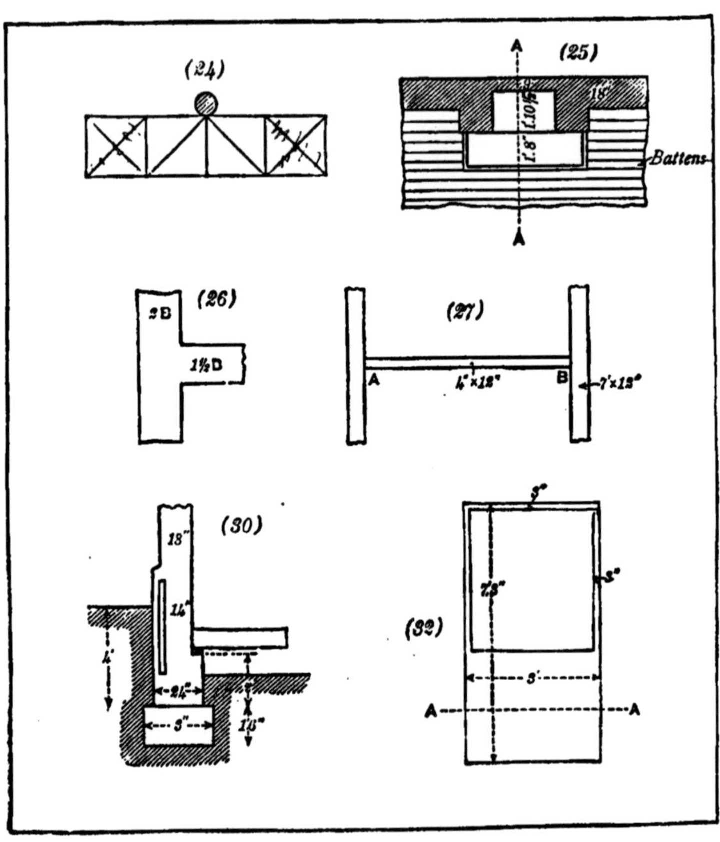
(24)
(25)
A
18"
1'.10½"
1'.8"
Battens
A
(26)
2D
1½D
(27)
A
4"×12"
B
7'×12"
(30)
18"
14"
4'
24"
3"
16"
3"
7.3"
3"
(32)
3'
A
A

window frame for 2¼" double hung sashes; the wall being of stone, 24" thick, finished inside with lath and plaster on battens, and square boxed shutters for a 4 feet opening. (18.)

## 1889.

### Second Stage or Advanced Examination.

INSTRUCTIONS.

*Read the General Instructions at the head of the Elementary paper. You are only permitted to attempt* SIX *questions.*

21. Describe the following bricks, stating the purposes for which they are suitable: Shippers, grizzles, malm cutters, blue Staffords. (12.)

22. What is the composition of the following stones? which would you consider the most durable, and why?—

York stone, Bath stone, Craigleith stone.

23. Explain what is meant by rich lime, poor lime, stone lime.

Which will carry the most sand, and why? (12)

24.* Diagram of a loaded truss.

Draw, to double the size, omitting as many members as possible, and marking with a × all the remaining members brought into compression by the load. (14.)

25*. Plan of a fireplace in a ground-floor room.

Draw, to a scale of 1/24 a section through A—A, showing all the detail of the construction. (14.)

26.* Plan showing the junction of a 1½-brick wall built in Flemish bond, with a 2-brick wall built in English bond.

Show, to a scale of ¾" to a foot, the arrangement of the bricks in two successive courses. (14.)

27.* Plan of a cross-beam framed into two girders.

Draw, to a scale of 1½" to a foot, sections through the joints, showing at A a shouldered or tusk-tenoned joint, and at B a chase-mortised joint.

Under what circumstances would the latter joint be used? (16.)

28. Give a part elevation and a cross section of a plate girder 2 feet deep, with a ½" web, connected to flanges, each consisting of two 12" × ⅜" plates; the rivets to be ¾" diameter, with a pitch of 4". (16.)

29. Draw, to a scale of 3 feet to an inch, an elevation of about half of a wooden roof truss for a 34 feet span, containing the following members:—

Tie-beam, 10" × 5".
Queen posts, 5" × 3½".
Principals, 5" × 5".
Straining beam, 5" × 6".
Braces, 4" × 2½". (16.)

30.* Vertical section through the base of the outer wall of a brick dwelling-house built on a damp site.

Draw, to a scale of ½" to a foot, showing the joints of the brickwork, and making any alterations or additions you consider necessary to prevent the damp from affecting the wall. (17.)

31. Give a cross section, to a scale of 1" to a foot, through the ridge of a slated roof, showing three courses of Duchess slates centre nailed on 3" × 1" battens, with 4" × 2" rafters, and a 9" × 1½" ridge-piece finished with slate ridging.

Also give a similar section showing the details of a lead ridge roll. (17.)

32.* Elevation of a 2" door, glazed above with nine panes and two panels below, bead flush outside and moulded inside.

Draw, to a scale of ¾" to a foot, the outside elevation; also a section through A—A, to double the scale. (18.)

## MAY AND JUNE, 1890.

### Second Stage or Advanced Examination.

INSTRUCTIONS.

*Read the General Instructions at the head of the Elementary paper.*
*You are only permitted to attempt* SIX *questions.*

21. What is the difference between single and double laths, and what does the first coat of plaster on ceilings ordinarily consist of? (12.)

22. When ought timber to be felled, and why?

What is American yellow pine chiefly used for? (12.)

23.* Sketches of two forms of mortar joints, one being known as *tuck pointing.*

Draw them to twice the scale, giving each its proper name, and state your views as to their merits, also making any alteration you think advisable. (12.)

24.* Cross section through part of a brick wall faced with ashlar.

Draw, to a scale of 1" to a foot, showing its construction. (14.)

25. Explain by sketches the meaning of the following terms: "fascia and soffit boarding to eaves," "dragging tie or dragon beam," "flitched girder," "torus moulded skirting." (14.)

26. Give an elevation and longitudinal section, one-half full size, of each of the following joints in a 1½-inch lead pipe: a wiped joint, a blown joint. (14.)

27.* Cross section of a hollow brick wall resting on a concrete foundation.

Draw to a scale of ¾" to a foot, showing the hollow space next the outer face, iron wall ties, and an asphalte damp course. (16.)

28.* Plan of a stair.

Draw to a scale of ½" to a foot, showing the handrail by double lines, and newels; also giving the name by which it is known and the names of its different parts.

Give, to a scale of 1½" to a foot, an end elevation of two of its steps showing return moulded nosings and a sunk and moulded string. (16.)

29.* Line diagram of an iron roof truss.

Draw to twice the scale, showing the members in tension by single lines and those in compression by double lines. (16.)

30. Elevation of a beam of a traveller running on a gantry.

Give an end elevation of the traveller, to a scale of ½" to a foot, showing how it is carried on the gantry. (17.)

31.* Plan of a double cover riveted joint in a ⅝" tie bar, showing the positions of the rivets.

State the nature of the joint, having regard to the arrangement of the rivets; and draw a section, one-third full size, through A—A, showing ¾" rivets to a 3" pitch, with snap heads above and pan heads below. (17.)

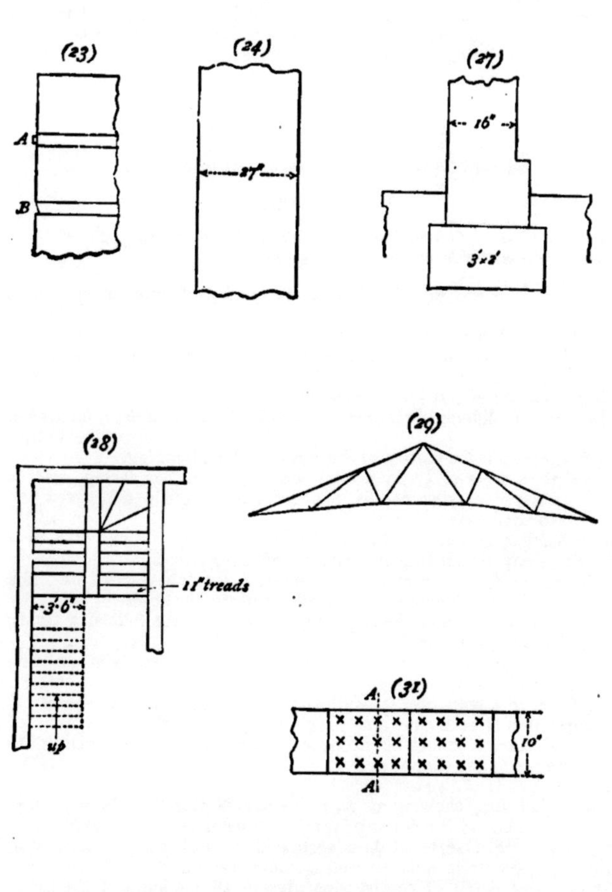
(23)
A
B
(24)
27"
(27)
16"
3'×2'
(28)
11" treads
3'-0"
up
(29)
(31)
A
10"
A

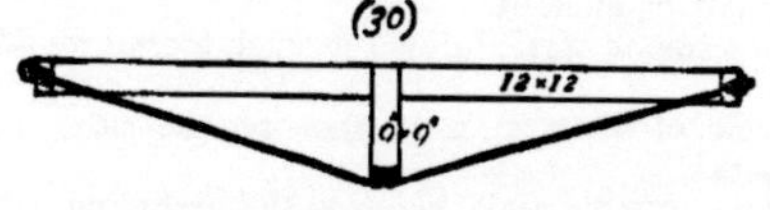
(30)
12×12
6×9"

32. Draw, to a scale one-sixth full size, a vertical section through a window back, showing a coursed rubble wall 12" thick, with both stone and wood sills, and the bottom rail of a 2½" double hung sash. The back lining to be 3' high to sash, with moulded panels, and to be box-framed, showing vertical sliding shutter in two 3' 6" leaves. (18.)

## APRIL AND MAY, 1891.

### Second Stage or Advanced Examination.

INSTRUCTIONS.

*Read the General Instructions at the head of the Elementary paper.*
*You are permitted to attempt only* SIX *questions.*

21. State how you would judge of the quality of different specimens of roofing slates. (12.)

22. Taking Roman and Portland cement, state which of the two is the heavier, darker in colour, quicker in setting, and stronger when set. (12.)

23. What is asphalte?

Name two of the best known varieties.

Mention two different processes by which asphalte is laid for traffic. (12.)

24.* Elevation of a portion of the end of a stone building.

Draw to a scale of ½" to a foot, showing an ashlar facing, laid in courses of varying depths, punched quoins, and a chamfered and rusticated base. (14.)

25.* Section, showing part of a brick wall carrying the end of a floor joist. State any objection to this method of construction.

Draw the section, to a scale of $\frac{1}{12}$, showing the joist carried on brick corbeling. The joints of the brickwork to be shown. (14.)

26. Show, by full-size sketches, the meaning of the following terms, as applied to mortar joints:—

Mason's joint; flat joint, jointed; struck joint, best and ordinary method; tuck pointing. (14.)

27. Give, to a scale of ¼, an ordinary section for a cast-iron beam 12" deep, supported at both ends, one flange being 7" × 1½".

State whether it would be stronger if fixed at both ends, giving the the reason for your answer. (16.)

28.* The ends of two iron rods.

Draw, full size, showing at A, a few square plus threads with a ¼" pitch; and at B a few angular minus threads with a ⅛" pitch. (16.)

29. Draw, to a scale of $\frac{1}{12}$, a section of a brick street sewer, 3' 9" high, to carry off storm water as well as house sewage.

Show every detail of construction, though all the joints of the brickwork need not be filled in. (16.)

30.* Section of a trench carried down through loose ground to a gravel foundation.

Draw, to a scale of 2' to an inch, showing the sides supported by poling boards.

Also draw a plan, to same scale, showing the timbering.

Give the dimensions and names of the different parts. (17.)

31.* Section of a window opening in a stone wall, lined with 4½" brickwork.

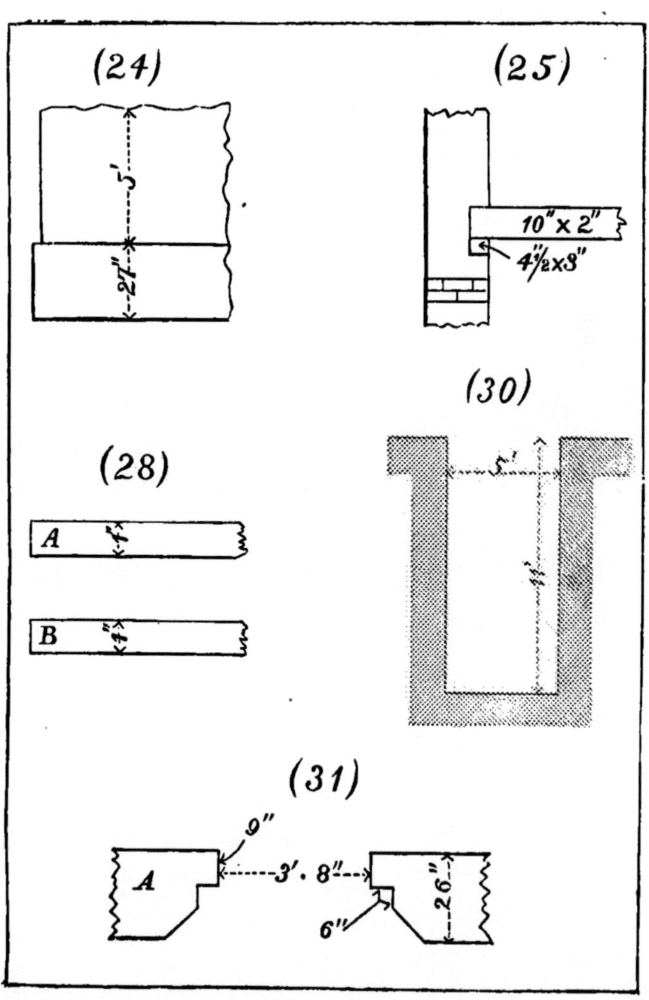
(24)
5'
27"
(25)
10" x 2"
4½x3"
(30)
5'
11'
(28)
A
4"
B
4"
(31)
9"
A
3'. 8"
26"
6"

Draw, to a scale of $\frac{1}{8}$, the side A, adding the details of a cased window frame, and the stile of a 2" top sash.

Show a paneled and moulded jamb lining, double-faced architrave, and wall finished with plaster. (17.)

32. Draw, to a scale of 8' to an inch, a line diagram showing an iron roof truss, suitable to a 43 ft. span. The compression bars to be shorter than the tension bars.

Give enlarged details of the joint at foot of truss, showing it secured to a stone template, resting on an 18" wall. The tie rod to be $1\frac{3}{4}$", and rafter 5" × $3\frac{1}{2}$" × $\frac{3}{8}$". (18.)

# INDEX.

Lightning Source UK Ltd.
Milton Keynes UK
UKOW051412060212

186753UK00001B/160/P